Paperbacks from Hell

The Twisted History of '70s and '80s Horror Fiction

Grady Hendrix

with Will Errickson

Quirk Books

Philadelphia

"CAREFULLY LAID-ON HORROR."
The New York Times
AVON/V2243/75¢
JOHN CHRISTOPHER'S Novel of pure terror
THE LITTLE PEOPLE

INTRODUCTION

Years ago at a science-fiction convention, I was flipping through the dollar boxes at a dealer's table when this Hector Garrido cover for *The Little People* brought my eyeballs to a screeching halt. I wasn't a book collector—I didn't even know who Hector Garrido was—but I knew what *this* was: the Mona Lisa of paperback covers. I bought it so fast my fingers blistered. I never expected to actually read the book . . . but three months later, I fished it out of my "To Be Read" pile and cracked it open.

I knew John Christopher's name from his Tripods science-fiction series, which had been serialized as a comic strip in the back of *Boys' Life* magazine. But this 1966 Avon novel was stronger stuff. In it, a gorgeous secretary inherits an Irish castle from a distant relative and converts it into a B&B to show her patronizing lawyer/fiancé that she can stand on her own. On opening weekend, the house is full of guests: an Irish dreamboat alcoholic, two bickering Americans with a hot-to-trot teenage daughter, and a married couple who met in a concentration camp, where he was a guard and she was a prisoner.

But some uninvited guests are lurking in the basement: the Gestapochauns.

The Gestapochauns live in the dark, battling their ancient rat enemies with teeny bullwhips. Shortly after we meet them, the author lets us know that these are not just any Nazi leprechauns. These are psychic Nazi leprechauns who enjoy S&M, are covered with scars from pleasure/pain sessions with their creator, were trained as sex slaves for full-sized human men, and are actually stunted fetuses taken from Jewish concentration camp victims. And one of them is named Adolph.

While all this information is being hosed into the reader's eyes like a geyser of crazy, this book rockets from 0 to 60 on the loony meter and overdelivers on practically every level. From the moment the Gestapochauns play a mean practical joke on the old Irish washerwoman who works in the kitchen to the moment that the lawyer/fiancé realizes exactly what the Nazi leprechaun named Greta is up to in his pants, it's one fifty-page freakout that's firing on every cylinder.

The book's original hardback cover by Paul Bacon featured merely a tiny foot.

Sadly, the Gestapochauns are completely absent from the last thirty pages of the book. The author devoted the remaining pages to a discrete psychic battle that takes place in the dreams of the non-psychic, non-Nazi, non-leprechaun members of the cast. In other words, the Boring People. Yet Christopher and his Gestapochauns fly so high and so far in those middle passages that they practically touch the sun.

No matter what book I read next, the Gestaopchauns clung to my gray folds, whispering to me in my sleep: *What else has been forgotten?* After some late-night googling brought me to Will Errickson's *Too Much Horror Fiction* blog, I blacked out. One year later, I woke up squatting in the middle of an aisle at Sullivan's Trade-a-Book in the heart of South Carolina, surrounded by piles of musty horror paperbacks. Apparently I was buying them. Apparently I was reading them. Apparently I was addicted.

The books I love were published during the horror paperback boom that started in the late '60s, after *Rosemary's Baby* hit the big time. Their reign of terror ended in the early '90s, after the success of *Silence of the Lambs* convinced marketing departments to scrape the word *horror* off spines and glue on the word *thriller* instead. Like *The Little People*, these books had their flaws, but they offered such wonders. When's the last time you read about Jewish monster brides, sex witches from the fourth dimension, flesh-eating moths, homicidal mimes, or golems stalking Long Island? Divorced from current trends in publishing, these out-of-print paperbacks feel like a breath of fresh air. Get ready to meet some of my new favorite writers: Elizabeth Engstrom. Joan Samson. Bari Wood. The Lovecraftian apocalypse of Brian McNaughton. The deeply strange alternate universe of William W. Johnstone. Brenda Brown Canary, whose *The Voice of the Clown* is one of the few books to actually make my jaw drop. You'll hear the dark whisperings of Ken Greenhall, the gothic Southern twang of Michael McDowell, the clipped British accent of James Herbert, the visionary chants of Kathe Koja, and the clinical drone of Michael Blumlein.

The book you're holding is a road map to the horror Narnia I found hidden in the darkest recesses of remote bookstores—a weird, wild, wonderful world that feels totally alien today, and not just because of the trainloads of killer clowns. In these books from the '70s and '80s, doctors swap smokes with patients while going over their ultrasounds, housewives are diagnosed as having "too much imagination," African Americans are sometimes called "negroes," and parents swoon in terror at the suggestion that they have a "test tube baby."

These books, written to be sold in drugstores and supermarkets, weren't worried about causing offense and possess a jocular, straightforward, "let's get it on" attitude toward sex. Many were published before the AIDS epidemic, at the height of the Swinging '70s, and they're unapologetic about the idea that adults don't need much of an excuse to take off their clothes and hop into bed.

Though they may be consigned to dusty dollar boxes, these stories are timeless in the way that truly matters: they will not bore you. Thrown into the rough-and-tumble marketplace, the writers learned they had to earn every reader's attention. And so they delivered books that move, hit hard, take risks, go for broke. It's not just the covers that hook your eyeballs. It's the writing, which respects no rules except one: always be interesting.

So grab a flashlight and come wander down these dark aisles. The shelves are dusty, the lighting is dim, and there's no guarantee you'll come back unchanged or come back at all. All you need is a map and you're ready to take a tour of the paperbacks from hell.

PROLOGUE

To appreciate the transformation that overtook horror fiction in the 1970s and '80s, let's consider the state of the genre a decade earlier.

More than any other genre, horror fiction is a product of its time, and the '60s were a runaway train, smashing through every social value, cultural construct, and national myth at 500 m.p.h., leaving smoking rubble in its wake. The United States officially entered the Vietnam War. A wave of assassinations killed President John F. Kennedy, Martin Luther King Jr., Malcolm X, and Robert F. Kennedy. Riots sparked by police brutality broke out in Detroit, Harlem, Rochester, and Philadelphia. More riots shook D.C., Chicago, Omaha, Minneapolis, and Baltimore. Buddhist monks set themselves on fire to protest the war; civil rights activists were dragged off buses and beaten; police dogs, tear gas, and fire hoses were turned on peaceful protestors; bombs killed children in churches while the corpses of civil rights workers were hauled out of the Mississippi mud. Birth control pills hit the market, the Vatican liberalized the Catholic Church, the New Pentecostal movement sparked outbreaks of glossolalia (speaking in tongues) in Ivy League colleges all over the Northeast. And a belief that we were living in the End Times spread across America almost as fast as Hugh Hefner was opening Playboy Clubs.

Horror movies responded with polite vampires in velvet capes. Mainstream movies were being mutated by the French New Wave and Akira Kurosawa's samurai spirit, while biker flicks flipped the bird at square society. Horror movies continued their zomboid shuffle, unaffected by the culture around them. Hammer Films offered dusty vampires shrouded in murky mist, and William Castle's hokey dime-store gimmicks were aimed squarely at kids. On TV, *The Munsters* and *The Addams Family* plodded through their paces to a mechanized laugh track, while the middle-aged vampires of *Dark Shadows* stalked cardboard sets.

But if horror movies and television shows were stuck in the '50s, horror publishing was trapped in the '30s. While mainstream publishers were on fire with

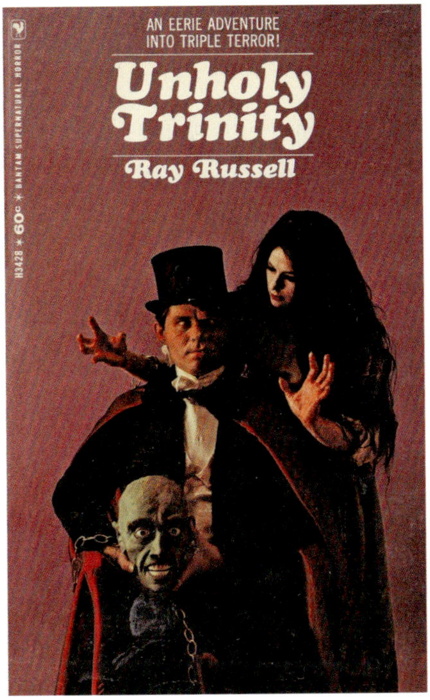

The '60s were rocking, but horror paperbacks got covers that were fusty, musty, and downright dusty.

books like Truman Capote's chilling true-crime shocker *In Cold Blood*, Jacqueline Susann's titillating *Valley of the Dolls*, and Joseph Heller's *Catch-22*, the horror genre was taking its cues from the pulps of yesteryear. These books rarely even used the word *horror* on covers, instead offering "eerie adventure," "chilling adventure," "tales of the unexpected," and "stories of the weird." Even the work of Shirley Jackson, the empress of American horror fiction, was sold with covers that made her books look like gothic romances.

It's not that people weren't buying books. After crashing in the 1950s, the paperback market surged back less than a decade later when college students turned Ballantine's paperback editions of *The Lord of the Rings* into a zeitgeist-sized hit. Bantam Books reprinted pulp adventures of Doc Savage from the '30s and '40s, adding lush, photorealistic, fully painted covers by James Bama. And there was an early-'60s "Burroughs Boom" when publishers discovered that twenty-eight of Edgar Rice Burroughs's books had fallen into the public domain. Suddenly, thirty-year-old Tarzan and John Carter of Mars novels were hitting stands, with new covers painted by Frank Frazetta and Richard Powers, alongside Conan reprints.

Yet for all that activity, horror appeared nowhere on best-seller lists. Horror was for children. It was pulp. If it was any good, it couldn't possibly be horror and so was rebranded as a "thrilling tale." Horror seemed to have no future because it was trapped in the past. That was all about to change, and already there were signs that something was stirring. They were found in the romance section of the bookstore.

Women Running from Houses

A terrified woman flees a dark house. One window glows against stormy midnight skies. Somewhere, someone is brooding. Between 1960 and 1974, thousands of these covers appeared on paperback racks as gothic romances became the missing link between the gothic literature of the eighteenth and nineteenth centuries and the paperback horror of the '70s and '80s.

It all started in 1959 when Ace editor Jerry Gross went to his parents' house for Sunday dinner and noticed that his mom was reading Daphne du Maurier's novel *Rebecca*. He asked why she was reading a book from 1938. "Honey," she said, "They don't write like that anymore."

Intrigued, Gross holed up in the New York Public Library and combed through *Book Review Digest*, studying the "gothic romance" category. He noticed that none of the books were currently in print, and none had ever appeared in paperback. He bought their paperback rights in bulk and in 1960 published *Thunder Heights* by Phyllis Whitney and *Mistress of Mellyn* by Victoria Holt, whose agent had pushed her to revive the gothic romances of the 19th century.

Gothic romances were adult fairy tales. Young governesses appeared at glowering ancestral piles and fell in love with the dark, brooding masters of the house. There was murder, confinement, and ancient curses. Dark secrets piled up at an alarming rate. In the end, the young governess fell into the arms of the dark lord, realizing that her confused feelings of attraction and revulsion could only be love.

Peak gothic was 1960 to 1974, and authors like Barbara Michaels, Victoria Holt, and Mary Stewart sold in the millions. But the tide began to turn in 1972 when Avon editor Nancy Coffey grabbed a manuscript out of the slush pile and

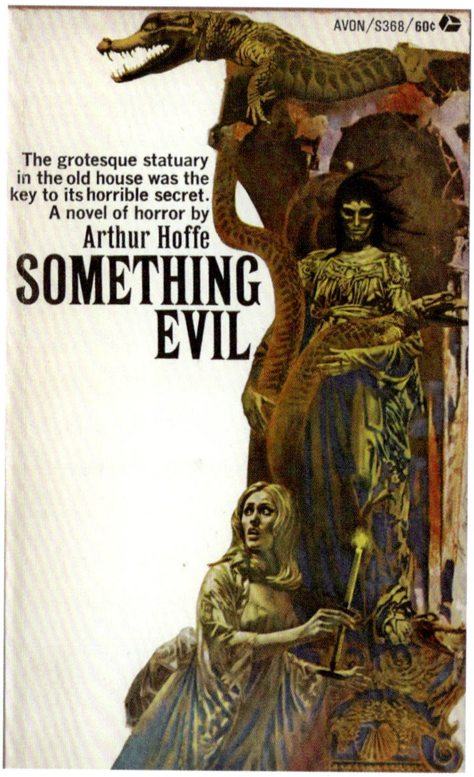

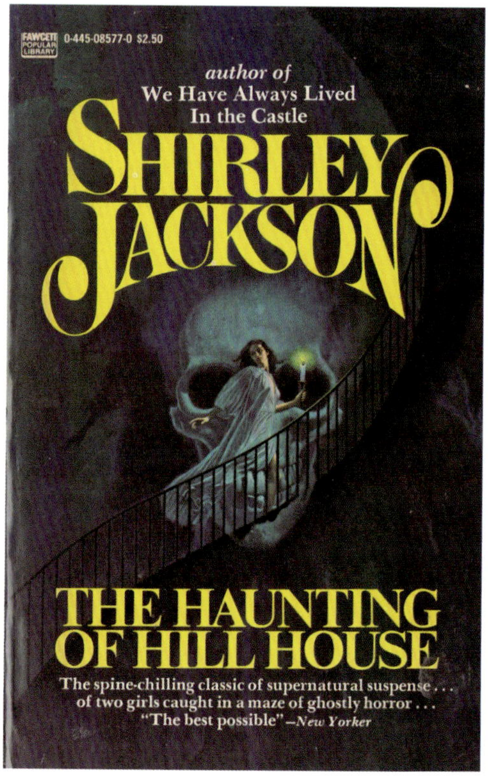

discovered she couldn't put it down. It was Kathleen Woodiwiss's *The Flame and the Flower*, and it became the first bodice ripper, a variety of historical romance featuring more explicit passion. It sold 2.6 million copies. By 1978 the gothic romance had been chained in the attic and starved to death by its younger, sexier competition.

When Gross came up with his idea to publish a line of gothic romances, he drafted a memo to his art director about the covers. "I want a category format that my mother and aunts would be proud to be seen reading," he wrote. "Make the heroine look like a very refined upper-class blond young woman with good cheekbones. . . . She's running towards you . . . behind her is a dark castle with one light in the window, usually in the tower. Make the tower tall and thick. Believe me, they'll get the phallic imagery."

Variations on this formula buried bookshelves for over a decade and had an enormous impact on the first wave of paperback horror covers. Women in diaphanous gowns holding candles, dark houses, stormy skies, and a reliance on the more ominous end of the color spectrum became trademarks. Hair, clouds, gowns, and landscapes dissolved into abstract swirls, light was luminous, darkness was tangible, compositions were dynamic.

Gothic romances seeded readers' imaginations for the horror boom that was on the horizon. Brooding, shadowy mysteries were relocated to the domestic sphere, turning every home into a haunted castle and every potential bride into a potential victim. The blood of the resilient gothic heroine would flow in the veins of '70s and '80s heroines fighting to save their souls from Satan, or were-sharks. And were-sharks were coming. Because over on the other side of the bookrack, pulp fiction was getting interested in the occult.

A Mod Approach to Demon-Fighting

The Guardians were pulp adventurers right out of the '30s, juiced with the trendy occult fascination of the late '60s, when suddenly everybody wanted to know your sign and Parker Brothers was selling Ouija boards in toy stores. Anton LaVey's Church of Satan opened its doors in San Francisco in 1966; a year later the Rolling Stones released *Their Satanic Majesties Request*, and the year after that came their song "Sympathy for the Devil." By 1969, the cover of *Time* magazine was talking about "Astrology and the New Cult of the Occult." Pulp was ready to cash in.

The totally macho moniker "Peter Saxon" was a group pen name for a bunch of British authors (W. Howard Baker, Rex Dolphin, and Wilfred McNeilly, among others) who churned out ersatz pulp novels with fully painted covers that looked like all the other pulp reprints on the stands. Baker had used the Saxon pen name to write some popular installments of the Sexton Blake detective series, and by many accounts he was the mastermind who ensured that his cabal of Guardian ghost writers hit their quota of nubile flesh, gratuitous violence, and sexy swinging.

The six Guardian books were about square-jawed, tweed-and-blackbriar-pipe types investigating haunted houses, underwater vampires, voodoo cults, and Australians. Sort of like *Scooby-Doo*, only with more orgies. Occult detectives had been literary superstars in the late nineteenth and early twentieth centuries, but this was their first major upgrade to Swinging London, and the books read like Hammer horror films gone mod.

On the frontlines of the fight against "Black Magic, Satanism, Necromancy, Witchcraft, Sorcery, Voodoo, Vampirism" was Steven Kane, the square-jawed occult expert and judo master. He was joined by hypochondriac private investigator Lionel Marks, Anglican priest Father John Dyball, and the exotic and alluring miniskirted psychic Anne Ashby, whose silver wrist cuffs gave her heightened psychic perceptions.

The Guardians logged their adventures in the *Journal of Evil* while their enormous cat, Bubastis, lurked about lapping up sherry. They discovered where evil dwelt by dowsing a road map, then zipped off in their Jaguars and Land Rovers to battle Scottish Death Dwarves, voodoo caverns located beneath the streets of London, and sinister covens of Glasgow beatniks. In *The Vampires of Finistere*, their best adventure, a young bride-to-be is abducted from under her boyfriend's nose during a mysterious pagan fertility festival in Brittany. Underwater vampires are to blame, and Steven Kane has to battle wolves and were-sharks and even lead an army of dolphins against the Drowned City of Ker-Ys before the climactic storming of an ancient castle.

The Guardians were transitional figures between pulp and horror, running around socking Satan worshippers in the jaw. But underneath their adventures runs a disquieting river of occultism that delivers moments of true horrific frisson. The Guardians were training wheels, getting readers used to horror as something everyday city dwellers might encounter rather than an outside force from another country, softening them up for the birth of the big demonic baby to come.

JEFFREY CATHERINE JONES

Jeffrey Catherine Jones, the artist behind these decadent covers, got her first gig on an Edgar Rice Burroughs book because she could imitate the dark, doomy dynamism of Frank Frazetta (whose hard-rocking art graced almost every book and album cover of the era). Jones eventually made art for everyone from *Screw* magazine to DC Comics. She found her own dreamy style, combining Art Nouveau influences with Frazetta's muscularity to depict liquid human forms in delicate landscapes that kept threatening to dissolve into purely abstract Rorschach blots. From 1975 to 1979, Jones shared studio space with Michael Kaluta, Barry Windsor-Smith, and Bernie Wrightson, and together the four of them helped reinvent American fantasy illustration. Jones was born male, but identified as a woman, and began hormone therapy in 1998. When she passed away in 2011, she had painted at least 150 covers.

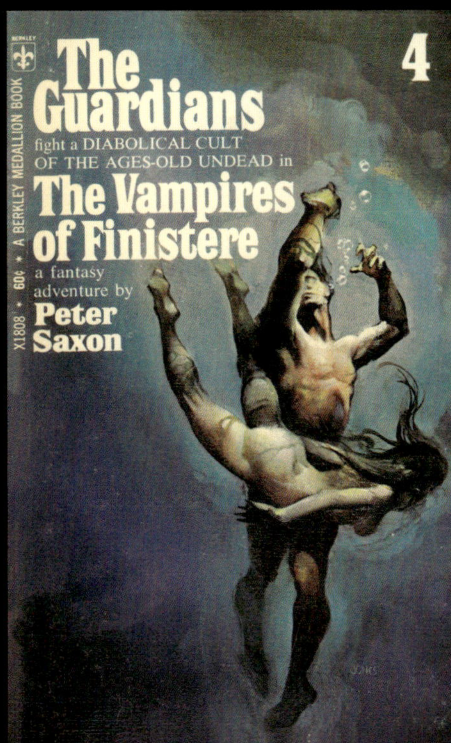

HAIL,

CHAPTER ONE

SATAN

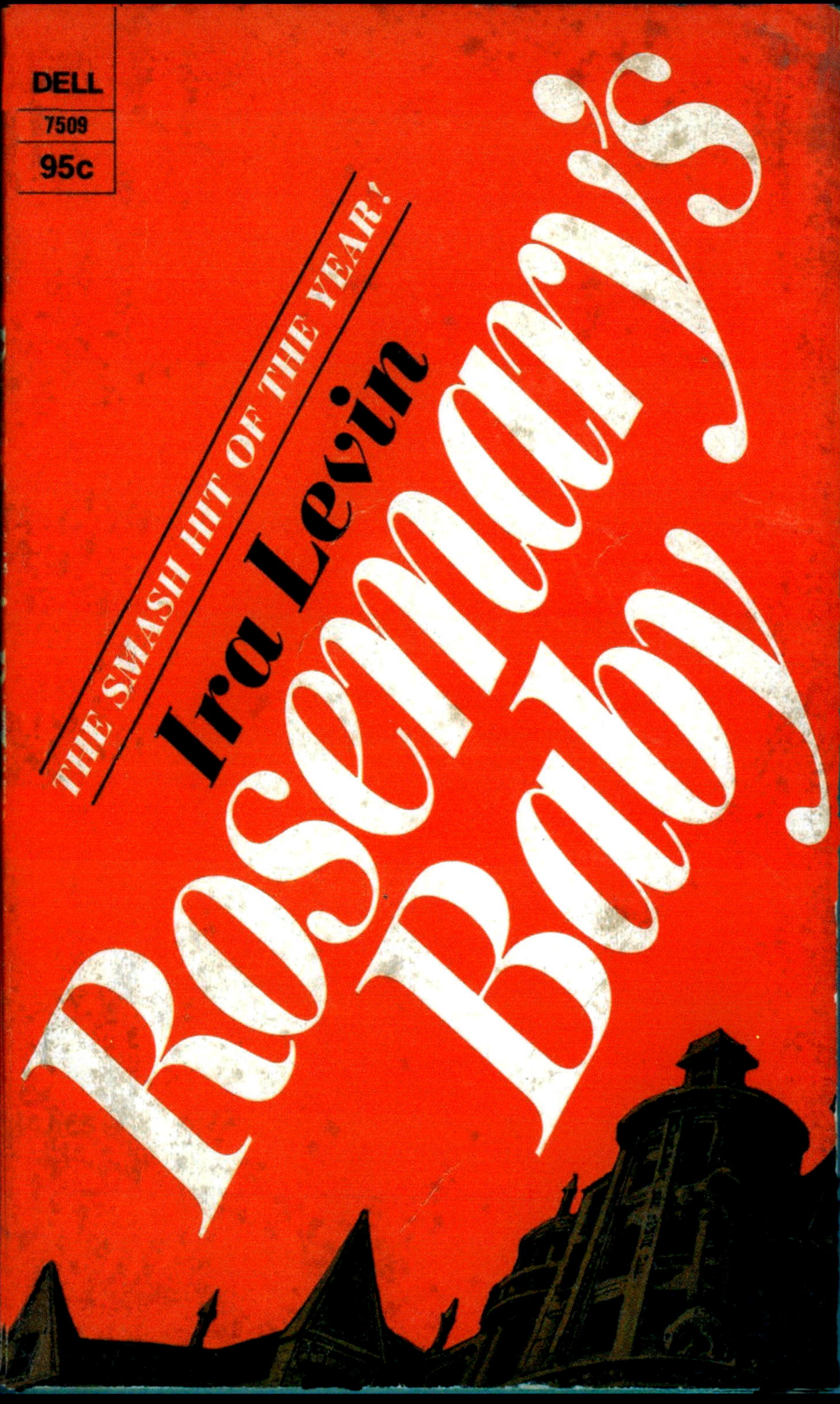
DELL
7509
95c
THE SMASH HIT OF THE YEAR!
Ira Levin
Rosemary's Baby

Unholy Trinity: *Rosemary's Baby* (1967), *The Other* (1971), and *The Exorcist* (1971) spawned a new era in horror fiction.

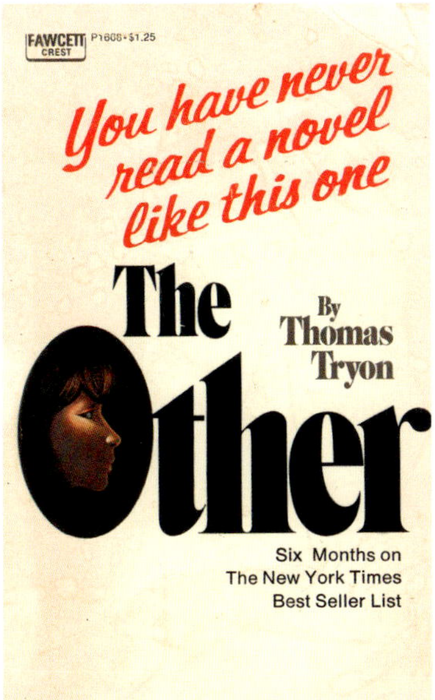

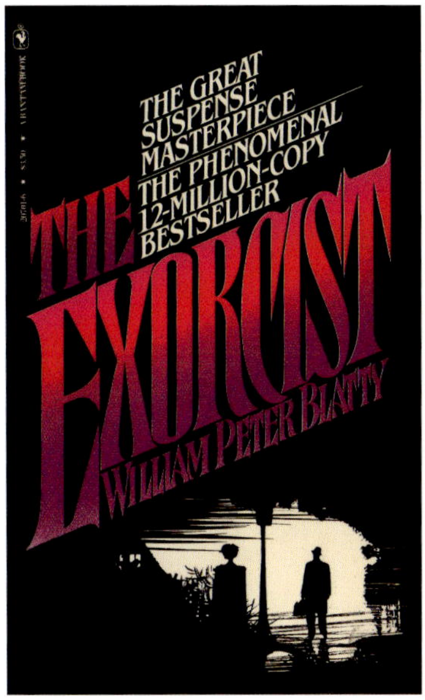

Between April 1967 and December 1973, everything changed.

In a little more than five years, horror fiction became fit for adults, thanks to three books. Ira Levin's *Rosemary's Baby*, Thomas Tryon's *The Other*, and William Peter Blatty's *The Exorcist* were the first horror novels to grace *Publishers Weekly*'s annual best-seller list since Daphne du Maurier's *Rebecca* in 1938. And except for three books by Peter "Jaws" Benchley, they'd be the only horror titles on that list until Stephen King's *The Dead Zone* in 1979. All three spawned movies and, most important, set the tone for the next two decades of horror publishing.

Horror was for nobodies when Ira Levin—a scriptwriter with a single book (1953's *A Kiss before Dying*) and a failed Broadway musical (*Drat! The Cat!*) to his name—sat down to write a novel about a woman who gives birth to the devil. A minimalist masterpiece written in deft, surgical sentences, *Rosemary's Baby* became a massive best seller. The film rights were sold before the book was even published. Four months after the book hit the stands, Roman Polanski rolled cameras on an adaptation that would earn an Oscar. The film, described as "sick and obscene" by the *Los Angeles Times* and given a "C for Condemned" rating by the Catholic Church, wound up saving Paramount Studios from bankruptcy.

Rosemary's Baby was a spark to the heart for horror fiction, but the corpse really began to boogie in June 1971, when Thomas Tryon's *The Other* and William Peter Blatty's *The Exorcist* simultaneously made the *New York Times* Best-Seller List. Fueled by amphetamines and written during a feverish ten-month spree, Blatty's book was dead on arrival in bookstores until a last-minute guest cancellation earned him a sudden appearance on *The Dick Cavett Show*. A blockbuster was born. For eleven weeks, *The Exorcist* and *The Other* held the #1 and #3 marks on the *New York Times* Best-Seller List. *The Other* slipped off after twenty-four weeks; *The Exorcist* would hold on for a whopping fifty-five.

Four million copies of *The Exorcist* were sold before William Friedkin's motion

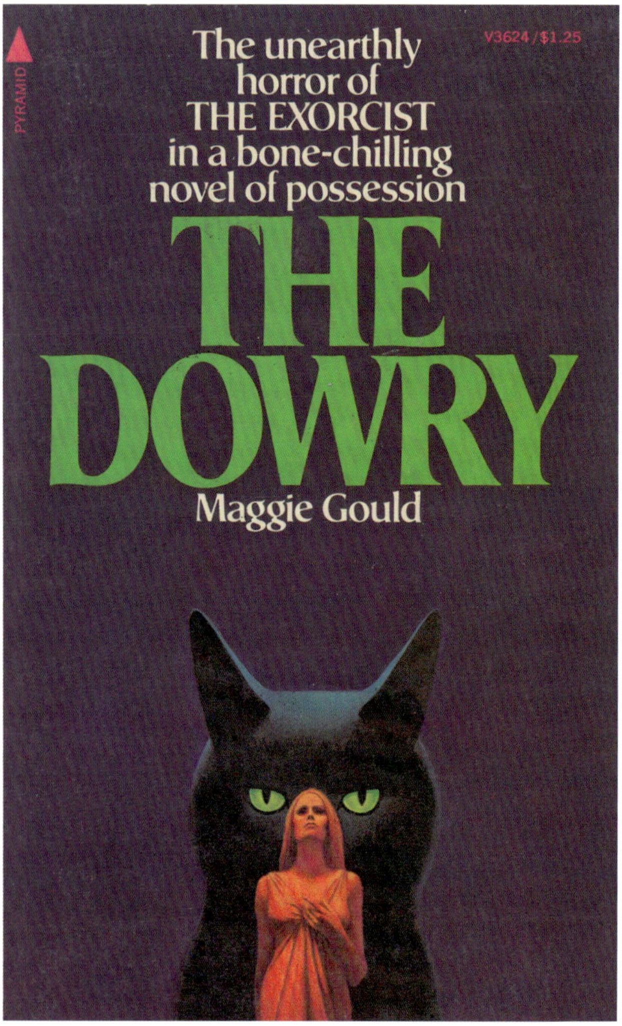

picture adaptation debuted in December 1973 and became a cultural landmark. The film was the second-highest-grossing movie of the year and won two Academy Awards.

Tryon had what *People* magazine called "a relentlessly mediocre acting career" before he starred in dictatorial director Otto Preminger's *The Cardinal*, an experience that drove the future author to a nervous breakdown and made him swear to become a producer so that he could always fire the director. No one cared about his treatment for a movie about evil twins called *The Other*, however, so he locked himself in a room for eighteen months and emerged having repurposed his screenplay into a novel. Working the promotional circuit like a pro, Tryon turned his book into the ninth best-selling book of 1971.

In contrast to *Rosemary's Baby*, both *The Other* and *The Exorcist* are overwritten. Tryon delivers an afternoon "spread lavishly, like a picnic on a cloth of light and shade," and Blatty begins his book, "Like the brief doomed flare of exploding suns that registers dimly on blind men's eyes, the beginning of the horror passed almost unnoticed." But Blatty writes excellent dialogue and he believes deeply in his material. For his part, Tryon underplays the horror so that it sneaks up on the reader, emerging from a thicket of epic-poetic descriptions of nature. By the time you're ambushed by Tryon's severed fingers, pitchforks hidden in hay lofts, and dead babies floating in jars, it's too late. Plus, the end includes a *Twilight Zone*–worthy twist that kept readers talking and has since influenced a hundred unreliable narrators.

These three books—one a precision thriller about the devil impregnating a woman on the Upper West Side, one a blood-and-thunder religious melodrama proclaiming that Satan wanted our children, and one a baroque and lyrical meditation about evil twins and killer kids—shaped everything that came after.

Rosemary's Baby started the pot boiling, but the publication of *The Exorcist* and *The Other* threw gasoline all over the stove. Whether it was a reprint from

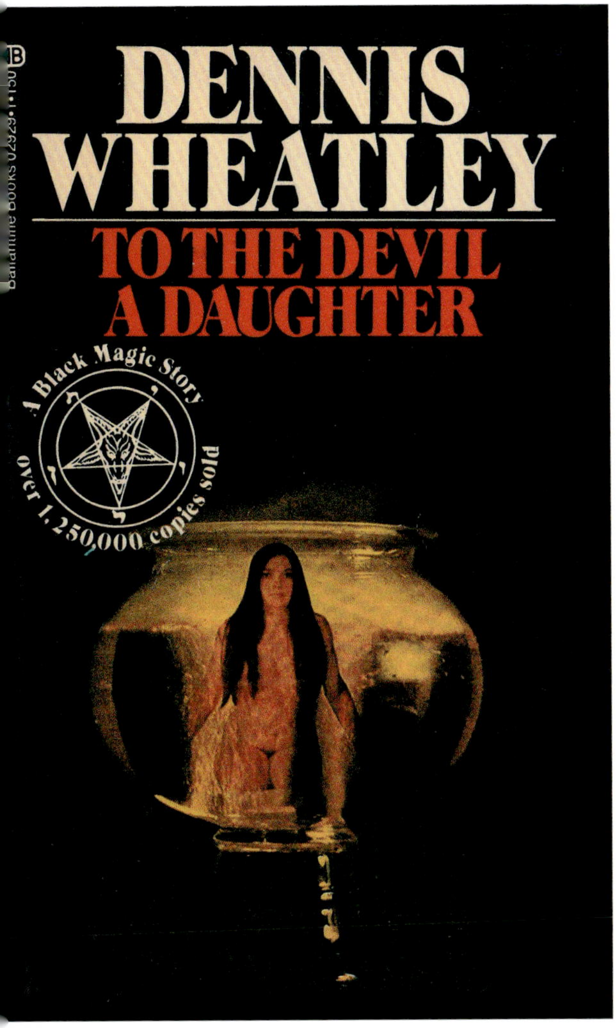

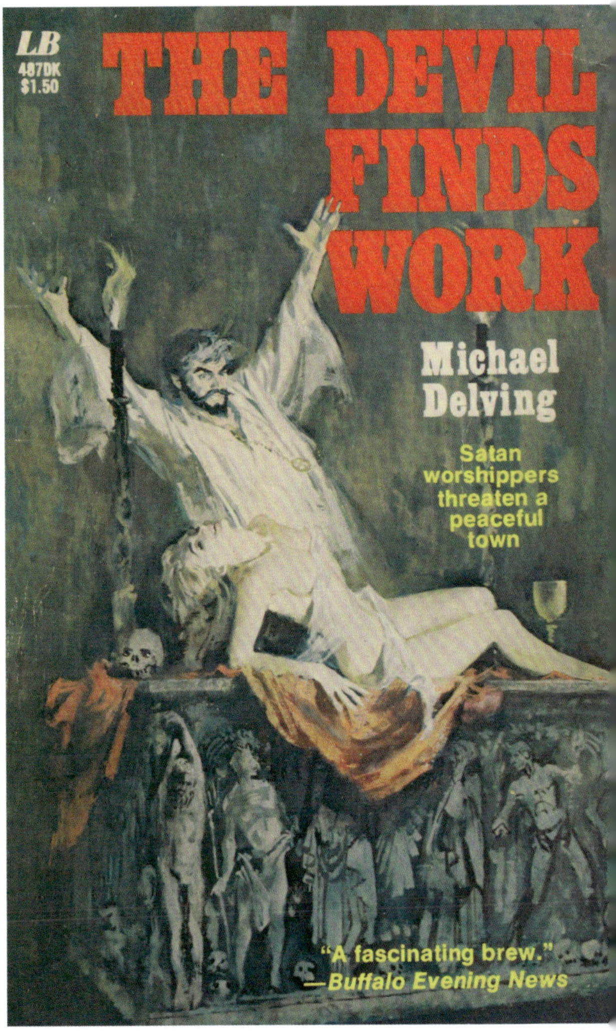

Satan sold, whether it was new covers slapped on old books (*The Dowry*, 1949; *To the Devil a Daughter,* 1953) or an occult cover applied to a mystery about antique collectors (*The Devil Finds Work,* 1968).

1949, a reissue of Dennis Wheatley black magic books from 1953, or a brand-new novel, soon every paperback needed Satan on the cover and a blurb comparing it to *The Exorcist* or *Rosemary's Baby* or *The Other*. It didn't matter if it was a murder mystery, an alternate-history sci-fi novel, or even an old pulp reprint—Satan was the secret ingredient that made sales surge.

Tryon's influence would take a few years to blossom, but after the one-two punch of *Rosemary's Baby* and *The Exorcist*, suddenly all anyone wanted to talk about was the Devil.

The Devil's Decade

Descended from the pulps, occult horror novels at the dawn of the '70s still felt like places where *The Guardians* would feel at home (see page 14). But after *The Exorcist* hit movie screens in 1974, horror fiction scraped its pulp influences off its shoe like a piece of old gum. These books still featured cults and black magic, but now Satan wasn't a threat that you met in remote mansions or on Jamaican plantations. Now the devil was within. Satan was no longer your next-door neighbor—he was you.

Marketing departments embraced Satan with gusto. The third novel from literary celebrity Beryl Bainbridge featured two creepy kids lurking beneath an enthusiastic comparison to *The Exorcist*, while avant-garde writer Hubert Selby Jr.'s book about a serial adulterer, *The Demon*, displayed a blurb comparing it to *Rosemary's Baby*. But a whole lot of authors willingly dipped their toes into the horror waters, with surprising success.

Classy Southern novelist Anne Rivers Siddons wrote *The House Next Door*, which remains one of the best haunted house novels in the genre. Joan Samson's sole book before her early death from cancer was *The Auctioneer*, another genre classic, and Mendal W. Johnson managed to write only *Let's Go Play at the Adams*' (page 62) before he passed away. Herman Raucher wrote the landmark coming-of-age novel *Summer of '42* before he delivered his only horror novel, the creepy *Maynard's House*, about a Vietnam vet taking on a witch in rural Maine. And William Hjortsberg stayed with literary fiction throughout his career . . . except for one influential sidestep: *Falling Angel*.

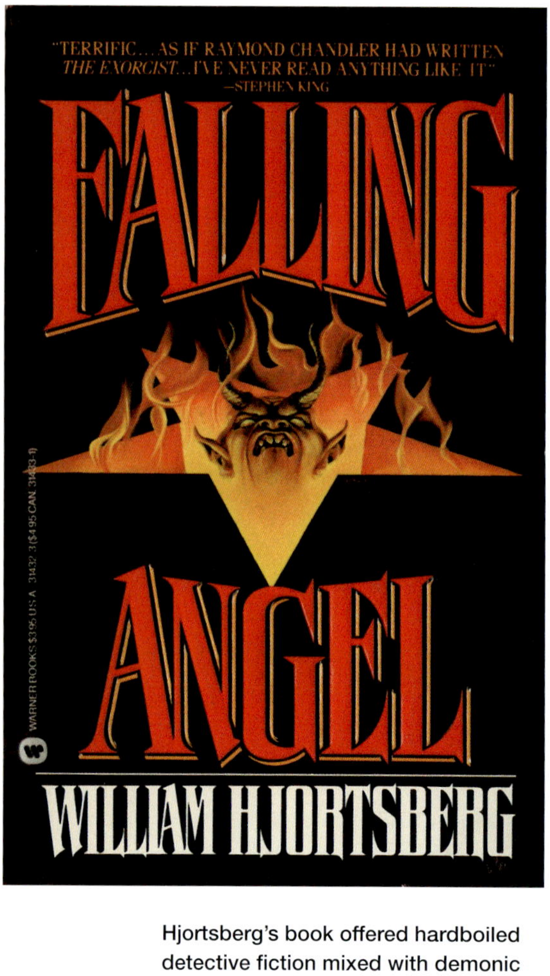

Hjortsberg's book offered hardboiled detective fiction mixed with demonic identity theft.

Somewhere between *The Guardians* and Michael Avellone's *Satan Sleuth* (page 25) in concept, Hjortsberg's novel depicts a private investigator who falls through the surface of the waking world into a nightmare of satanic sacrifice. The '70s saw the reinvention of the classic private-eye character by everyone, from Jonathan Fast in his shaggy dog novel *The Inner Circle* to Joseph Hansen and his gay detective Dave Brandstetter. But Hjortsberg delivered his hardboiled noir straight, tongue nowhere near cheek.

P.I. Harry Angel is hired to find a missing jazz singer, Johnny Favorite, who may be trying to pull an insurance scam. As Harry closes in on his target, everyone he interviews is murdered. It seems that Favorite sold his soul to the devil—and is maybe trying to welch on the deal. And maybe Johnny Favorite is really Harry Angel.

If you can get past the surface silliness—like people meeting at 666 Fifth Avenue and Satan stand-ins with names like Louis Cyphre—the result is a doom-choked detective story that's one part Philip Marlowe, one part *Oedipus Rex*, and one part *Satanic Bible*. The horror isn't that Harry Angel might be Johnny Favorite, or that Johnny Favorite might have sold his soul, but that Harry Angel might not be who he thinks he is. He may not be a brave World War II veteran. He might in fact be a murderer. Everyone in this book has a double identity, leading to the chilling matter at the heart of all satanic possession fiction: if Satan can get inside us, then maybe we aren't who we thought we were. Maybe we're much, much worse.

As '70s Satan bought and sold souls on the open market, some trends emerged. The bad guys were cultured and elegant. They had violet eyes, black dogs, and vast libraries of antique tomes, and when they died their souls slipped into good guys' bodies. Struggling reporters got a chance to become famous concert pianists, flailing movie distributors got their dream apartment, traumatized car crash survivors got freedom from their guilt and a new lover, all in exchange for giving away their identities, their selves, their souls.

Every book was "better than *Rosemary's Baby*," "more terrifying than *The Exorcist*," and "in the tradition of *The Other*!" Read in the right order, the titles painted a grim portrait of Satan marching from free-spirited young demon to middle-aged ennui: *Satan's Holiday, Satan's Gal, Satan's Seed, Satan's Child, Satan's Bride, Satan Sublets, The Sorrows of Satan, Satan's Mistress, Satan: His Psychotherapy and His Cure*.

Publishers deployed desperate gimmicks in order to stand out. Fred Mustard Stewart's *Mephisto Waltz* came with a 45 rpm recording of the titular "Mephisto Waltz" by Franz Liszt. TV ads ran for Joan Samson's *The Auctioneer* and John Saul's *Suffer the Children*. Cover art got bigger, gaudier, and racier, expanding into die-cut covers with stepback art. Inside those covers, authors competed to see who could be a more turned-on, now-era, groove daddy. *Exorcism* (page 27) featured possession by LSD, *The Inner Circle* (page 28) was all about Beverly Hills and movie stars, and *The Stigma* (page 27) saw a witch choked to death on a three-foot-long demon dick.

The history of sixteenth-century Scotland, where witches were hung every Monday, Wednesday, and Friday, was the basis for this last as well as early folk-horror novel *Satan's Child* and Jane Parkhurst's *Isobel* (next page), which was based on the life of Isobel Gowdie, the only witch ever to freely confess to her crimes.

Demonic incubuses and succubuses slithered out of Italian discotheques to send entire apartment buildings into sexual frenzies and to impregnate women with their demon seed. And the most turned-on, now-era, groove daddy of them all was a forgotten hero known as the Satan Sleuth.

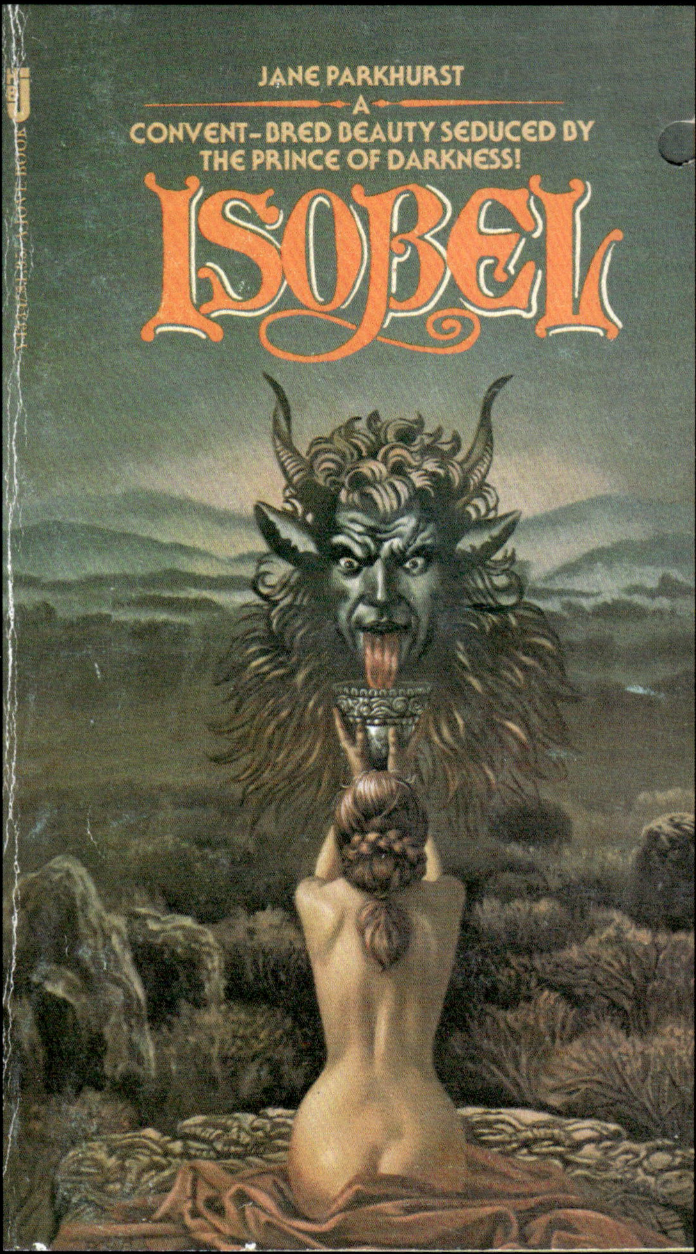

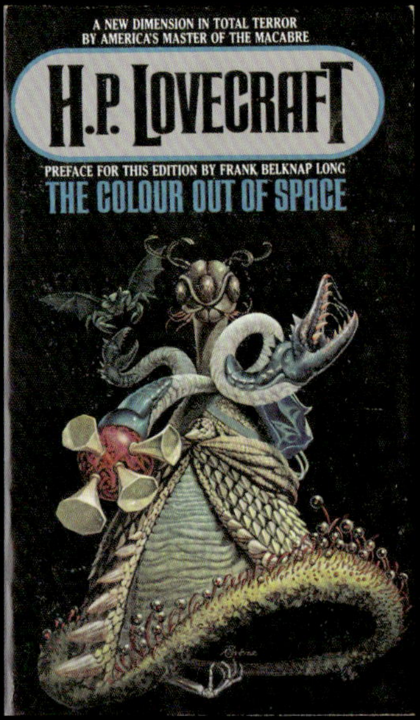

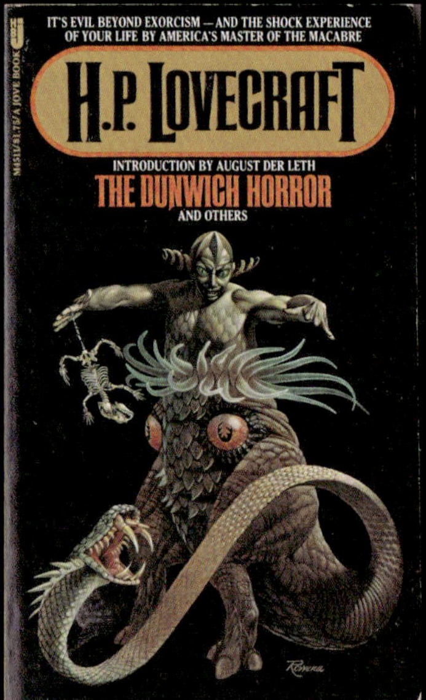

Isobel's electrifying cover painting is the first horror art sold by Rowena Morrill, one of the all-time greats. Better known for her work in science fiction and fantasy, Morrill also painted covers for a freaky series of Lovecraft reprints from Jove. And she remains the only artist in the field whose work has graced not only the cover of Metallica's greatest bootleg album (*No Life 'til Power*) but also the walls of one of Saddam Hussein's love nests.

The Greatest Man in the Whole Entire World

Call him Troy Conway. Call him Vance Stanton. Call him Edwina Noone, or Dorothea Nile, or Jean-Anne de Pre, or any of the seventeen pseudonyms he used to write his more than two hundred novels. He was Michael Avallone, and by his own estimation he was the "King of the Paperback" and the "Fastest Typewriter in the East." Avallone wrote detective fiction, and gothics, and *Partridge Family* tie-ins, and the novelization of *Friday the 13th Part III* in 3-D. And when Satan got hot, he wrote all three slim volumes of *The Satan Sleuth* series for Warner Books, published between November 1974 and January 1975.

Avallone's protagonist Philip St. George III "makes even Robert Redford look vapid." He is "one hundred and eighty-five pounds of whipcord muscles" with "a mind bordering on Einstein IQ." St. George has "scaled Everest, mastered the Matterhorn, [and] located a lost tribe of headhunters in the Amazon," but now he receives a phone call that his fiancée Dorothea Daley has been murdered. The killers? Three devil worshippers who are "really sick, demented, half-mad creatures from another universe. Some other planet. They were not human."

When he sees the carnage (worse than "the Tate-Manson killing orgy of '68"), St. George develops two white streaks in his hair. "The bastards!" rages his lawyer. "They should fall into Hell with no clothes on." St. George knows who the culprits are: "Hippies, drop outs, draft dodgers, left-wing radicals, right-wing militants, Jesus Freaks, Devil worshippers, generation gappers, motorcycle weirdos—the whole shebang." He balances the scales with these cultists (one of whom is "as gay as a green goose when the asses were down") using LSD and hand grenades.

Avellone planned two more Satan Sleuth novels—*Vampires Wild* and *Zombie Depot*—but Warner Books never bought them, so he never wrote them. But Philip St. George III lives forever in our hearts, and in our remainder bins.

The Satan Sleuth used karate to take on werewolves and dynamite to take out chic but satanic fashion designers obsessed with short women.

A CHILLING NOVEL OF SEXUAL POSSESSION, AND AN EVIL OLDER THAN TIME...
THE NIGHT VISITOR
LAURA WYLIE
PINNACLE BOOKS 40-398-4 ★ $1.95

DELL • 17716 • 2.25
HER KISSES ARE LIKE FIRE.
HER TOUCH HOLDS THE PROMISE OF HEAVEN.
BUT HELL HAS NO FURY LIKE...
The Succubus
A Gripping Novel of Supernatural Terror
Kenneth Rayner Johnson

CARLYLE CS7058-T
SATAN SUBLETS
JACK YOUNGER

TERROR AWAITS—FOR THOSE WHO SURVIVE A MODERN-DAY PLAGUE...
DARK ADVENT
BRIAN HODGE

1-55817-088-X

Hip chicks with LSD are gateways to Hell in *Exorcism*, while demons with deadly wieners feature in *The Stigma* and *Incubus*. *The Succubus* is based on the Manacled Mormon, a kidnapping case that rocked London in 1977. *Son of Endless Night* is a satanic legal thriller and, despite the cover, *Dark Advent* is a postapocalyptic novel with no Satan at all.

Putting the Cult in Occult

The 1968 Manson murders and the 1970 trial of the Manson family so shocked America that we couldn't wait to get our hands on *Helter Skelter*, the 1974 book by prosecutor Vincent Bugliosi. The biggest best-selling true-crime book in history, its tale of life with Charlie was also a gift for horror novelists, providing a new and timely antagonist: the satanic cult. Until then, satanic covens met in basements or wooded glades, slapping at mosquitos who flew up their black robes. They marched around in circles, hailing Satan the way New Yorkers hail a cab, muttering curses and spells in barely remembered high school Latin.

But thanks to *Helter Skelter*, ritual murder became the highlight of the satanic social season. Consider Joy Fielding's *The Transformation* (which she has since disowned), published only five years after Charles Manson was sentenced to death. In it, young actresses on the make fall under the influence of their great god Tony, who says things like, "To love your family, you must kill them."He encourages his glamorous disciples to break into homes and poop on the carpets. At the book's climax, he sends them to murder every other major character in a genuinely shocking Tate/LaBianca–style home invasion.

In Barney Parrish's *The Closed Circle* thinly veiled versions of Robert Redford, Elizabeth Taylor, Ann-Margret, and Jackie Gleason pick up hitchhikers and murder them to praise Satan and stay famous. And they would have gotten away with it, too, if not for a darn psychic pursuing a "university-level" course in weaving who can tune into their telepathic wavelength. Cannibal cultists in upstate New York kidnap young women in *The Sharing*, and in *The Sacrifice*, fabulously wealthy elbow-patch types obtain extended lives via human sacrifice and are defeated only when a fanatically loyal Yale professor becomes enraged that they stole a book from the university library.

One thing all these books had in common, besides a fanatical devotion to the forces of darkness and a phobic fear of private clubs, was that their characters were as white as the driven snow. Why was Satan only bothering white people? Turns out he wasn't.

Cults are inclusive. The Inner Circle worships the Aztec jaguar god, Tezcatlipoca.

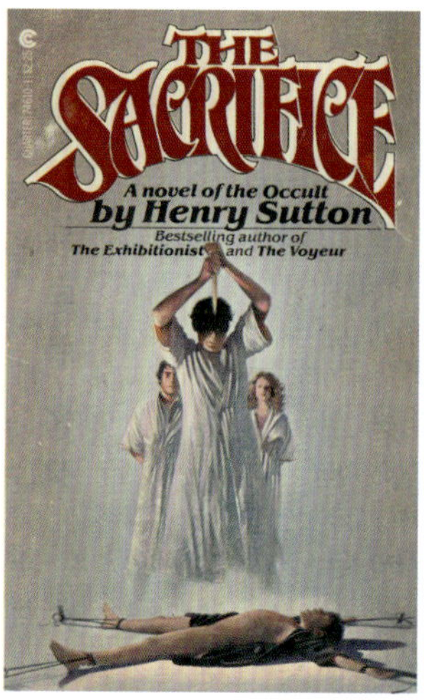

He didn't belong to a cult of kill-crazed Hollywood stars, but he certainly painted the covers of books about them. *The Transformation* and *The Closed Circle* both sport cover art by Ron Sauber, whose gauzy, fluid artwork was a favorite of art directors. Sauber was born and educated in California and then moved to New York City in 1979. Arriving on Halloween, he almost immediately began working for clients ranging from *Twilight Zone* magazine to children's book publishers. He later expanded into painting collectible plates—probably not bearing scenes of cult activity—for which he won great recognition.

Satan Gets Woke

In 1971 another one-two pop culture punch reshaped the era when a pair of low-budget movies, *Sweet Sweetback's Baadasssss Song* and *Shaft*, grossed millions at the box office. Blaxploitation was born! Ready to ride the wave was Holloway House, a cheapjack publisher founded by two white Hollywood publicists in 1959. The company radically changed direction after the Watts riots in 1965, when management saw an underserved audience in the ashes and started cranking out mass-market paperbacks for African American readers.

Holloway House was run with all the ethics of Blackbeard the Pirate, and its iconic authors like Iceberg Slim and Donald Goines earned pennies while the publishers made millions. The company published twelve magazines, including *Players*, an African American version of *Playboy* that was a huge financial success and, for a time, functioned as a soapbox for black liberation. Until the bosses actually read an issue and insisted on removing every article about politics and making the models look as white as possible.

Joseph Nazel was an author, activist, and journalist who edited *Players* for a year and hated every minute of it. Slugging down Jack Daniels, a pistol in his desk drawer, he jammed out a tornado of pulp fiction in a blaze of fury, all of it published by Holloway House. Capable of producing a book in six weeks, Nazel wrote novelizations of blaxploitation flicks like *Black Gestapo* and hardboiled pulp like *Black Fury*. And he never, as far as anyone knew, sent a single submission to another publishing house, remaining weirdly loyal to the people who least valued his talents. In his blaze of pulp production, Nazel had a blaxploitation version of *The Exorcist* ready to smack the racks nine months after the movie premiered in theaters. Meet *The Black Exorcist*.

Barbados Sam and his woman, Sheila, are high priest and priestess of a satanic voodoo cult on the outskirts of Los Angeles. Their pitch is simple: "What the hell has that jive white God and jive honkie religion done for them?" But in a cynical twist, the cult is in fact a front for the Mafia, with Barbados Sam and Sheila forcing true believers to assassinate mob targets. Every inch of Sam and Sheila's scam is fake until they murder a cult traitor (and possible police informant). Sheila's eyes glow green and she becomes possessed by the real Satan. "It was time to move beyond murder for hire. It was time to slaughter at random," the Dark Lord enthuses, dreaming of a race war.

Opposing them is righteous soul brother Reverend Roger Lee, assistant pastor of Resurrection Church of Christ, who used to be a pimp working the streets until he found God. Sheila sprouts cloven hooves and tries to seduce Lee; when that fails, she squats to urinate on his Holy Bible and he whips her bare butt with his belt, driving her into the streets. Meanwhile, a young cultist trying to kick his satanic habit tosses his grandma out the third-story window of a hospital.

Nazel lifts gags from *The Exorcist*, giving them a quick coat of gritty ghetto grime, and there's plenty of padding as mamas spend five pages wailing for their dead babies. But Nazel was an African American man deeply tied to his community, and so *The Black Exorcist*

Holloway House published only two other horror novels: *Devil Dolls* and *The Rootworker*.

BH463 $150

The Black Exorcist

Voodoo rituals and human sacrifices spawned by a cult of Black devil worshippers grips a town in a nightmare of terror!

by JOSEPH NAZEL

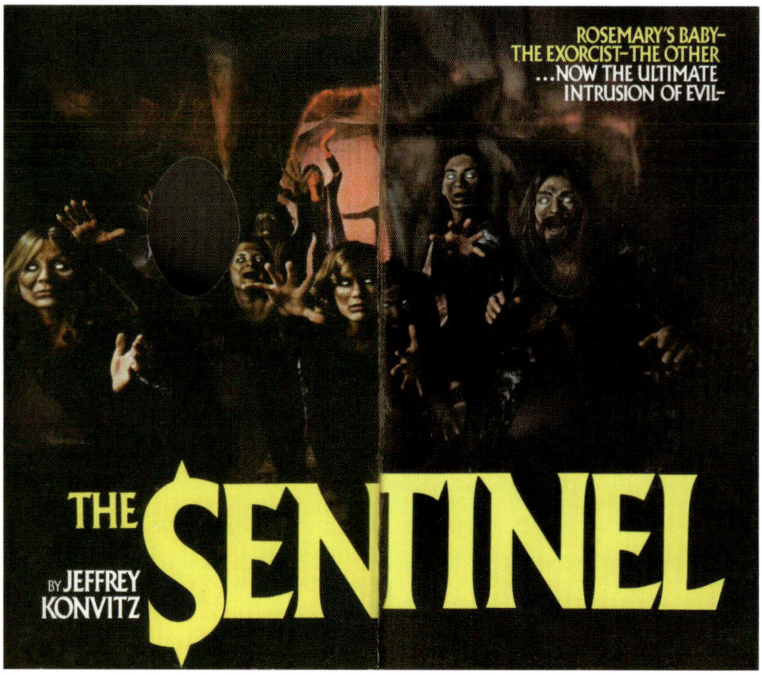

has a real feel for L.A. street life. And any book that gives us a climax where the protagonist is stabbed to death in the face as his cult chants "White is the color of death! Black is life and power!" knows how to deliver the goods to its small sector of the literary marketplace.

Hot under the Collar

Readers couldn't get enough books about spooky Catholics. In the wake of *The Exorcist*, a cry went up from paperback publishers: "Send more priests!" And, lo, did the racks fill with demonic men of the cloth and scary nuns.

For unto us, in 1974, three horror novels were born: *The Black Exorcist* (see previous page), *The Search for Joseph Tully*, and *The Sentinel*. As discussed, *The Black Exorcist* is its own wild West Coast jam, while *Joseph Tully* and *The Sentinel* are set in isolated apartment houses in desolate New York neighborhoods. *Tully* became a cult classic, conjuring up gloomy gothic Gotham atmosphere and delivering a still-potent sting. But *The Sentinel* was a bona fide money train thanks to a moderately successful movie version that featured an all-star cast (John Carradine is Father Halloran! Burgess Meredith is Charles Chazen! Christopher Walken is Detective Rizzo! Jeff Goldblum is Jack! And Ava Gardner is "the Lesbian"!) It also featured a grotty urban hellscape, courtesy of director Michael "Death Wish" Winner, and a famous climax in which the gates of hell spring open and vomit forth a legion of demons played by sideshow freaks, actors with disabilities, and amputees.

Invoking the holy trinity of *The Exorcist*, *Rosemary's Baby*, and *The Other* on its inside cover, *The Sentinel* tells the story of Alison Parker, a top model in New York City who, like all beautiful women in 1970s paperbacks, is troubled by a dark past.

After flying home to attend daddy's funeral, Alison returns to New York

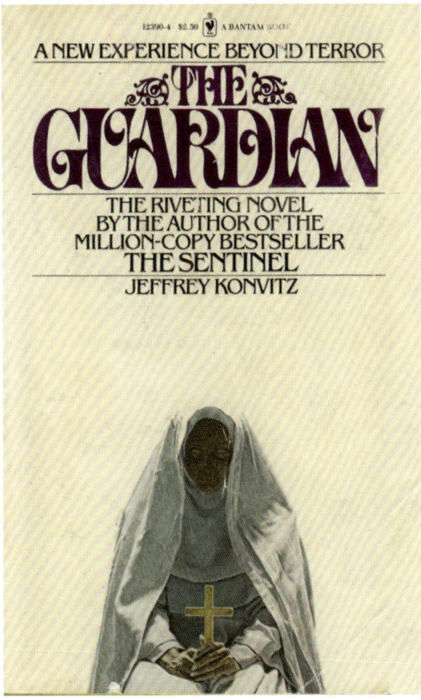

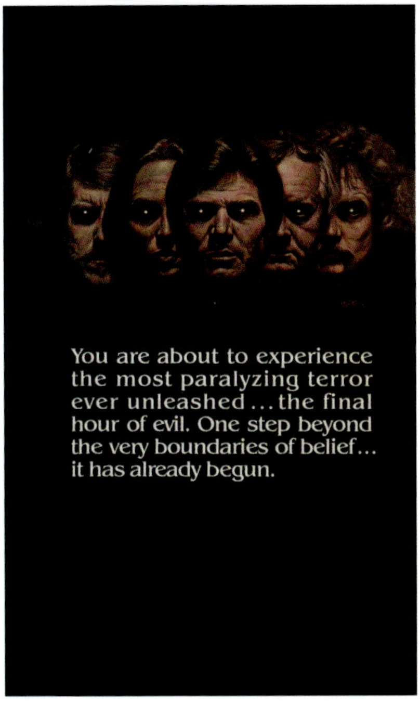

The Guardian featured big action, psychic warfare, and séances gone wrong, but its tired transsexual-panic plot twist left it feeling as flat as a communion wafer.

determined to make a fresh start, move into her own apartment, and forget about sins of the past. She finds a dream pad in an old brownstone that comes complete with antique furniture and creepy neighbors, like lovable old busybody Charles Chazen and his black and white cat Jezebel; the Norwegian lesbians in 2A; and Father Halloran, who sits in his unfurnished apartment on the top floor staring out the window with blind eyes.

After being shocked by her lesbian neighbors ("Masturbation and lesbianism. Right in front of me!") Alison takes to fainting randomly. A doctor excavates the dark secret behind her multiple suicide attempts: when Alison was a kid, she walked in on her father having sex . . . with two women at the same time!!! Young Alison ran away but her father chased her down and tried to strangle her with a crucifix necklace, sending her into a fainting, barfing frenzy that ended only when she kicked him in the nards and renounced the church.

What happens next is that Alison is attacked by the naked ghost of her father, her mind shatters, and her lover confines her to the loony bin like some eighteenth-century country squire chaining up his wife in the attic. After Alison is released, her delicate grasp on sanity slips completely when she confronts the realtor who rented her the apartment.

"Why, Alison," the realtor says, "no one lives in that building but you and Father Halloran."

Alison never stood a chance, thanks to a Catholic conspiracy to groom her as Father Halloran's replacement. The poor guy is ready to retire from guarding the gates of hell, which happen to be conveniently located in this delightful brownstone with period details. The book ends with Alison taking the job and the brownstone being torn down and turned into luxury condos. Which sounds like a cheap punchline until a couple years after the movie, when Konvitz wrote a sequel, *The Guardian* (1979), set in the same high rise.

Readers were particularly fascinated by the priestly vow of celibacy. Surely,

Fifty million American Catholics provided a ready audience for two-fisted tales of priests taking on Satan *(In the Name of the Father)*, heretical cults *(The Night Church)*, and possessed kids *(Shrine)*.

they reasoned, a total denial of sex must mask total sexual perversion. *In the Name of the Father,* by John Zodrow, wallows in the sweet spot where fascination blurred into fetishization. Peter Stamp is the youngest priest in church history, and he's haunted by his vows of celibacy, scourging himself in private and exercising constantly to burn off his dangerous sexual energy. Miraculously able to find water in drought-stricken countries, Father Stamp advocates tirelessly for the liberation of oppressed peoples. But wise readers will instantly see through his lies. Turns out, all Stamp's talk about liberating Central America and the Middle East masks his true agenda: he's the anti-pope, whose liberal Marxist theology will destroy the Church and bring about the apocalypse.

Real-world Vatican infighting always makes for a good plot. Whitley Streiber's *The Night Church* depicts a Catholic Church split between a secret cult of Cathars, who are breeding the antiman to wipe Homo sapiens off the map, and the last surviving vestiges of the Inquisition, who use gruesome blowtorch torture to snuff out the Cathars before their mind-controlled subjects can hump mankind into extinction.

Horror stalwart James Herbert took the Roman Catholic Church to task in *Shrine*: a mute child performs miracles and, before you know it, the holy fathers are ignoring scary nuns, ghosts, and animated statues of the Virgin Mary and instead falling all over themselves to capture the media spotlight. Here the Church is less concerned with helping the poor than with recruiting new congregants to fill its empty pews. Which means the clergy are caught completely off guard when the little girl turns out to be possessed not by the Holy Spirit but by yet another ghost of yet another murdered English witch. It's a theological failure that can only be resolved when an army of zombies claw their way out of the grave during a televised healing session and murder pretty much everyone on live TV.

In 1978, after the thirty-three-day reign of Pope John Paul I, the Catholic Church elected its first non-Italian pope in four hundred years. Pope John Paul II became an instant international celebrity, drawing crowds wherever he went.

The fascination with priest sex met the adoration of JP2 in *Dark Angel*, 1982's overheated hothouse of a novel that tells the story of how the Pope was stalked by a flesh-hungry succubus and how one lone wolf Irish American priest risked everything to slake the she-demon's insatiable thirst for man flesh and save John Paul's celibacy.

Joe O'Meara, a tough Irish kid born to Pennsylvania steelworkers, became a college football star known as "the Wolf" before attending seminary in Boston. Now he functions as valet and bodyguard to Cardinal Ricci, the Pope's right-hand man, who gets humped to death by a succubus in Vatican City. Whoops.

Full of thick-blooming flowers and ripe nightmares wherein hugely pregnant nuns give birth to clawed monsters with the face of Cardinal Ricci, *Dark Angel* exists in a state of maximum hysteria. As for the succubus, Angela Tansa, she drives Porsches and must have sex every seven days in order to stay alive. Her latest Romeo is a Eurotrash aristocrat who says things like, "I want to fuck that fatness out of you!" as Angela gorges on artichokes and Mexican food . . . because she's carrying Cardinal Ricci's baby!

This is the kind of book in which a priest resists fleshy temptation by jamming a nail through his hand, people vomit their souls into toilets, and succubuses ooze black breast milk. And when Joe discovers that the succubus can be destroyed only if she's decapitated at the moment of orgasm, you know this book is about to go so far over the top it achieves orbit.

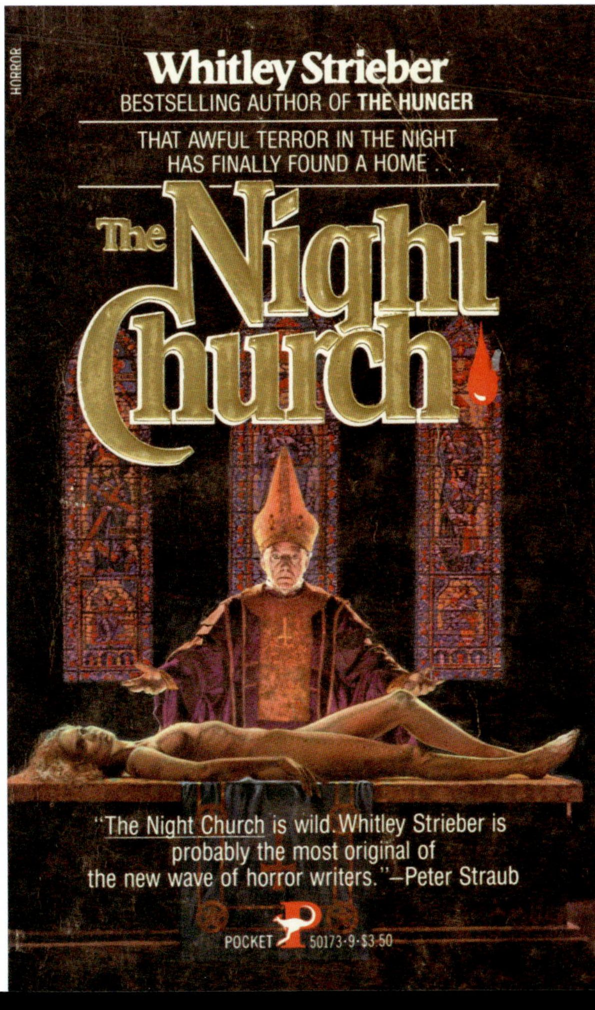

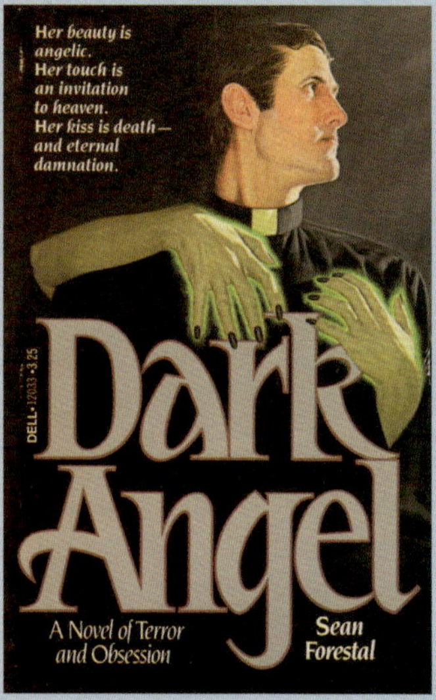

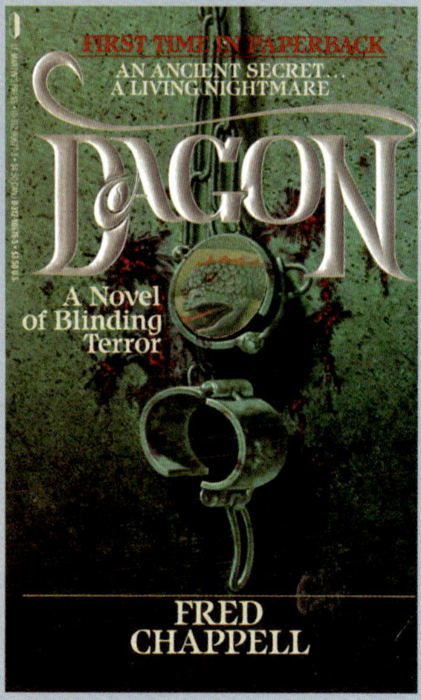

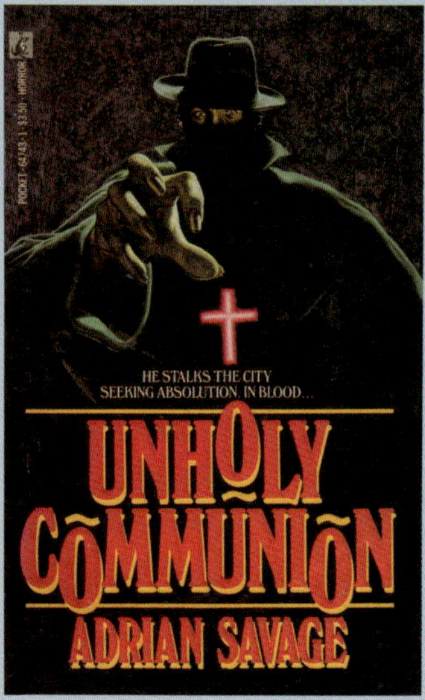

Catholic priests looked so good on covers, it didn't matter what was inside. William Peter Blatty's *Exorcist* sequels, *The Ninth Configuration* and *Legion*, were Catholic enough, and *Unholy Communion* was about a priest who becomes a horny werewolf. But *Dagon* was a Southern Gothic by way of H. P. Lovecraft.

Jim Thiesen is famous for his fully painted, beautifully textured book covers for such authors as Brian Lumley and Chelsea Quinn Yarbro. He's also known for his work on Doubleday's reprints of Stephen King's first four novels and his iconic H. R. Giger–inspired cover for Richard Matheson's *I Am Legend* (which Tor cropped, digitally blurred, and altered, much to Thiesen's dismay). But nothing can alter the power of his cover for *The Gilgul,* which is based on a monstrous head he sculpted, lit, and photographed himself. There's nothing else like it in horror paperbacks, and it is truly a staggering work of heart-breaking horror genius.

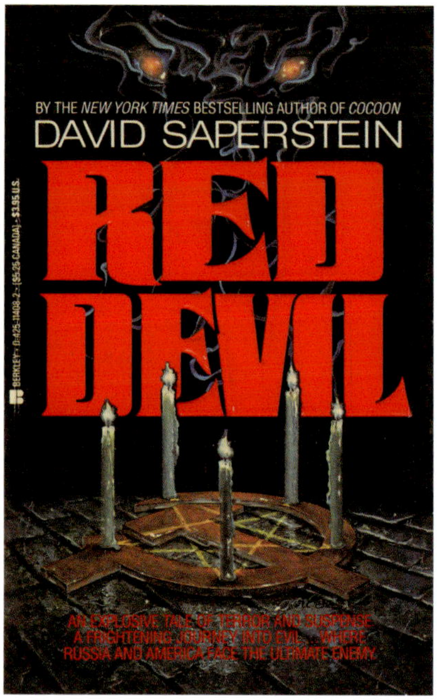

A Jewish historian and an ancient evil fought Nazis in *The Keep*, which spawned five sequels, while the KGB teamed up with Mossad against Satan in *Red Devil*.

One from Golem A, One from Golem B

Catholics weren't hogging all the horrific fun. Jewish horror is a small but strong subset of the paperback horror boom. In fact, this tiny ethnic enclave punches above its weight and includes one of the best covers of the decade, as well as one of the best books in the whole boom. Even F. Paul Wilson's *The Keep* got the big-budget Michael Mann Hollywood movie treatment. But it was Henry Hocherman's *The Gilgul* that ruled bookstore shelves, thanks to its amazing cover (see page 37).

The Gilgul doesn't quite live up to the promise of its cover, however. It honors the beautiful traditions of the Jewish people with the story of a young possessed bride who sprays blood from her nipples. When her future groom witnesses her finger-banging a nurse in the local nuthouse, he flees for Miami to swill Jack Daniels and pick up every hooker he can find. The memory of the Holocaust is evoked by a touching scene in which an army of Jewish concentration camp victims comes back from the dead in a Bay Shore living room and ascends into the heavens while singing. And an American psychiatrist is tied up and injected with HIV-infected blood by two of his patients, a bisexual Puerto Rican and a black pimp, after they sneak a peek at his notes stating that people who get AIDS do so because they lack the self-control to put on a condom. (Don't judge. It was the '80s.)

Coming the same year that the Berlin Wall fell and the Soviet Union started to disintegrate, David Saperstein's Cold War thriller *Red Devil* is a book no one was in the mood for. The premise: Satan (actually Shaitan, the Arabic jinn who refused to kneel before Adam), ditched the Nazis when they lost World War II and assumed the identity of a dead Soviet intelligence officer. Now a higher-up in Soviet military intelligence, Shaitan has recruited a cadre of loyal Satan worshippers and is planning a coup. It's up to a band of loyal KGB agents, allied with

Israeli intelligence, to arm themselves with super-shofars that can blast demonic spies and prevent World War III.

Red Devil is Yiddish Cold War camp of the highest order, but it feels like yesterday's cold kugel next to Bari Wood's deeply felt immigrant love song *The Tribe*. Wood started her career as an editor for the medical journal *CA: A Cancer Journal for Clinicians*, which sounds like the most depressing job ever. Later she had hits with *Twins* (1977), which was adapted into David Cronenberg's film *Dead Ringers* (1988), and *Doll's Eyes* (1993), adapted into the Neil Jordan film *In Dreams* (1999).

The Tribe's opening sequence is guaranteed to make readers' hearts sink: a prologue set during World War II. In Nuremberg. If you've read five horror novels from the '80s, then you've read four prologues set during WWII. But this one asks a question whose answer is intriguing: how did the Jews in Barracks 554 of the Belzec concentration camp survive the war while the SS officers guarding them were starving to death?

Cut to Brooklyn, 1981. On Flatbush Avenue, a Jewish philosophy professor named Adam Levy is stabbed to death by a gang of kids who can barely grow mustaches. His best friend, Roger Hawkins, an African American cop on the rise, gets the grim task of telling the family their son is dead. Roger and Adam are practically brothers, and their surrogate father is Jacob Levy, Adam's father, who survived Belzec and now functions as the revered elder of a tight-knit group of Holocaust survivors who, unfortunately, hate Roger because he's black. Before Roger can track down the kids who killed Adam, an enormous stranger tears them to pieces. Roger suspects the survivors have something to do with it, but his suspicions drive away Jacob and Rachel, Adam's widow.

Years later, the Levys have ditched Brooklyn for Long Island, raising Adam's son in the safe suburbs. But when a black family moves into the neighborhood, the Jewish homeowners panic over potentially plunging property values. Then another murder is committed by an enormous stranger who leaves his African American victims torn to shreds. Suddenly the past is bubbling up through the floorboards: Adam's murder, Brooklyn, Belzec, Barracks 554, all the way back to the village in Dabrowa where Jacob Levy was born. The war never ended, and it's hauled its stinking carcass onto Long Island.

A true novel of New York City, *The Tribe* is about gentrification, urban blight, and super-rabbis.

This is a book about tribes—found families who put their backs together and face outward, defending themselves against invaders—and how toxic they can become. It's also a book of grace notes and details. A broken bottle of perfume whose scent still haunts a garage thirty-five years later. An incongruous flowered curtain that acquires menace as the reader slowly realizes what it conceals. And a murdered man whose last thoughts, as he's stabbed to death on Nostrand

Avenue, are not of fighting back but of a trip he once took with his wife. The way she looked, paddling clumsily at the bow. Of her profile as she turned to smile at him. He's dying, and all he can think about is that impossibly perfect afternoon a long, long time ago.

Welcome to Porn Country!

These three novels were published by Carlyle, the slightly more respectable imprint of Beeline Books, which published straight-up, no-holds-barred dirty books like *Paris Sex Circus*, *The Wife Who Liked to Watch*, and *High School Orgy Society*. But in 1977 the publishers saw horror novels all over drugstore racks and asked one of its authors, Brian McNaughton, to rip off the recent hit *The Omen*. When he turned in his sex-free manuscript, the head of the company ordered him to put in more "quivering breasts" and "stirring pricks."

In *Satan's Love Child*, Marcia Creighton is a reporter for a small-town newspaper in New Jersey, happy to lead a normal life after spending her teenage years in a hippie love cult attending Satanic orgies she'd rather forget. Now she's a mother of three, and all is well except for her selfish alcoholic husband, their family's disappearing black dog Lucifer, and a corpse strolling around the local morgue. But hey, that's not so weird for New Jersey. Then a bunch of hippies moves into the area and, before you know it, Marcia's oldest daughter is falling into trances and having nightmares. Invisible monsters show up, people get killed, there is a lot of sex and . . . it's actually pretty great.

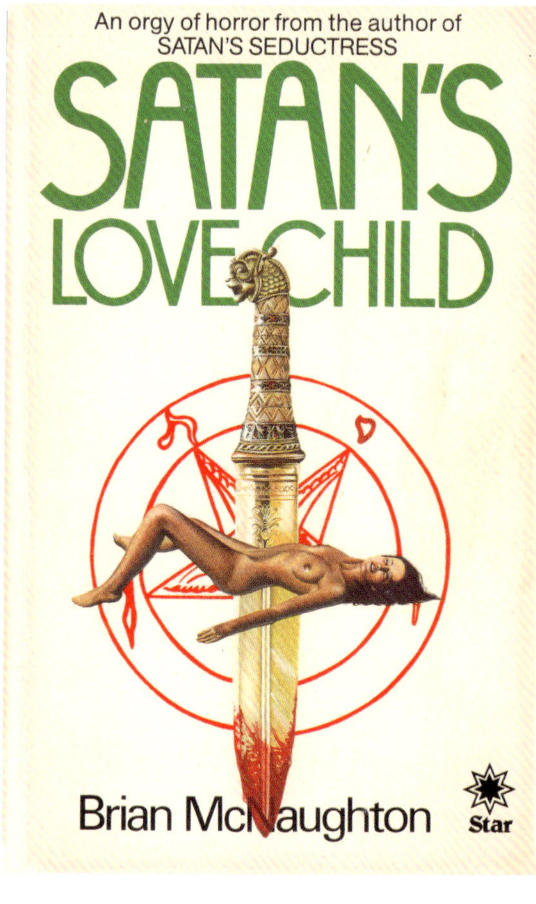

The explicit sex scenes are so cut and pasted they barely obscure McNaughton's cracked cosmic vision. See, these hippies aren't trying to summon Satan. They worship witches trapped in the fourth dimension. Described as the "Older Gods," they're cousins of H. P. Lovecraft's Elder Gods, and the plot twists and turns like a snake as they force their way into our earthly plane.

Satan's Love Child was one of Carlyle's biggest sellers, and the publisher rapidly greenlit two more, this time giving McNaughton a free hand. *Satan's Mistress* and *Satan's Seductress* are practically sex-free, twisted up in each other's chronologies, with echoes of *Mistress* reverberating through *Seductress* in a way that's downright masterful. If you can call a book that features so many trans-dimensional slime monsters masterful.

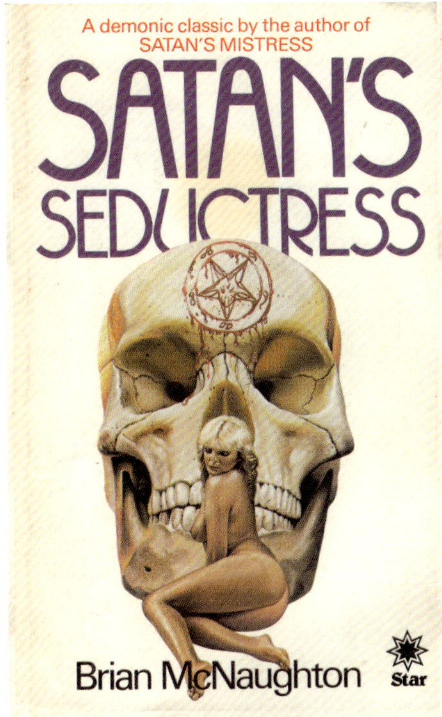

A fourth book in the series, *Satan's Surrogate*, took McNaughton's literary experimentation to its hallucinatory limits.

McNaughton's essential subject is failed families led by crummy parents who've given up trying to raise their kids; sort of like Rick Moody's *The Ice Storm* with more shoggoths. *Satan's Mistress* features another hippie housewife, another lousy husband, a "conspiracy of scholars, literary men, and theoretical physicists" hiding the truth about the fourth-dimensional witches, and mass murder. *Satan's Seductress* picks up years later, when a survivor of *Mistress*'s climactic massacre moves back home and cautiously tries to pick up the pieces of her shattered life. Then time loops, undying witches, and books inside books stomp the protagonist's delicate recovery into shards, reminding us that McNaughton is writing about a Lovecraftian universe that shows no mercy for fragile humans and their petty emotions.

The icy heart at the center of McNaughton's trash fiction masterpieces is the new world promised by the Older God Zurvan. He will eliminate all contrasts and contradictions, making Earth a planet with no prisons, no mental hospitals, no darkness, and no war. Sounds good, until you realize that he will also eliminate the difference between good and evil; life and death will blur, and there will be no more freedom, because it will also be slavery.

Zurvan is a vampire of life's essence, the great leveler, the same-maker. He is the ultimate expression of the hippie summer of love: the loss of self, the destroyer of conflict. He embodies the existential fear at the heart of Satanic cult books and possession novels, the fear that we are losing our individual identities to become servants of another's will. Have a Coke and a smile. Zurvan is here.

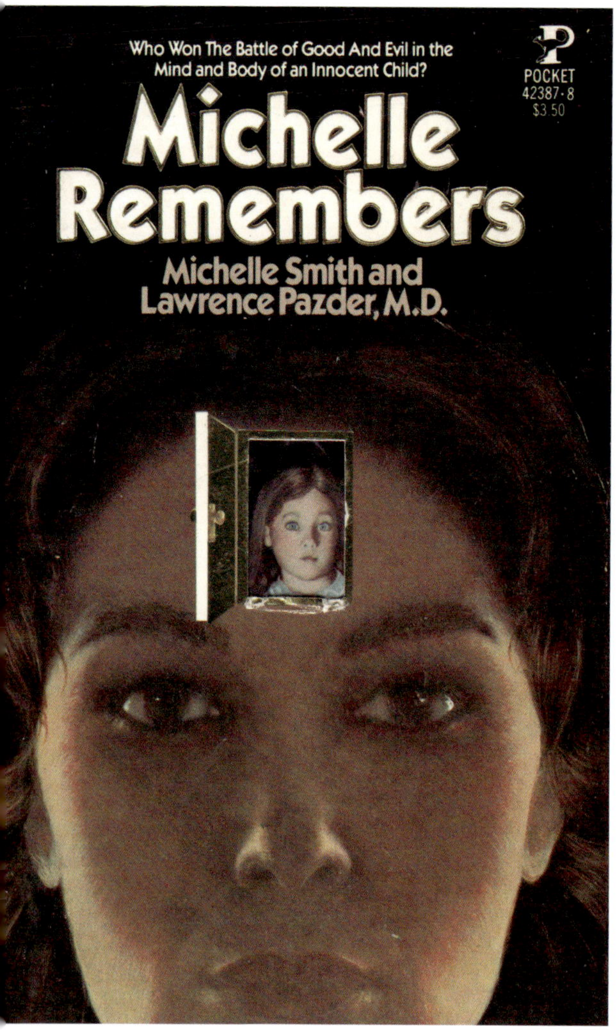

Michelle Misremembered

In 1977, real-life Canadian housewife Michelle Smith suffered a miscarriage and sank into depression. She began therapy with Dr. Lawrence Pazder, who revealed that her problems stemmed from repressed childhood memories. Together, they recovered these traumatic memories—which revealed that in 1955, when Michelle was five years old, her mother turned her over to a Satanic cult that used her as the centerpiece in an 81-day ritual known as the Feast of the Beast. During this marathon orgy, Michelle was raped by snakes, defecated on a Bible, watched her playmates being murdered, saw kittens crucified, had a devil tail and horns surgically grafted to her skeleton, got her teeth knocked out, and ate human flesh while being rubbed all over with dead babies. At the finish line, the Virgin Mary and the Archangel Michael appeared and healed her, miraculously erasing all physical evidence of these crimes.

It sounds like a Brian McNaughton novel, but Smith claimed it was all true. To warn the world, she and Pazder wrote *Michelle Remembers*, a blockbuster memoir that helped spark America's Satanic Panic in the 1980s. People who should have known better became convinced that Satan lurked under every heavy-metal album cover and operated day care centers across the country. Smith and Pazder left their respective spouses and married each other; they appeared on *Oprah*, went on a national book tour, popped up in *People* magazine, and shopped around a movie adaptation of their book, which was kept out of theaters thanks only to threats of a lawsuit from both the Church of Satan's Anton LaVey and Smith's father.

Michelle Remembers was a foundational text that brought recovered-memory syndrome and Satanic Ritual Abuse into the mainstream, updating for the '80s lurid, turn-of-the-century conspiracy theories about white slavers running an international network of sin. The Satanic Panic posited a cradle-to-grave satanic network that indoctrinated children into sex and drug rings, using Saturday morning cartoons and He-Man action figures, with New Age occultists wielding crystals behind it all. Eighties America was ready for conspiracy theories, no matter how silly, and we're about to meet a man named Russ Martin who had a few for sale.

He's Hurting Me All Over!
His Eyes Are Scaring Me!
They Look Crazy!
Where's My Mommy?

But it was her Mommy, a disturbed, peculiar woman who had yielded up 5-year-old Michelle Smith to a cult of devil worshippers for The Feast of the Beast.

And in that dreadful 3 month ritual, innocent little Michelle was tortured, imprisoned, and used most evilly as an instrument to raise Satan himself.

And they did raise him.

And only a divine intervention saved Michelle from the supreme terror.

22 Years Later

A troubled woman begins visits to a gentle, compassionate psychiatrist, and finally the long-buried memory of a childhood agony comes screaming forth with terrifying clarity.

The stuff of fiction? Perhaps.

But it all really happened to Michelle Smith.
And, at last...
Michelle Remembers

"FASCINATING!...A PAGE TURNER!"
—Flora Rheta Schreiber, author of Sybil

PRINTED IN U.S.A.

ISBN 0-671-42387-8

Could the demonic ordeal described by Michelle Smith possibly be real? *(Spoiler alert: No.)*

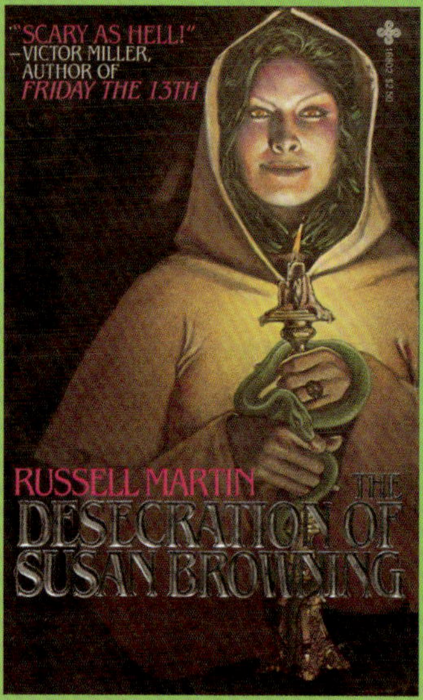
"SCARY AS HELL!"
—VICTOR MILLER,
AUTHOR OF
FRIDAY THE 13TH
RUSSELL MARTIN
THE DESECRATION OF SUSAN BROWNING

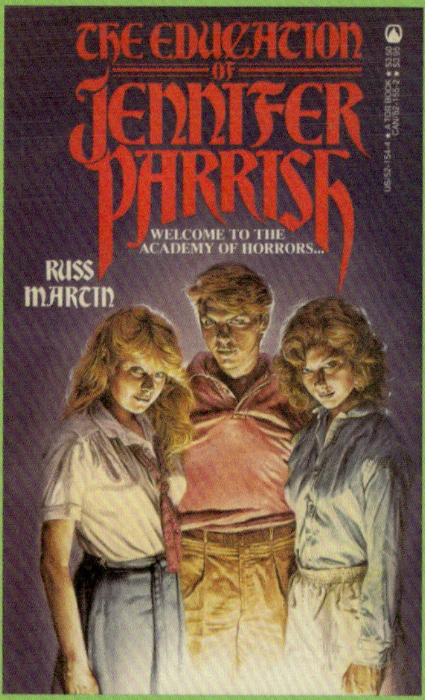
THE EDUCATION OF JENNIFER PARRISH
WELCOME TO THE ACADEMY OF HORRORS...
RUSS MARTIN

NOTHING CAN PROTECT YOU FROM
THE VASTLY EVIL SENSUALITY OF
THE OBSESSION OF SALLY WING
RUSS MARTIN
AUTHOR OF THE POSSESSION OF JESSICA YOUNG

AN EXTRAORDINARY SENSUAL NOVEL
OF VAST AND ORGANIZED EVIL.
THE POSSESSION OF JESSICA YOUNG
RUSS MARTIN

16683 $2.50
A NOVEL OF
UNHOLY PASSION
RHEA
BY RUSS MARTIN

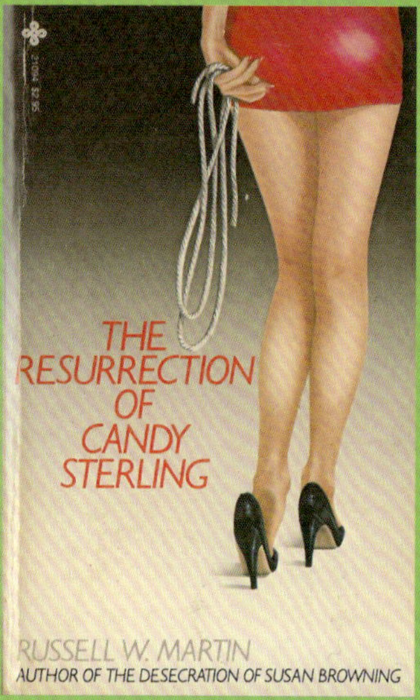
THE
RESURRECTION
OF
CANDY
STERLING
RUSSELL W. MARTIN
AUTHOR OF THE DESECRATION OF SUSAN BROWNING

Russ Martin's Conspiracy of Kink

Between 1978 and 1984, Russ Martin wrote seven books about the Satanic Organization, a global conspiracy dedicated to the Devil and run by the elite 0.01 percent who rule society and use mind control and body swapping to destroy their enemies. *Rhea* is an outlier: nothing more than the straightforward story of a cheating Hollywood executive, the witch who seduces him, and the wife who ends up impaled on Satan's ice-cold, two-pronged penis.

After that, he stepped firmly into the new decade with *The Desecration of Susan Browning*. Susan and Marty are young actors in Los Angeles about to make it big when Marty saves a wealthy woman named Wanda Carmichael from being raped. Wanda is intrigued by this young stud, and soon Marty has disappeared, filed for divorce, and is living with Wanda on her fabulous estate. The Satanic Organization has made him Wanda's love slave using an obsession spell. As he tells Susan, if Wanda asked him to kill his ex-wife, he'd do it in a heartbeat.

This was Satanic Panic fan fiction, updating the *Michelle Remembers* fever dream of a global satanic conspiracy to the yuppie-infested '80s and giving it a kinky twist. In the next five books, Martin returns obsessively to certain themes: betrayal by authority, body swapping, mind control, and an ever-shifting power exchange as obsession spells bounced from character to character like pervy pinballs. Lisa Black, a minor character in *Susan Browning*, takes center stage in *The Devil and Lisa Black*. In *The Possession of Jessica Young* we meet Stephen Abbott, head honcho of the Satanic Organization, locked in a psychic war with Jessica Young, whose powerful abilities spell trouble for Satan. Abbot mind-controls Jessica's sister, Jessica teams up with a cop to stage a rescue, the cop betrays Jessica, and then Jessica's sister betrays Jessica, too.

And so it goes: betrayal bleeds into betrayal in an endless blur of sexualized dominance and submission. Nine-year-olds are trapped in adult bodies. Powerful women are turned into French maids. Psychic vampires from Hong Kong murder children in Washington, D.C. The final installment takes place at a military academy, which is also a secret base for swapping the minds of older Satanic Organization loyalists into the bodies of teenaged cadets. The only ones who can resist the mind control are virgins. Lest one think this is too kinky for mainstream publishing, know that when Playboy Press shut down in 1982, Tor instantly picked up the rest of Martin's series.

Underneath all the pseudosexual silliness was the message that a decadent elite controlled everything. In Martin's world, everyone was either a master or a slave. Satan was the force that made your dreams come true at the price of your soul. Satan was the cause of all corruption. Satan was the reason things never worked out. Resistance was futile. The game was rigged before you were ever *born*.

The horror of these books is that Satan always wins. Just look at the world. The evidence is everywhere.

Logically, Playboy Press published most of Martin's kinky, cynical, psychosexual books.

CREEP

CHAPTER TWO

Y KIDS

SIGNET•451-J8180•$1.95
THE 3½ MILLION COPY BESTSELLER!
A TERRIFYING SHOCKER
OF SUPERNATURAL EVIL FROM
20TH CENTURY FOX!
THE
OMEN
666
DAVID SELTZER
2000 YEARS AGO
HIS BIRTH
WAS FORETOLD.
NOW HE IS FIVE
AND HIS TIME
HAS COME!
WITH 8 PAGES OF
FILM SCENES!

All the way back to Henry James's *Turn of the Screw,* with its little creeps Flora and Miles, kids in fiction have been trouble. In the '40s, Agatha Christie's *Crooked House* featured a twelve-year-old psychopath named Josephine, and Ray Bradbury's 1946 short story "The Small Assassin" gave us a baby out to murder his parents. But the '50s were the true decade of the terrible tyke. The decade kicked off with Richard Matheson's short story about a spider baby, "Born of Man and Woman." In 1953 came Jerome Bixby's classic "It's a Good Life," with its all-powerful, bratty three-year-old psychic god Anthony. It has been adapted three times for *The Twilight Zone* (the original series, the reboot, and the feature film) and once for *The Simpsons.*

The next year saw the arrival of the twin masterworks of killer-kid literature: William Golding's *Lord of the Flies* and William March's *The Bad Seed.* John Wyndham rounded things out with *The Midwich Cuckoos* in 1957, which was adapted for film as *Village of the Damned* in 1960. For the next ten years, evil kids belonged on film. *Turn of the Screw* became director and cinematographer Freddie Francis's dripping, doomed, black-and-white chiller *The Innocents* (1961). *Lord of the Flies* hit the silver screen in 1963, and then Jack Hill gave us Ralph, Virginia, and Elizabeth Merrye, three murderous adults with the minds of children in 1964's *Spider Baby,* followed by the game-changing satanic fetus of *Rosemary's Baby* and in 1970 Freddie Francis did it again with *Girly.*

As discussed in Chapter 1, Thomas Tryon's 1971 evil-twin best seller *The Other* inspired the horror boom of the '70s, with its underage murderers playing big brother to the most infamous killer child of them all: Damien Thorn. Wanting to cash in on the success of *The Exorcist,* producer Harvey Bernhard hired screenwriter David Seltzer to write *The Omen,* a smash that spawned two sequels and numerous remakes (as well as popularizing 666 as the "number of the beast").

A few weeks before the movie debuted, Seltzer wrote a novelization of his screenplay that ran a slim 202 pages and it became a surprise hit, selling 3.5

million copies. It's one of the better movie novelizations, with the film's big scenes all present and accounted for. Seltzer adds even more details, such as gutter journalist Keith Jennings being so lonely that he creates a friend by sticking a cooked chicken on a root beer bottle and making it dance. There's also a nutty backstory in which one of the priests selected to kill Damien reminisces about doing missionary work in Africa, where he fell in love with a young man and was forced to watch his lover eat his own testicles before being flayed alive.

Unlike David Seltzer, Joseph Howard isn't even credited on the cover of the 1978 novelization *Damien: Omen II*. His book isn't terrible, but it pales compared to the original. Characters communicate mostly by reciting long passages from the Book of Revelation or shouting, "Your child is the Antichrist! He must be destroyed!" Nevertheless, it sold about 1.5 million copies.

The third novelization (and the last to correspond to a motion picture), *Omen III: The Final Conflict* (1980), was written by Gordon McGill, whose name appears on the cover but who had nothing to do with the screenplay. Damien's character, now the head of Thorn Corporation, talks as if he was raised in a German military academy ("Pleased to meet you, Miss Reynolds. You are the Barbara Walters of the BBC, perhaps?"), recites death metal lyrics ("Birth is pain. Death is pain. Beauty is pain."), and waxes rhapsodic over, as he charmingly puts it, "the gaping wound of a woman." A bunch of priests are on a holy suicide mission to stab the now-adult Damien to death with the Seven Sacred Daggers of Megiddo; after Damien makes love to the Barbara Walters of the BBC, the priests manage to stick one of these magic Ginsu knives in his back. That seems to be curtains for Damien, and it certainly was for the film franchise.

Not so for McGill, who returned in 1982 to write an *Omen* novel not based on a film, *Omen IV: Armageddon 2000*, which opens with a scene of rectal childbirth. The Barbara Walters of the BBC ushers Damien's son, Damien Jr., into the world via her anus before dying (probably of shame). Cut to seventeen years later, in the futuristic year 2000: Thorn Corporation is run by Paul Buher, a relatively

The Final Conflict wasn't so final—Damien Thorn's progeny kept the family business going for two more installments.

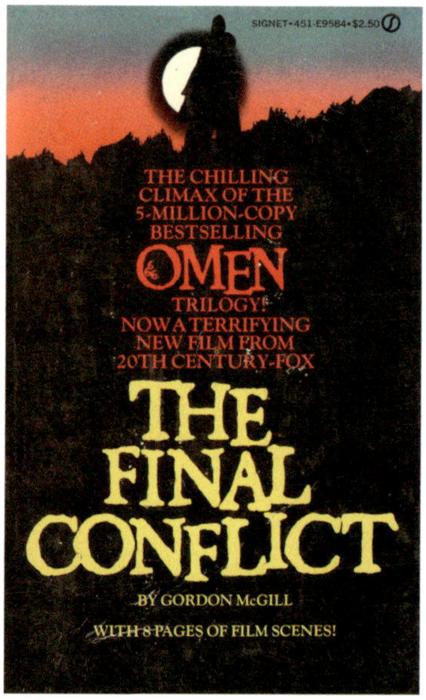

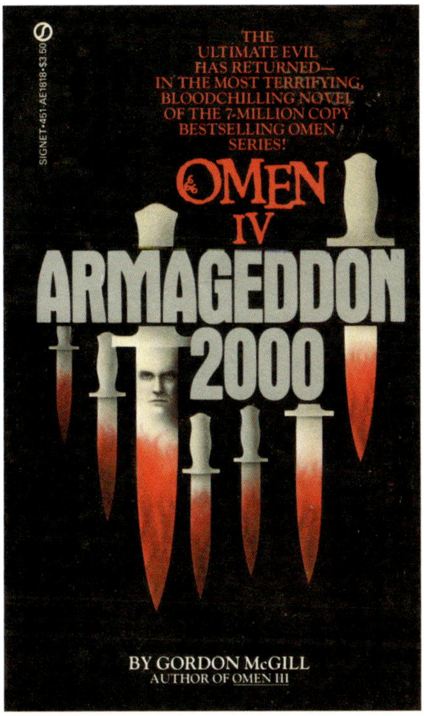

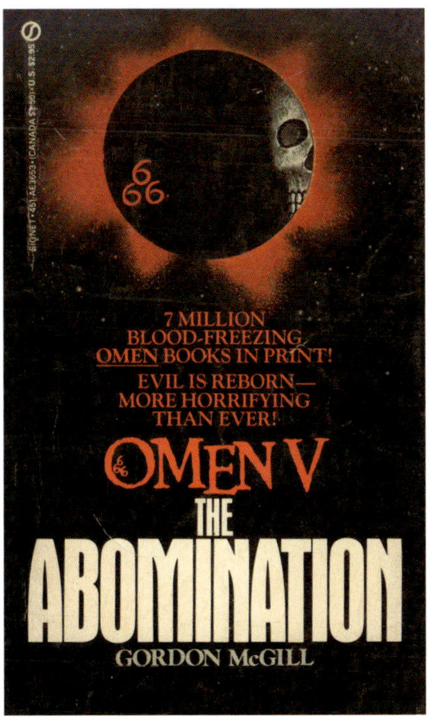

minor character from the series who keeps teenage Damien Jr. isolated on the grand old family estate, Pereford, where Dad's embalmed corpse stands like a mannequin in the black chapel.

This book revolves around yet another attempt to insert the Seven Sacred Daggers of Megiddo into the spawn of Satan. Chief among those trying to turn the Antichrist into a knife block is Philip Brennan, the American ambassador overseeing Arab-Israeli peace talks, which fall apart when an Israeli politician clocks a Syrian representative with an ashtray. Then Brennan's devil-worshipping wife stabs her husband before he can stab Damien with his Christian cutlery, and World War III breaks out.

Omen V: The Abomination (1985) picks up a few years after this nuclear exchange. Opening with a list of the thirty-one characters slaughtered in the series so far, it follows Pulitzer Prize–winning writer Paul Mason and his intrepid researcher Anna as they write a book about the Thorn family and how all their friends die a lot. Damien Jr. becomes head of the Thorn Corporation and starts engineering the apocalypse again. Anna is brainwashed into becoming Damien's slave shortly after she interviews Philip Brennan's backstabbing wife from the previous book, who has since taken a knife and mutilated her vagina as penance for her betrayal.

Everyone converges on Pereford for a satanic orgy, where Anna betrays Paul, who tries to kill Damien Jr. The series concludes with Damien Jr. crushed by a massive falling crucifix ridden by Philip Brennan's mad wife, who lands on Damien crotch-first, and we're informed that the last sight Damien Jr. sees is "the mutilation of Margaret Brennan." THE END.

Or is it? In the epilogue, Paul Mason sits down to write his book and types . . . the first lines of the first *Omen* novelization by David Seltzer.

What to Expect When You're Expecting (a Hell Baby)

The 1960s and '70s spawned a million myths about babies as everyone tried to keep up with the changing rules of reproduction. The Pill hit the market in 1960, IUDs appeared in 1968, abortion was legalized in 1973, and the first successful IVF was carried out in 1978. Massive changes in contraception and fertility technology had phrases like *test tube baby* and *sperm bank* on the lips of every American. A lot of fear emerged surrounding pregnancy and childbirth, but fortunately horror paperbacks were there to address every new parent's fears with a resounding "Yes!" Yes, having sex will cause your baby to die, especially if that sex involved female orgasm (*Crib*, 1982). Yes, having a baby will cause a woman's breasts to look "as though a vandal had defaced a great work of art" (also *Crib*). Yes, you will be confined to a locked mental ward after giving birth (too many books to list). Yes, if you have an abortion the remains will be buried in a shallow grave behind the hospital, where they will be struck by lightning and reanimated as brain-eating babies who telekinetically explode your womb (*Spawn*, 1983).

Many women make their way through this minefield of potential hazards with the guidance of their doctor. But the horror novels of this era warn women that their doctors were less likely to write a prescription than to hire a hitman to run them over because they threatened to blow the lid off their baby mill operation. The horror-novel OB/GYN is remote and cold. His name is Dr. Borg or Dr. Kabel, and he works at the Karyll Clinic, which sounds like a location in a David Cronenberg movie. He spends Christmas Day alone, and he's probably having an incestuous affair with his sister. If you are visiting a fertility clinic that has a conveyor belt running directly from the delivery room to what everyone refers to as "the Off-Limits Building," find another doctor.

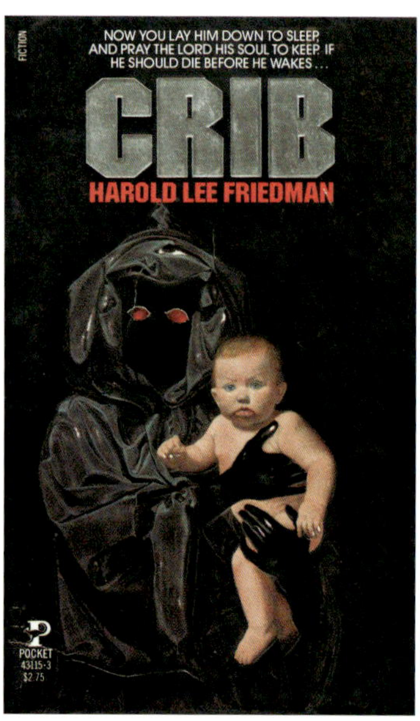

The floating unborn became a recurring image on horror novel covers, even for books like *The Jonah* and *The Reaping*, which didn't feature a single evil fetus.

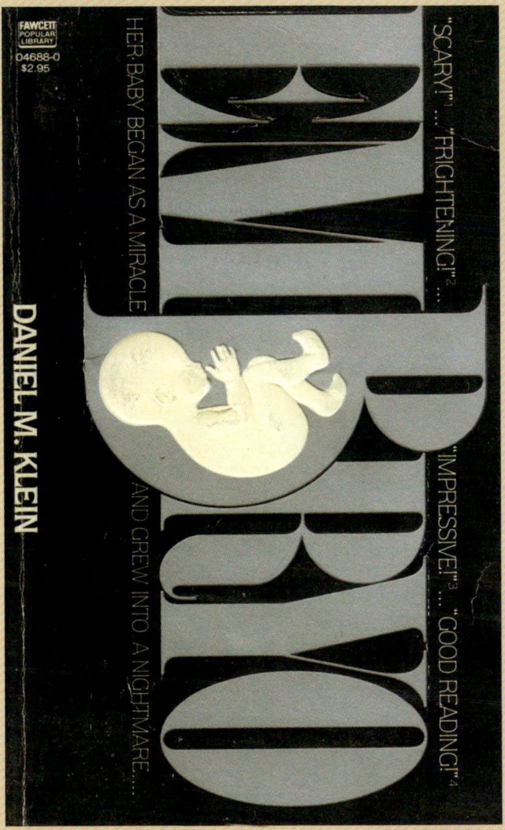
FAWCETT POPULAR LIBRARY
04688-0
$2.95
EMBRYO
"SCARY!"1 ... "FRIGHTENING!"2 ...
"IMPRESSIVE!"3 ... "GOOD READING!"4
HER BABY BEGAN AS A MIRACLE
AND GREW INTO A NIGHTMARE....
DANIEL M. KLEIN

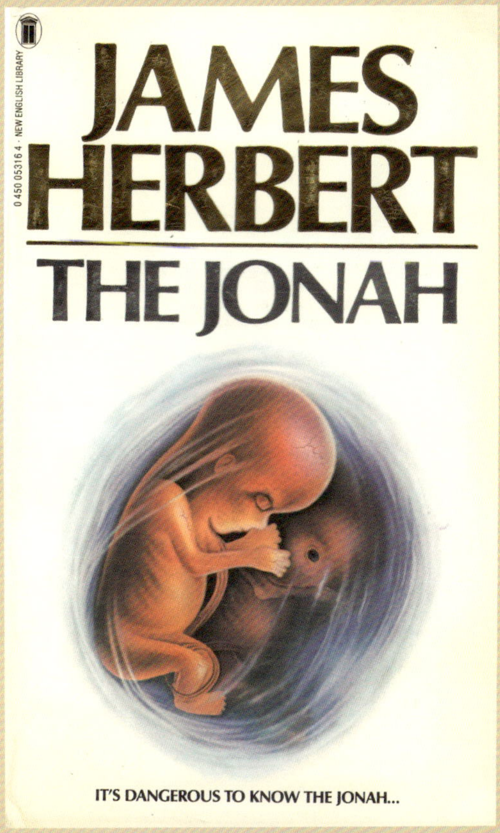
0 450 05316 4 · NEW ENGLISH LIBRARY
JAMES HERBERT
THE JONAH
IT'S DANGEROUS TO KNOW THE JONAH...

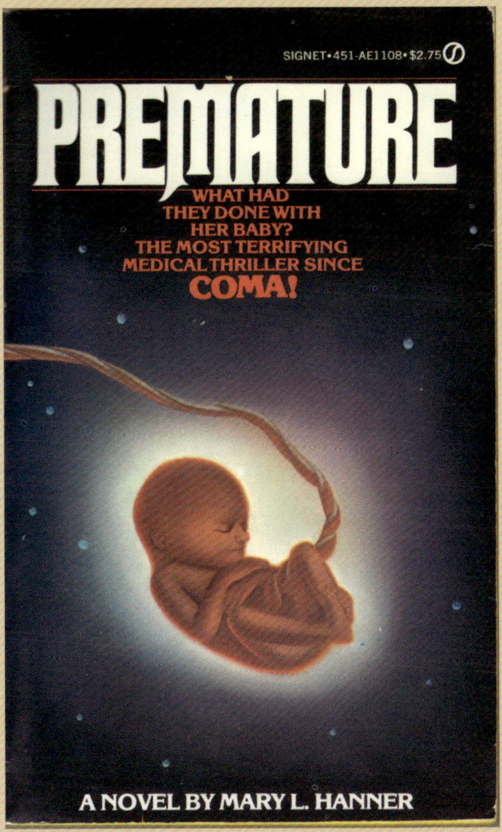
SIGNET•451-AE1108•$2.75
PREMATURE
WHAT HAD THEY DONE WITH HER BABY?
THE MOST TERRIFYING MEDICAL THRILLER SINCE
COMA!
A NOVEL BY MARY L. HANNER

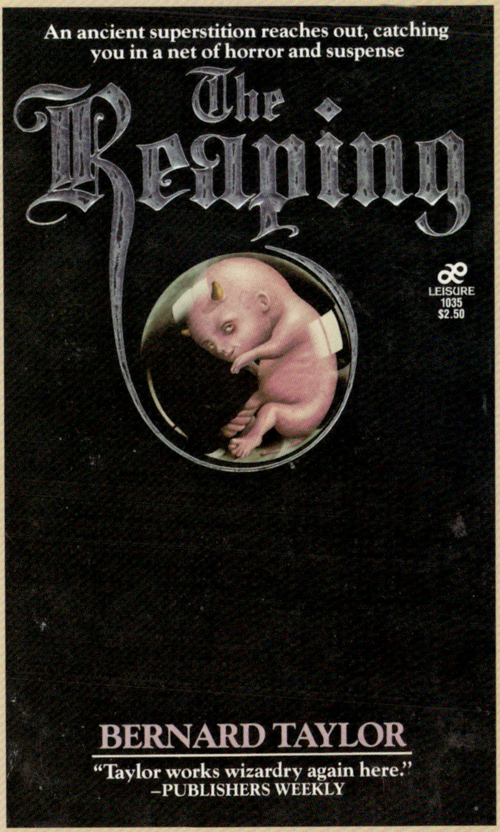
An ancient superstition reaches out, catching you in a net of horror and suspense
The Reaping
LEISURE 1035 $2.50
BERNARD TAYLOR
"Taylor works wizardry again here."
–PUBLISHERS WEEKLY

As readers soon learn, a woman is never more vulnerable than when she's pregnant or in labor, especially if the hospital happens to be conducting illegal experiments on living human fetuses. Essentially medical thrillers in the vein of *Coma* (more about that book in chapter 5), these novels stopped at every station of the genre and genuflected deeply. A doctor always gave a lecture about the virtues of playing God, someone was always sneaking around the hospital's off-limits area, an insider involved in the experiments was always unable to live with the guilt and volunteered vital information to the main character but was killed before their secrets could be revealed. That death was always made to look like a suicide. And, just as surrogate mothers always turned out to be crazed murderers, there was always a previous victim who seemed insane but who might be telling the truth if everyone would stop dosing her with Thorazine for a second and listen.

The message seemed to be that women should have babies by finding them in a cabbage patch or receiving them from a stork, the way nature intended, rather than using their dangerous, weird-looking wombs. But for those who insisted on doing things the hard way, these novels were full of long descriptions of medical procedures like amniocentesis and culdoscopy. Books like *Embryo* (1980; page 53) served, on the one hand, as thrillers about insane gynecologists trying to produce a master race of identical Swedish babies, and on the other as racy versions of *What to Expect When You're Expecting.*

The terrifying truth about childbirth is that carrying the fetus to term is merely the first step on the long road to having your house to yourself again. Every fetus eventually turns into a child, and, as so many wise men and women in the horror paperback industry know, terror toddles on two chubby legs.

In the world of horror paperbacks, child-rearing has few rewards. If you manage to avoid the deranged surrogate mothers who orgasm during labor and want to steal back their baby and send it to heaven with its brothers and sisters (*Hush Little Baby*, 1982), *and* you can dodge the secret cult stealing Jewish babies and selling them for $50,000 a pop (*Crib*, page 52), you still must care for the infant itself, which comes with its own challenges. Babies can be fussy, and the fussiest babies have a body count.

Of course, every mother thinks her baby is perfect, but at some point, as her home fills with dead bodies, she has to face facts and admit that the fruit of her womb is a face-eating beast spawned from the deepest recesses of hell. If Whitney Houston is right, and the children are indeed our future, then we need to approach our future with maximum caution.

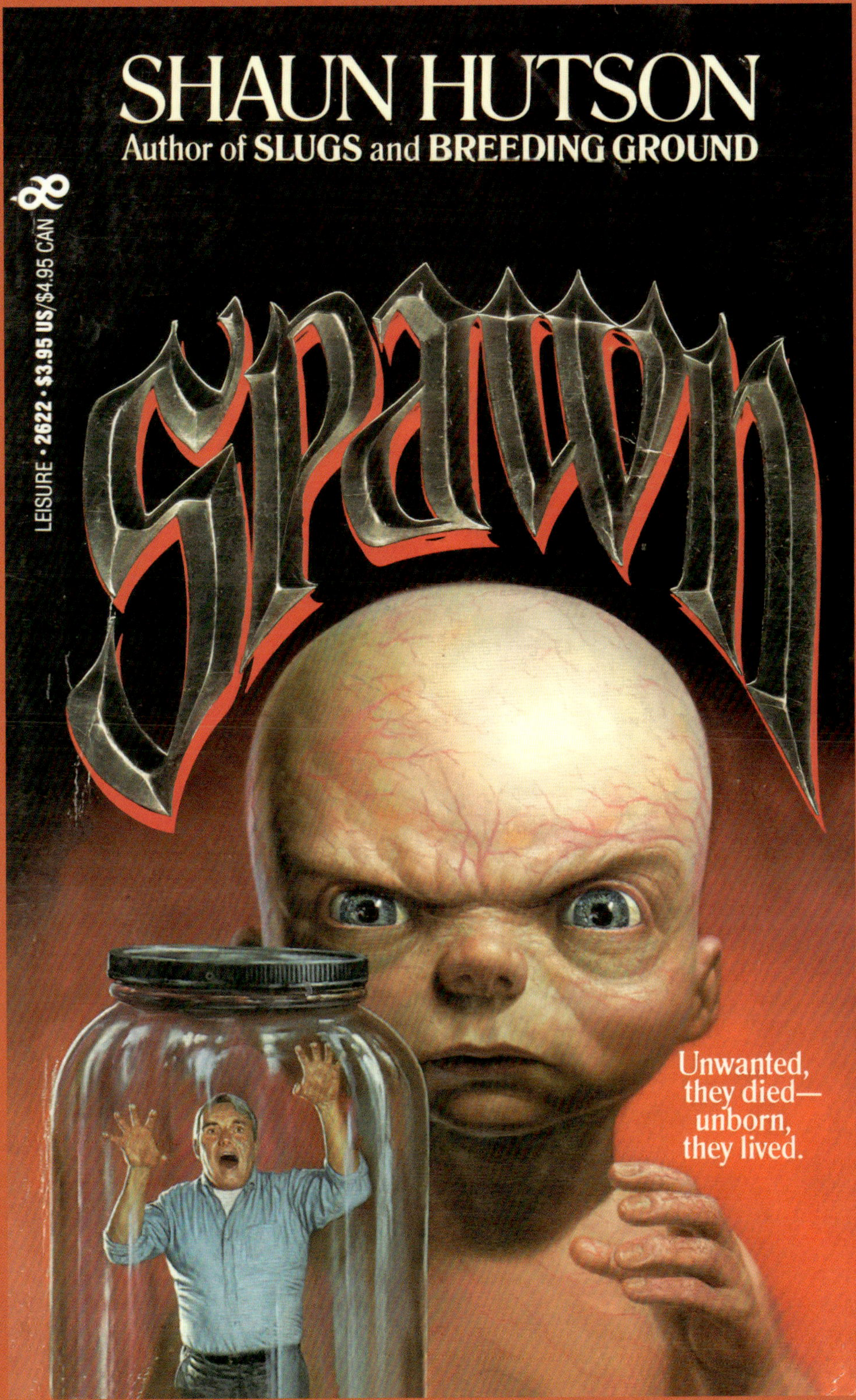
SHAUN HUTSON
Author of SLUGS and BREEDING GROUND
LEISURE • 2622 • $3.95 US/$4.95 CAN
Spawn
Unwanted,
they died—
unborn,
they lived.

Parenting the Homicidal Child

As long as they belong to someone else, homicidal children can be a joy. They're highly accomplished, respectful to those they're not murdering, and when they're finally arrested, you're left feeling that much better about your own little under-achievers, whose terrible table manners suddenly seem like a testament to their normalcy rather than your poor parenting.

But what to do if the sinister suckling lives under your roof? How does one parent the homicidal child? First, make sure that what you're dealing with is in fact a child and not just, say, a slow-growing adult who shaves his pubic hair to appear prepubescent (*The Next*). Second, it's important to determine what kind of homicidal child you have:

a) adopted (*The Godsend*, 1976)
b) chemically altered (*Childmare*, 1980)
c) possessed (*The Moonchild*, 1978)
d) reincarnated (*The Children*, 1982)
e) poorly parented (*Mama's Little Girl*, 1983)
f) inappropriately violent for no good reason (*Prissy*, 1978)
g) in possession of psychic powers (*The Savior*, 1978)
h) Satan spawn (*Seed of Evil*, 1988)

Adopted or chemically altered children should be destroyed immediately because they cannot be reformed. No matter how hard you try, they probably will, at some point, go on a rampage and murder all your other children. Possessed children are usually pawns of a revenge-seeking spirit and, helpfully, often come with instructions for how best to lay the spirit to rest and return your child to normalcy, albeit with a few murders on the little angel's rap sheet. Reincarnated children are tricky. Seek professional help.

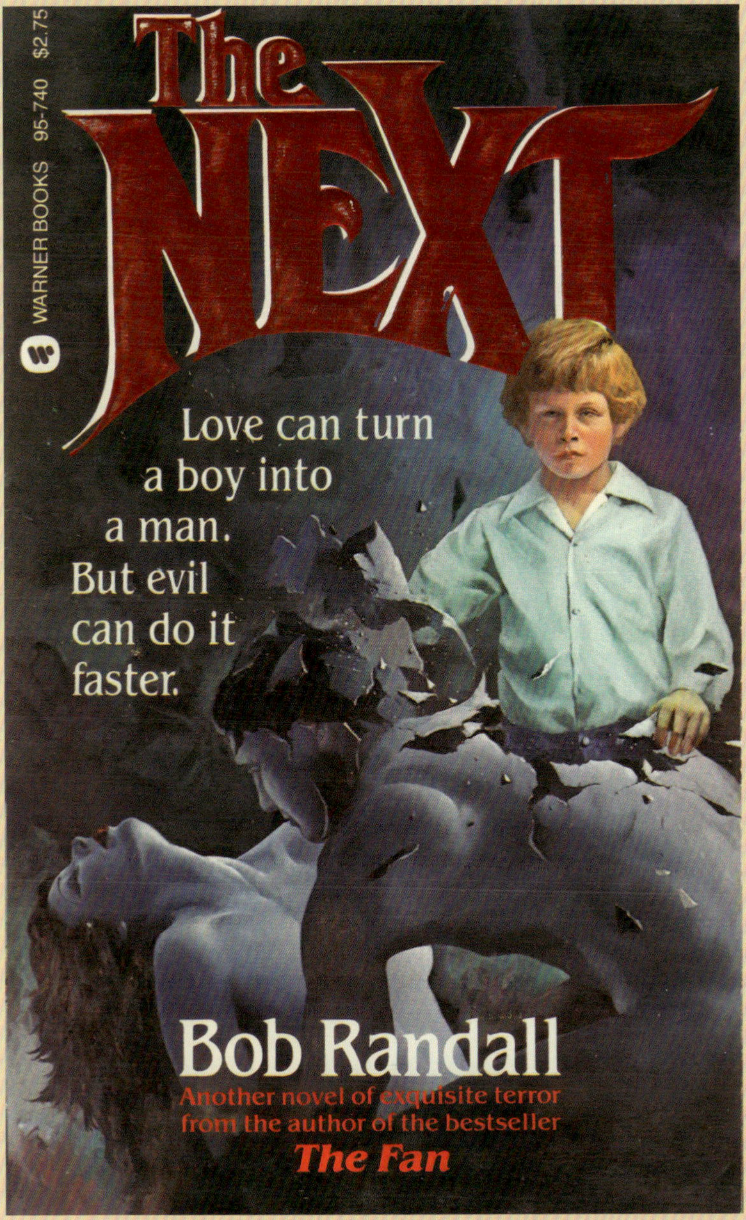

Kids can be a handful, especially if they aren't actually kids (*The Next*), control reality via a dollhouse (*Kate's House*), or catch on to the fact that you're practicing human slavery (*The Sky Children*). But as long as you keep them away from leaded gasoline (*Childmare*), don't let them grow monster arms (*The Moonchild*), and don't kidnap them (*Prissy*), you should survive.

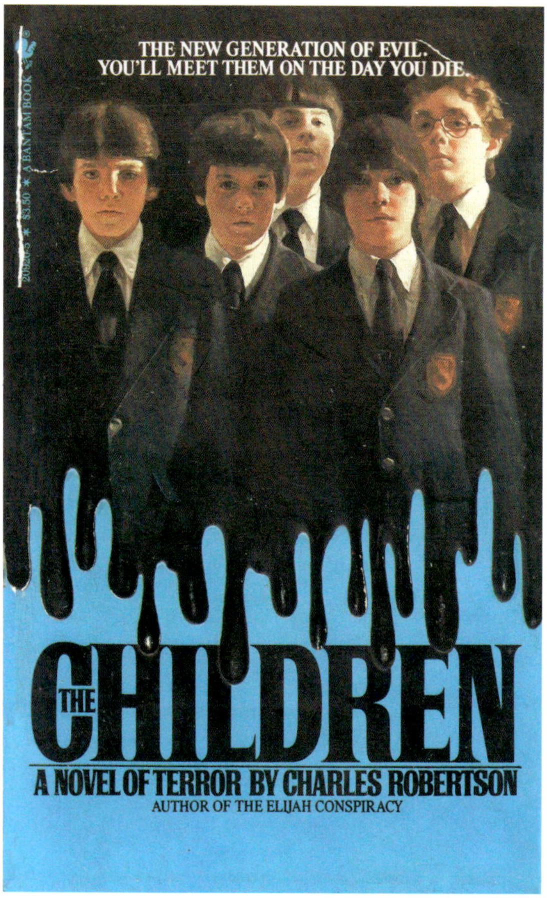

Some crossover exists between poorly parented children and children who are inappropriately violent for no good reason, but it's best to stay out of the way of either type. Same for children in possession of psychic powers.

The most important thing to remember is that it is not your fault. Many children are born evil and must be taught to be good. As the famous French writer Alain Robbe-Grillet said, "What do little girls dream about? Knives and blood." Or, as Erma Bombeck said, "A child needs your love most when he deserves it least." For example, after he has murdered a news anchor by shooting him in the face (*The Children*) or as he's lighting your wife's teenaged lover on fire (*Tricycle*, page 187).

Some parents will feel helpless. "How can I possibly stop my child from murdering strangers with a hammer because she thinks they are demons from hell?" you might wail (*Mama's Little Girl*, page 61). Fortunately there are some practical, commonsense steps you can take to lower the body count. Most important, try not to have sex with Satan. Fornicating with the incarnation of all evil usually produces children who are genetically predisposed to use their supernatural powers to cram their grandmothers into television sets, headfirst. "But how do I know if the man I'm dating is the devil?" I hear you ask. Here are some warning signs learned from *Seed of Evil*: Does he refuse to use contractions when he speaks? Does he deliver pickup lines like, "You live on the edge of darkness"? When nude, is his body the most beautiful male form you have ever seen, but possessed of a penis that's either monstrously enormous, double-headed, has glowing yellow eyes, or all three? After intercourse, does he laugh malevolently, urinate

on your mattress, and then disappear? If you spot any of these behaviors, chances are you went on a date with Satan. Or an alien.

Even if, despite these precautions, you have given birth to the spawn of Satan, all is not lost. Look on the bright side: deadly children are the best-dressed children. A coat and tie on your wee whippersnapper (*Seed of Evil*) says either "tiny funeral director" or "psychopath." A young lady wearing a bow at her neck or wearing a lacy party dress reads as either "I am a living Victorian doll," or "I will murder you the minute your back is turned." Some parents try to deal with the difficulties of dressing homicidal children by sending them to a school that requires them to wear a uniform, which is an excellent idea. Nothing looks smarter, or more fashionable, than hordes of schoolchildren dressed in matching navy blazers rampaging across the British countryside, slaughtering everyone in sight (*Childmare*, page 56).

Last, but not least: never be home on Halloween. For some reason, that's when the little cherubs absolutely lose their minds. Disregard these warnings and end up like the town of Elliot, Pennsylvania, where, in *Piper* (1987), hundreds of children under the age of thirteen, dressed as adorable witches, pirates, and cowboys, murder three thousand adults one All Hallow's Eve. On the glass-half-full side, the whole town works together and brings their psychotic progeny under control, with local Vietnam and Korean War vets teaming up to machine-gun the little ankle biters into kibble.

As they say: it takes a village.

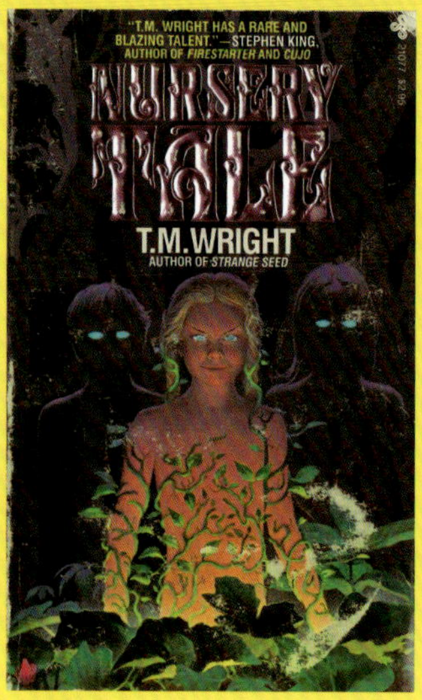
"T.M. WRIGHT HAS A RARE AND BLAZING TALENT." —STEPHEN KING, AUTHOR OF FIRESTARTER AND CUJO
NURSERY TALE
T.M. WRIGHT
AUTHOR OF STRANGE SEED

THE GODSEND
THE CHILD... THE OBSESSION... THE NIGHTMARE...
"IF YOU LIKED THE EXORCIST, THE OTHER & ROSEMARY'S BABY, THE GODSEND IS FOR YOU."
HARTFORD COURANT
BERNARD TAYLOR

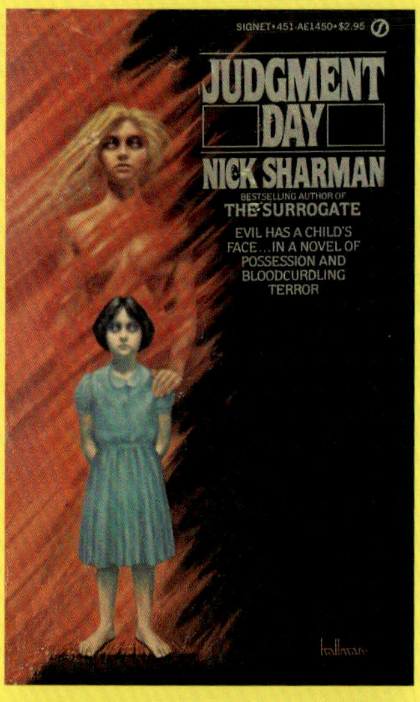
SIGNET•451-AE1450•$2.95
JUDGMENT DAY
NICK SHARMAN
BESTSELLING AUTHOR OF THE SURROGATE
EVIL HAS A CHILD'S FACE...IN A NOVEL OF POSSESSION AND BLOODCURDLING TERROR

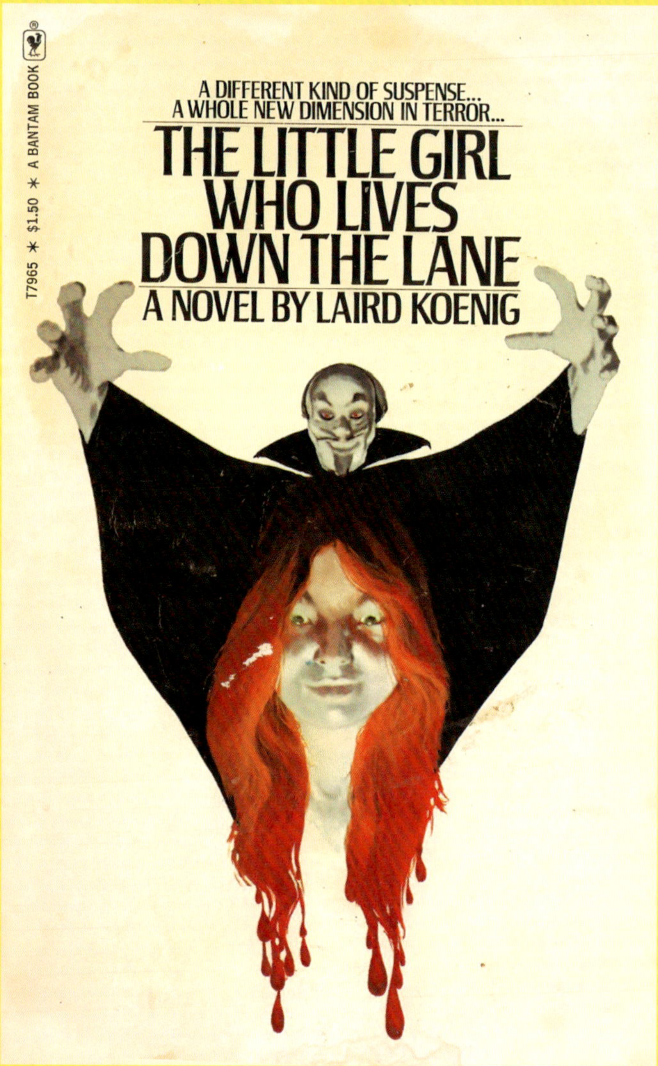
T7965 ★ $1.50 ★ A BANTAM BOOK
A DIFFERENT KIND OF SUSPENSE... A WHOLE NEW DIMENSION IN TERROR...
THE LITTLE GIRL WHO LIVES DOWN THE LANE
A NOVEL BY LAIRD KOENIG

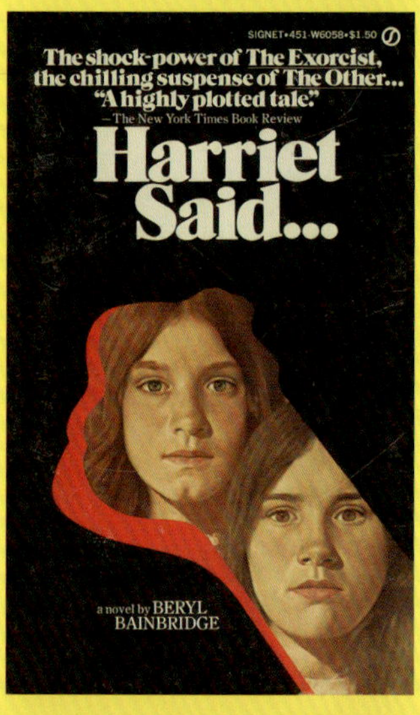
SIGNET•451-W6058•$1.50
The shock-power of The Exorcist, the chilling suspense of The Other... "A highly plotted tale."
—The New York Times Book Review
Harriet Said...
a novel by BERYL BAINBRIDGE

THE FUTURE IS HERE...THE HORROR IS NOW
THE SENDAI
A NOVEL BY
WILLIAM WOOLFOLK
POPULAR LIBRARY

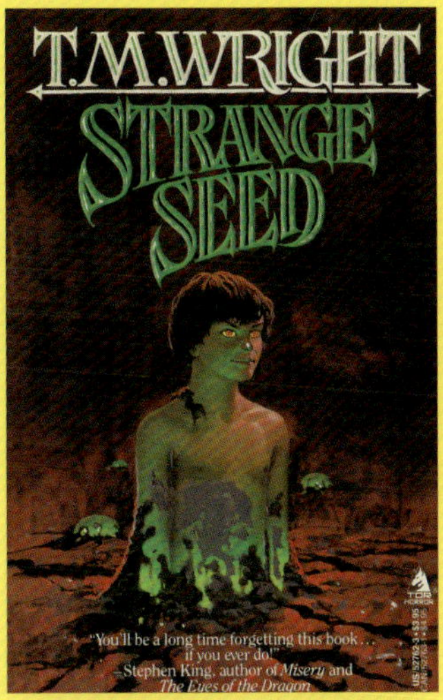

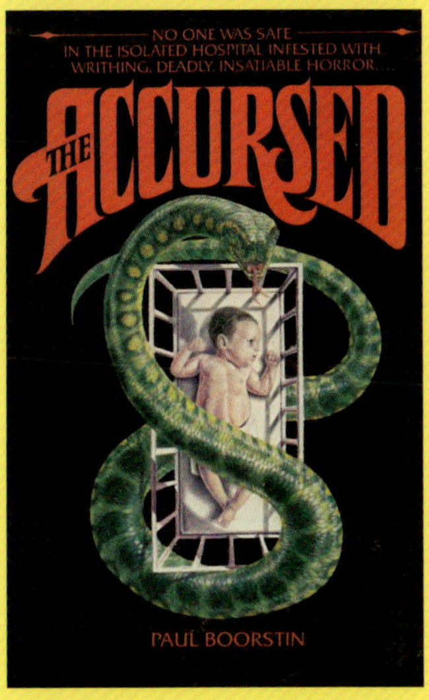

Why do children act out? They might be nature creatures (*Nursery Tale, Strange Seed*), possessed by a vengeful spirit (*Judgment Day*), covering up a murder (*The Little Girl Who Lives Down the Lane*), or plotting a murder (*Harriet Said...*). Maybe they're an ape-human hybrid (*The Sendai*), getting attacked by snakes (*The Accursed*), a hammer-wielding hellion (*Mama's Little Girl*), capable of raising the dead (*The Savior*), or juggling a second personality that's probably a demon (*Smart as the Devil*).

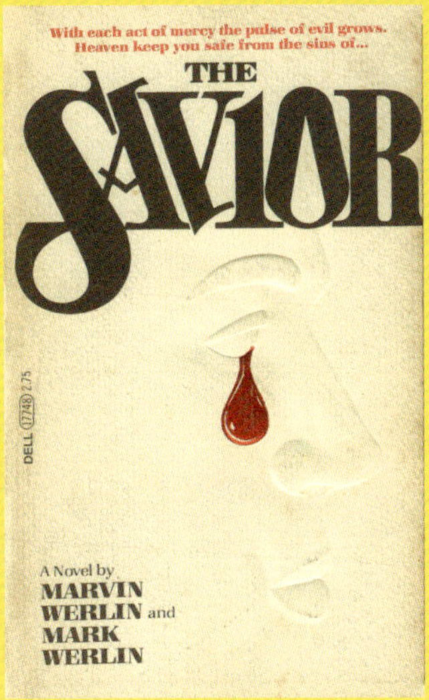

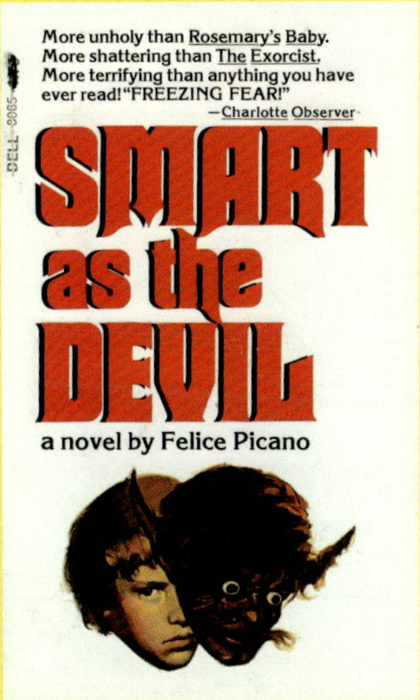

It's All Fun and Games Until . . .

The only book written by Mendal W. Johnson, who died two years after it was published, 1974's *Let's Go Play at the Adams'* still elicits passionate loathing. Search online and you'll find readers who describe destroying the book after finishing it, who write about being left ill, about how sick the author must have been. They call it "misogynistic" and "loathsome." Yet people remember it vividly decades later. It's been published from Australia to Turkey and has inspired two self-published sequels (both available online). The book has serious flaws, but it also sticks with you.

Summer in Maryland. Barbara is 20 years old and she's come to babysit for the Adams children—Bobby, age 12, and his sister Cindy, age 10—while their parents are in Europe for two weeks. Neighborhood kids stop by and go swimming and everything feels like a dream. Then Barbara is chloroformed and wakes up tied to the bed. The neighbors, Dianne (age 17), Paul (age 13), and John (age 16), have decided it would be funny to play games with the babysitter.

Days pass and Barbara is kept bound. Gradually the kids begin to do things to her. As Cindy giggles, "Paul likes girls' feet . . . He's the best at torturing." Barbara's confinement reduces her to her essential self. She's horrified that people she thought were her friends have "no ability or desire to project themselves into her situation or imagine how much she hurt." They treat her like a Barbie doll, and we all know what kids eventually do to their Barbie dolls.

The torture gets worse, and it ends exactly where you're dreading it will, but the sleaziness one would expect isn't there. Instead, the conclusion is suffused with an existential grief. Why the kids do this, no one knows. The closest we come to an answer is when Dianne screams at Barbara, "Somebody has to win, and somebody has to lose." Barbara demands to know what game they're playing. "The one everyone plays . . . The game of who wins the game," Diane answers.

A completely nihilistic vision of the world, *Let's Go Play at the Adams'* doesn't deny the possibility of goodness, or beauty, or grace. It merely points out that those are the things we kill first. As Johnson writes in his final, lyrical chapter: "Goodness, go out of the world."

14139-2 ★ $2.50 ★ A BANTAM BOOK
TONIGHT THE KIDS ARE TAKING CARE OF THE BABYSITTER
LET'S GO PLAY AT THE ADAMS'
A NOVEL OF LINGERING HORROR BY
MENDAL W. JOHNSON

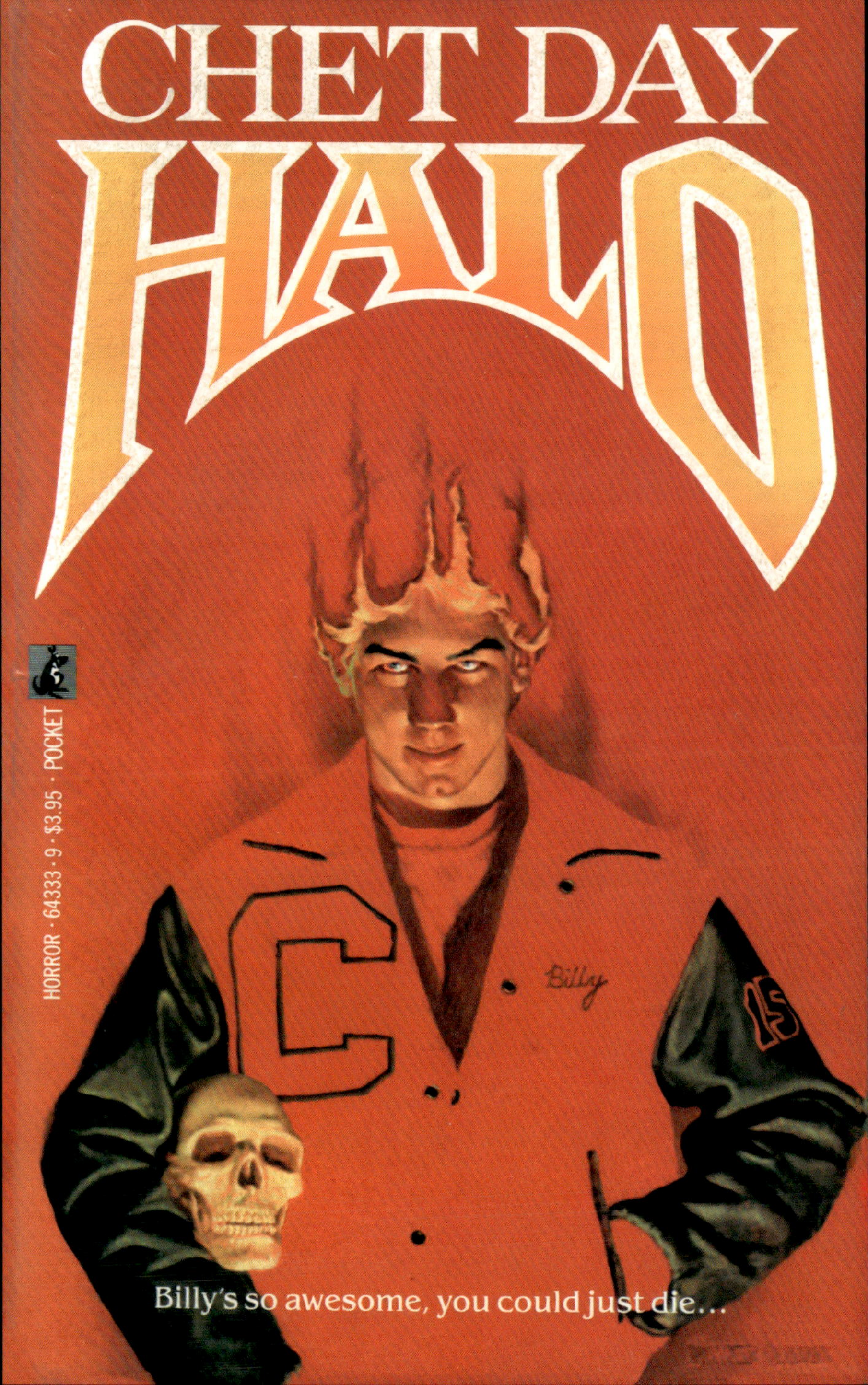
CHET DAY
HALO
HORROR · 64333 · 9 · $3.95 · POCKET
Billy
15
Billy's so awesome, you could just die…

Like a Shane Black movie, it's always Christmas in these books. Even *Halo*, which climaxes at graduation, saves its most sadistic set piece for Christmas vacation.

Attack of the Killer WASPs

In horror fiction, every culture has its own supernatural menace. African Americans get voodoo. The Chinese get fox spirits. And WASPs (white Anglo-Saxon Protestants) get the all-American boy sporting a varsity letter jacket and blinding-white smile that mask the howling maniac on the inside.

Living in exclusive Connecticut neighborhoods or affluent New Orleans suburbs, these families have names like Stuyvesant and Scarborough. The fathers are successful doctors, lawyers, and insurance brokers; the mothers run fashionable boutiques or, preferably, don't work at all. The children attend only the best schools. They love to ski, and their problems are handled by therapists with German accents and names like Dr. Reisenkönig.

Everything is perfect, everyone is privileged, and every single son is hopelessly insane. *Such Nice People* (1981) and *The Sibling* (1979) unfold over that holiest of WASP holidays, Christmas, its silly seasonal anxieties contrasted with sheer horror. In *Such Nice People*, one son sobs helplessly in the toolshed as his imaginary God, SOLA, screams that he must steal a gun and shoot his family. In *The Sibling*, another son disappears into a fantasy world where he must steal pieces of cadavers from a morgue and leave them as love offerings for his little sister.

Halo (1987) takes us into a Reagan-era nightmare set in New Orleans, as quarterback, senior, and class valedictorian Billy Halo writes a motivational to-do list that morphs from "Study hard, get a Porsche, go to Stanford" to "Kill my English teacher, kill my ex-girlfriend, go to Stanford," his charming grin hardening into a death's-head rictus.

What happened? *Such Nice People* blames mental illness. *The Sibling* blames sibling rivalry. *Halo* blames Billy's parents for being oblivious and withholding. These families are all so committed to everything being perfect that they look the other way while their sons murder neighborhood pets, develop Nazi fetishes, and curb-stomp weaker kids. By the time they can no longer ignore the monster in the house, it's too late.

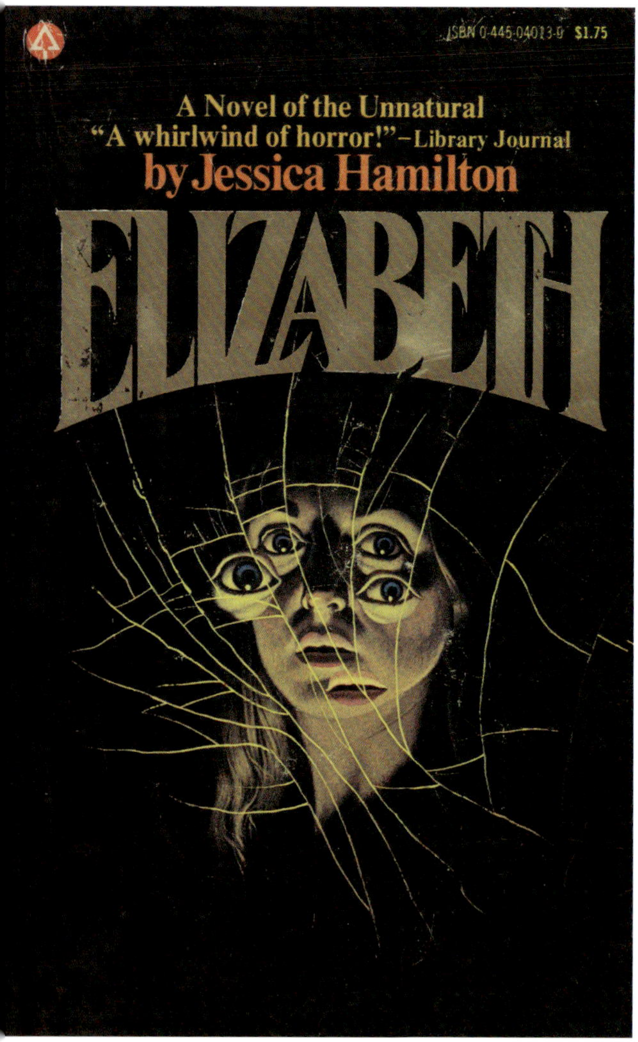

The Whisperer in the Darkness

Subtlety and understatement are not words normally associated with a genre whose covers feature skeleton cheerleaders and hog-tied babysitters, but those qualities are the hallmarks of the six books written by Ken Greenhall (including two under the pseudonym Jessica Hamilton). His characters sit down across from you and tell their stories in measured, reasonable tones. Greenhall writes about animal attacks, witchcraft, serial killers, human sacrifice—and of course, homicidal children—without ever raising his voice.

"When I was younger I saw James, my father's brother, look from our dog to me without changing his expression. I soon taught him to look at me in a way he looked at nothing else." So begins *Elizabeth* (1976). Elizabeth's voice is calm and sophisticated, winding its way around the events of the book as sinuously as a snake. The fourteen-year-old explains how she murdered her parents with witchcraft and started an affair with her uncle, thanks to the assistance of Frances, a long-dead relative and witch executed in the sixteenth century who appears to Elizabeth through mirrors. Or maybe she doesn't. Maybe Elizabeth's parents

Ken Greenhall's books were quieter than his covers . . . and more disturbing.

drowned in a storm. Maybe Elizabeth is insane.

Born to British immigrants in Detroit in 1928, Greenhall graduated from high school at age 15. After serving in the army he moved to New York City, where he lived for the rest of his life, editing encyclopedias. He wrote *Elizabeth* out of the blue, just to see if he could (he also taught himself to play the piano and harpsichord), using his mother's maiden name as a pseudonym. *Elizabeth* landed him an agent but he never felt like part of the New York publishing scene. He was appalled by the cover Zebra Books gave *Hell Hound* (1977), but he was desperate—no other publisher would touch the book. He wrote *Childgrave* (1982) next, trying to deliver a novel that contained slightly more human sympathy, but it still came out dark. Its secrets are best kept safe, for it revolves around the idea that, as one character notes, "Maybe God is not civilized."

Greenhall's next book, *The Companion* (1988), was told from the point of view of an angel of death working for, and occasionally murdering, the elderly. Then came *Death Chain* (1991), about a cognac salesman surrounded by murder. At some point, Greenhall's agent vanished, but when the author went looking for new representation, everyone told him he was too old. Undefeated, he went home, sat down, and wrote *Lenoir* (1998), an elegant historical novel about the black man who posed for Rubens's *Four Studies of the Head of a Negro*. The book was Greenhall's favorite, and his ability to flawlessly evoke the voice of an abducted African slave stranded in seventeenth-century Amsterdam is nothing short of astonishing. But a patronizing review in the *New York Times* broke his heart and he never wrote again. He passed away in 2014.

Greenhall is gone, but his characters—Elizabeth, Baxter, Lenoir—go on talking. They sit across from us, chatting calmly, explaining the madness that infects their lives, and eventually it begins to infect our lives, too. We only have to listen.

Toys 'R' Death

If the house you just moved into has a basement stuffed with old mannequins, run. If it has a "toy room" filled with clown puppets, run faster. Because the only things scarier than children are their toys. In *Keeper of the Children* (1978; page 71), a stuffed Smokey the Bear lays waste to an entire house with its ax, a witch marionette uses part of a bannister as a club, a department store mannequin shows up at the front door holding a golf club, and a superstrong scarecrow comes to kill, leaving "little broomstick footprints" in its wake. Eventually the family dog hurls himself out the second-story window, preferring the sweet release of death to this toybox of terror.

Automatonophobia is the name smug people who've never been chased by witch marionettes give to the irrational fear of inanimate objects that resemble human beings: puppets, robots, mannequins, dolls. But can it be called an irrational fear if dolls can actually kill you? And are in fact eager to do so? From *Ghost Child* (1982) by Duffy Stein:

> *Marionettes surged forward from their pegs along the wall, as if a spring released them, alive, demonic, an army at war, their faces screaming masks. Their cloth bodies swarmed against the girls, covered their noses, their mouths. Their manipulating wires wrapped snake-like around the girls' necks, pulled taut, tore tender skin, severed arteries, closed off windpipes, and strangled and mutilated their defenseless victims.*

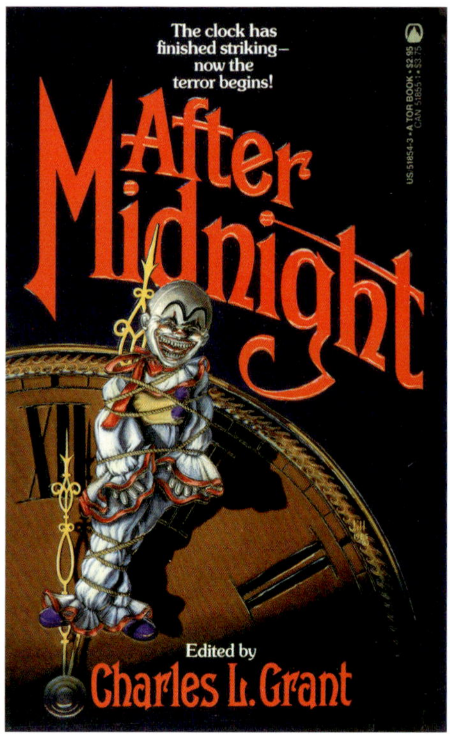

Clown marionettes are bad, but *real* clowns are worse. Since time immemorial, humankind's greatest natural predator has been the clown. Stephen King terrified readers with Pennywise in *It* (1986), but that was centuries after most mammals had learned to flee in terror at the sound of floppy shoes.

Our murderous mountebanks arrive courtesy of the anarchic Harlequin in sixteenth-century commedia dell'arte, followed by the seventeenth-century's insanely violent Punch and Judy puppet shows. The first white-faced, full-makeup-wearing clowns appeared in the nineteenth century. In England it was Joseph Grimaldi, a horribly abused child who became a clown, then retired at age 45 when his tortured joints crumbled to dust. His son, also a clown, drank himself to death at age 30. France's first clown, Jean-Gaspard Deburau, once beat a child to death in the street (he was acquitted).

Dead White's experimental cover caused a stir—and cleverly concealed its cackling horde of killer clowns.

Fictional clowns come with a body count. Edgar Allan Poe's *Hop-Frog* (1849) was a dwarf forced to be a jester who burned eight courtiers to death. *Pagliacci* features opera's most famous clown, a sad sack who stabs his cheating wife to death onstage. In the early 1980s, clown panics erupted in Boston, Omaha, and Pittsburgh when rumors circulated that clowns were luring children into white vans.

Clowns are part of the holy trinity of horror paperback iconography, along with skeletons and dolls, yet few books deliver death jesters. Some of horror fiction's only blood-smeared Bozos appear in Alan Ryan's *Dead White* (1983), the charming Christmas tale of killer clowns riding a circus train of death to a snowbound Catskills community. Obscured by veils of billowing snow, they stay offstage for the most part, appearing only a few times—but that's enough. "The last things Evan Highland saw were the grinning, wide-eyed, red-lipped face of a clown and gigantic white hands that were reaching for his head." And "The clown's grin broadened at once into a merry smile. It tightened its grip on Sally's neck, and then it began to twist her head to the side." Too many more killer clowns than that and the book cover would need a warning label.

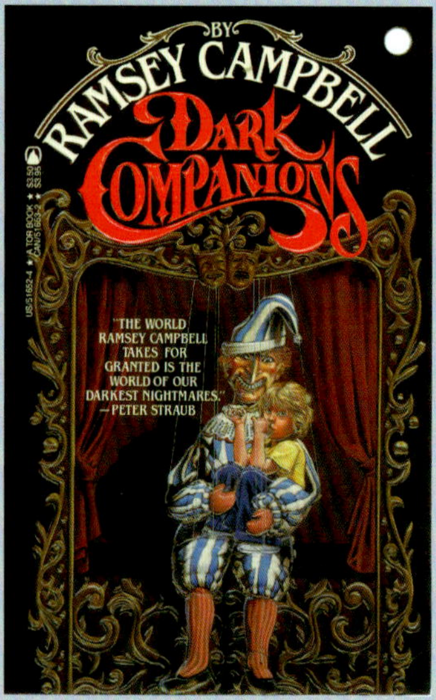

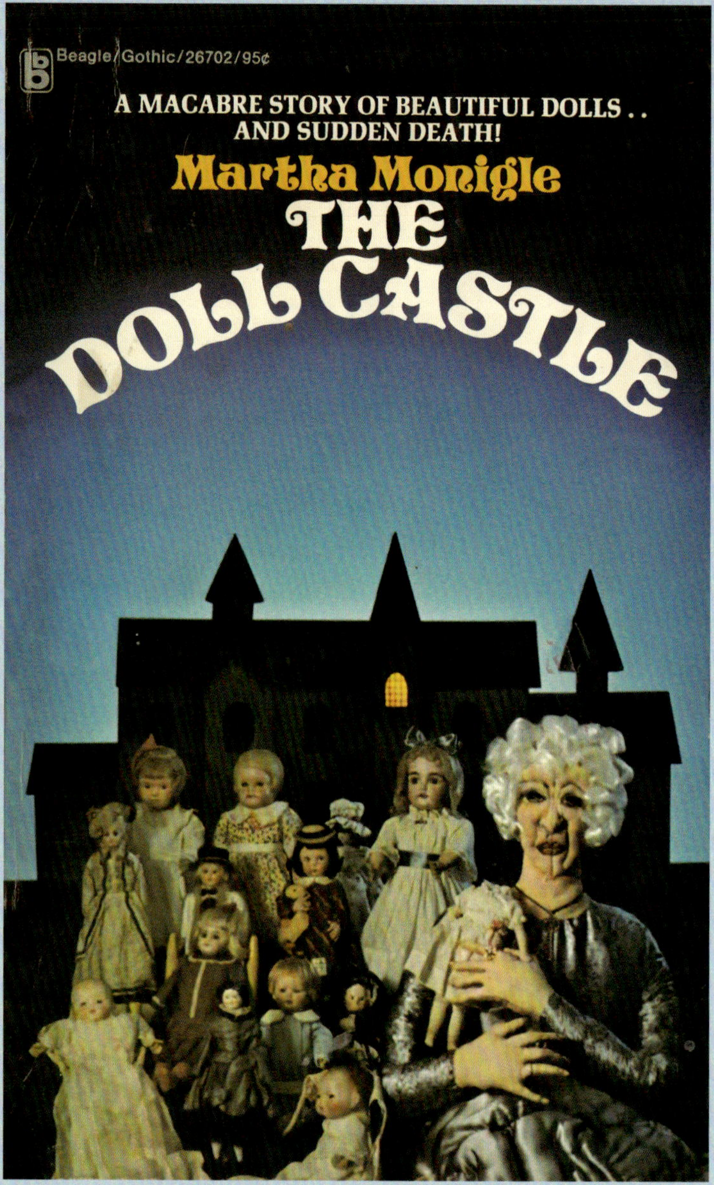

Sometimes a doll on the cover symbolizes possessiveness (*Possession*) or general creepiness (*The Doll Castle*, *Dark Companions*). But in *The Surrogate*, an actual doll gleefully strangles humans, and the ghost kid of *Somebody Come and Play* lures children to their doom with a playroom full of gendered toys: dollhouses and play kitchens for girls, action figures and toy cars for boys. And in *Keeper of the Children*, it's not just a teddy bear with an axe, but also a witch marionette, a mannequin with a golf club, and a scarecrow that gleefully murder humans.

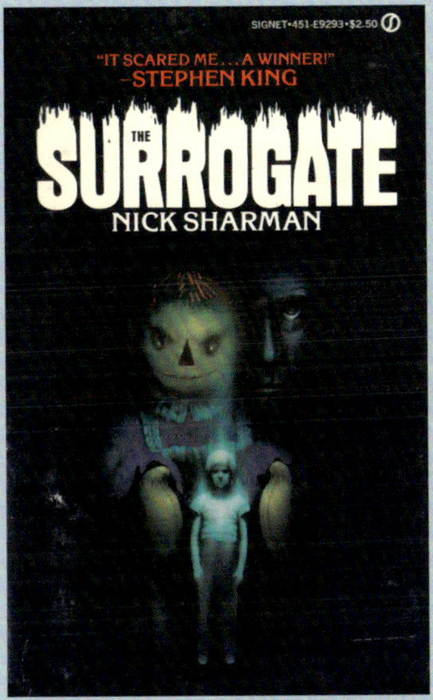
SIGNET•451-E9293•$2.50
"IT SCARED ME . . . A WINNER!"
—STEPHEN KING
THE SURROGATE
NICK SHARMAN

CLARE McNALLY
Bestselling author of Ghost House and Ghost House Revenge
SOMEBODY COME AND PLAY
Death lurked in Nicole's inviting smile!

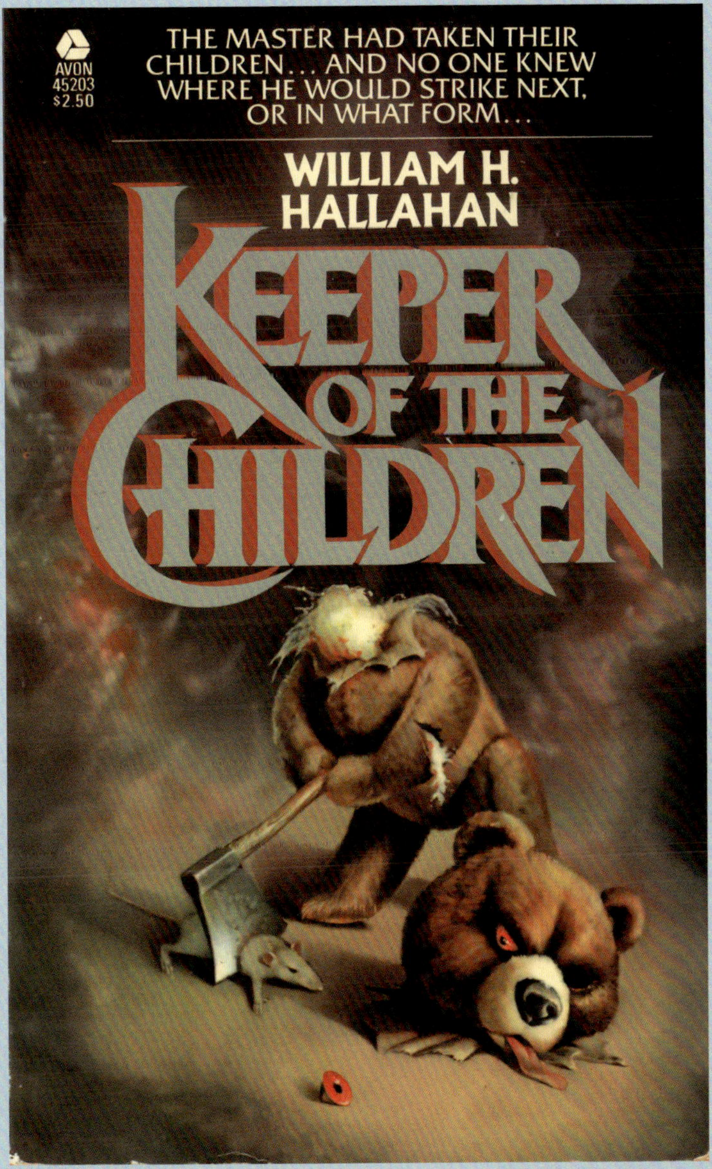
AVON
45203
$2.50
THE MASTER HAD TAKEN THEIR CHILDREN... AND NO ONE KNEW WHERE HE WOULD STRIKE NEXT, OR IN WHAT FORM...
WILLIAM H. HALLAHAN
KEEPER OF THE CHILDREN

If all the knife-wielding kindergarten kids, psychic preschoolers, and homicidal high-school students from this chapter were in a school picture, *The Voice of the Clown* (1982) would be the snarling six-year-old standing slightly to the side, staring into the camera, clutching a clown doll. Her name is Laura, and she sees right through you. Whatever tricks you try to make her like you, she and her clown are ready.

Laura lives in Oklahoma with her daddy and his new family, and she's had her clown doll ever since she was born. It's one of those childhood security objects that just appears in the crib one day and sticks around. But there's one problem: "Her clown hated her mother."

Well, that isn't very comforting. Laura's mother killed herself long ago, and her father's new wife fits right into the fairy-tale tradition of wicked stepmothers, although she doesn't seem to have done anything bad enough to earn the ire of a clown. After Stepmom forces Laura to attend first grade (which ends badly), Laura and her clown declare full-scale war. They start with gaslighting, but when Stepmom gets pregnant and gives birth to what Laura describes as "the screaming mud-baby," things go full psycho. You will have moments when you need to put this book down and walk away.

Later chapters involve some Native American woo-woo, but in the face of the carnage of the final pages, that's a minor speed bump on the highway to hell. This book teaches us one thing about kids: you can't live with 'em, you can't kill 'em. But they sure can kill you.

Clown dolls (*The Voice of the Clown*) and ordinary dolls (*The Kill*) are the hardest working cover models in the horror paperback biz, along with skeletons.

JILL BAUMAN

When Jill Bauman painted the cover for Alan Ryan's *The Kill* she took a doll into the woods, shooting it in as many different poses as possible before draping it over a wooden fence like a corpse. Refusing to depict dead bodies in her paintings, she's since painted dozens, if not hundreds, of dolls on book covers ranging from Elizabeth Engstrom's *When Darkness Loves Us* (page 167) to Edmund Plante's *Garden of Evil* (page 100).

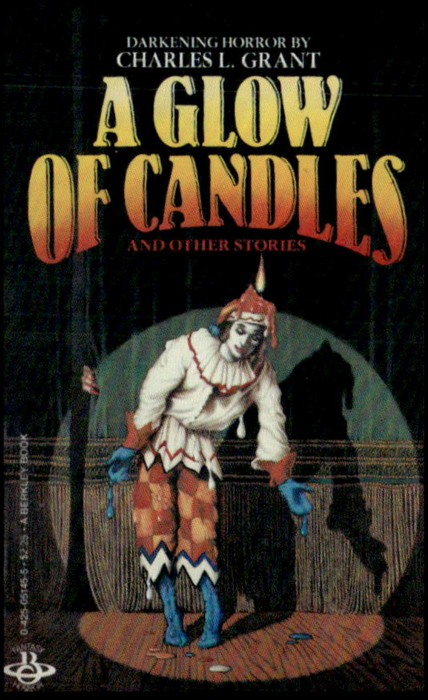

A self-taught painter from Brooklyn, New York, and now living in Queens, Bauman was working as a studio assistant for the painter Walter Velez when he lost his agent. He made her a deal: if she represented his work, he would teach her how to paint. His only condition: she couldn't show her portfolio to anyone for two years. She agreed and two years later she was ready to rock. One of her first covers was for Charles L. Grant's *A Glow of Candles*. "It was my birthday," she remembers. "I thought everybody forgot it, and I was doing this cover, and no one was calling, so I put the candle on top of (the doll's) head. That was my birthday present to myself."

Deeply tied to New York's horror community, Bauman has painted covers (and dolls) not just for Charles Grant's books but for Harlan Ellison, Ramsey Campbell, and everyone in between.

The Only Good Magician Is a Dead Magician

Hating clowns is a waste of time because you'll never loathe a clown as much as he loathes himself. But a magician? Magicians think they're wise and witty, full of patter and panache, walking around like they don't deserve to be shot in the back of the head and dumped in a lake. For all the grandeur of its self-regard, magic consists of nothing more than making a total stranger feel stupid. Worse, the magician usually dresses like a jackass.

Stephen Gresham's *Abracadabra* (1988) manages to be about something even worse than the unholy child/clown alliance: the child/magician union. Meet eleven-year old Olivia Jayne Smith, known as Juice, who loves magic. Juice dances around like a beam of sunshine, dusting her sentences with adorable phrases like "Gosh o'Friday" and "Crime-a-nitly." By the time her alcoholic mom calls her "little bitch mouth," you're kind of on Mom's side.

Juice's pa-nah (what normal people would call Grandpa) belongs to the Sleights-of-Hand, a group of elderly men who love magic so much they gather at one another's homes every month and force their tricks on each other. Juice attends the meetings, showing the men her own pathetic, half-baked tricks, which they indulge because they're too frail to hold a pillow over her face until she stops struggling.

One day, while milling around near the Wilner Theater on the local college campus, Juice stumbles into the basement and opens an old trunk with a skeleton key Pa-Nah gave her, releasing Robert LeFey, a sexy young man who, to cut through a lot of crap, was an evil magician back in the whenevers and got imprisoned in the trunk by the Sleights-of-Hand. He has come back to seek revenge and the Sleights must rally to defeat him.

The fact that the Sleights' master plan to dispose of their dangerous enemy was to lock him in an unguarded trunk and shove it in the basement of the local college drama department gives you an indication of the masterminds we're dealing with. Then again, LeFey can't even lift Pa-Nah's magical skeleton key off a simple-minded girl whose biggest dream is to wear fishnet stockings and wash dove shit out of top hats. This is hardly a battle of titanic intellects.

In the end, the Sleights are rendered helpless when they accidentally lock themselves inside a closet, or something, and Juice must confront LeFey alone. Does she conjure the spirit of Houdini to lend her strength? No. She calls upon the magic of the Rubik's Cube, then she and Pa-Nah and the Sleights use the power of love to zap LeFey with a heavenly spotlight. He disappears into nothingness, leaving behind his clothes.

Because, as *Abracadabra* tells us, "Real magic is people."

And please note, "people" does not include magicians, witches, witch marionettes, clowns, clown dolls, or children. We'd all be a lot safer without any of them.

NOTHING COULD SAVE HER FROM THE HORROR,
NOT EVEN THE MAGIC WORD—
ABRACADABRA
STEPHEN GRESHAM
ZEBRA/0-8217-2350-2 (CANADA $4.95) U.S. $3.95

Toll of the Dice

"Last night I cast my first spell . . . this is real power!"

"Which spell did you cast, Debbie?"

"I used the mind bondage spell on my father. He was trying to stop me from playing D&D. . . . He just bought me $200 worth of new D&D figures and manuals. It was great!"

Ladies and gentlemen, welcome to 1984, the year Jack Chick published his infamous anti-RPG (role-playing game) tract *Dark Dungeons*, claiming that these dice-and-paper games were a gateway to satanism and suicide. But the moral lather that Chick and groups like B.A.D.D. (Bothered About Dungeons and Dragons) worked themselves into stemmed from a very real tragedy: the suicide of a child prodigy named James Dallas Egbert III.

First, the facts. In 1979, Egbert disappeared from his dorm room at Michigan State University and was traced to the steam tunnels that ran beneath the campus. There the trail went cold. His parents hired private investigator and tireless self-promoter William Dear to look into the case. Dear knew that Egbert played Dungeons and Dragons, and he heard that some of the Michigan State students LARPed in the steam tunnels (LARP stands for live-action role-playing, a type of game in which costumed players interact in character.) Dear knew absolutely zilch about D&D, so he told a reporter that the game might have had something to do with the disappearance. That was all the press needed to declare Egbert a victim of a D&D game "gone wrong," igniting a media maelstrom.

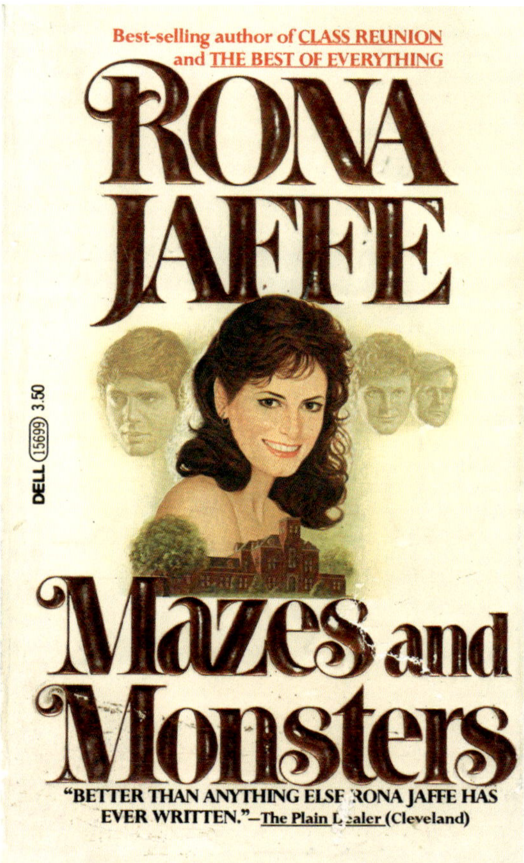

It turns out the only monster in this book is ill-informed writing.

Egbert showed up six months later living in Louisiana under an assumed name, but by then Dear's colorful version of events had taken hold and two relevant books were already on their way to market. The first was from Rona Jaffe, the extremely famous author who, back in 1958, had published the proto–*Sex and the City* best seller *The Best of Everything*. Her subsequent *Mazes and Monsters* (1981), released in the wake of the Egbert scandal, was a book about RPGs written by an author who knew nothing about them—and cared even less.

Jaffe did mint two conventions that

Will a D&D-type game make a high school student more popular, or more murdery? The answer won't surprise you.

became staples of RPG panic books. The first was that each player turns to RPGs because something is broken inside them (usually, divorced parents are to blame). The other is that the games are deeply silly. ("Kate was Glacia, the fighter, Jay Jay was Freelik the Frenetic of Glossamir, a Sprite, and Robbie was Pardieu, a Holy Man.") *Mazes and Monsters* is best remembered today for its TV movie adaptation, which aired in 1982 and featured Tom Hanks in his first leading role, as Pardieu the Holy Man, freaking out on the streets of New York before trying to jump off the World Trade Center.

It's an unwritten rule that if you're going to make a quick buck off a young person's alleged suicide attempt, you should at least be entertaining. Jaffe broke that rule, but John Coyne would not repeat her mistake with his *Hobgoblin* (1981).

Protagonist Scott Gardiner is exactly the kind of kid Jaffe warned us was vulnerable to RPGs' lurid lure: brilliant, creative, socially awkward, and with a dead dad. He's also into a truly terrible RPG called Hobgoblin that may be only slightly less ridiculous than Mazes and Monsters. In a deeply unrealistic touch, Scott became wildly popular after introducing this RPG to Spencertown, his fancy boarding school. But as the story begins, he's not popular anymore. After his dad died (while Scott was playing Hobgoblin, of course) he was sent to public school, where his skill as the 25th level paladin, Brian Boru, makes him not an object of admiration, but a creep.

After ambling along like a slow-moving character study for eighteen chapters, the book delivers a gibbering, blood-drenched climax at the school's Halloween dance as almost every secondary character is gruesomely slaughtered. In a brief epilogue, Scott decides that murdering a man makes him a grown-up and he no longer needs to play Hobgoblin. Ironically, while Jaffe and Coyne posited RPGs as an escape from reality, they're the ones running from the truth, fabricating a fear of games that hadn't harmed anybody, based on false information about a missing person case. Who's the hobgoblin now?

WHEN A
ATT

CHAPTER THREE

NIMALS

ACK

A BANTAM BOOK ★ $1.95 ★ Y8500

#1 SUPERTHRILLER

A NOVEL OF RELENTLESS TERROR

JAWS

BY PETER BENCHLEY

In the early '70s, being killed by Satan or his spawn seemed a lot less likely than being killed by some corner-cutting, penny-pinching, midlevel employee at a giant corporation. In 1967, the captain of the oil tanker *Torrey Canyon* took a short cut on his way to Wales and hit Pollard's Rock, 15 miles off the coast of Cornwall, spilling 25 million gallons of crude oil and unleashing a lethal 270-square-mile slick. In 1969, a blowout on Union Oil's Platform A off the coast of California coated 30 miles of shoreline with black sludge. Ohio's Cuyahoga River was so polluted with industrial runoff that it burst into flames. The toxic water of Lake Erie was devoid of life.

Suddenly, everyone noticed we were destroying the planet, and so in 1970 the Environmental Protection Agency was created, the same year the first Earth Day was held and Greenpeace was founded. The Clean Air Act of 1970 was followed by the Clean Water Act in 1972, and then the Endangered Species Act in 1973. It was clear that nature needed to be protected from us. But who would protect us from nature?

H. G. Wells had written about vast armies of ants eating Brazilians in 1905, and Daphne du Maurier and Alfred Hitchcock had introduced audiences to death from the skies in *The Birds* (1963), but 1974 was pop culture's Year of the Animal. First came *Jaws* by Peter Benchley, a novel about a stressed-out great white shark suffering from portion control issues. It sank its teeth into the *New York Times* Best-Seller List and hung on for an astonishing forty-five weeks. In the summer of 1975, Steven Spielberg's big-screen adaptation became an *Exorcist*-sized blockbuster, ensuring that a generation of children would be so terrified of sharks, they'd fish them into near extinction over the next three decades.

Watership Down was already a hit in England, but in April 1974 it debuted in the United States, where Richard Adams's saga of brave bunnies outsold Peter Benchley's angry shark, remaining on the *New York Times* Best Seller List until January 1975. In the United Kingdom, the first animal rights groups were standing trial for carrying out raids on animal-testing laboratories. And over in a grungy part of London, a 28-year-old advertising copywriter named James Herbert was writing his first novel, all about his deepest childhood fear. It was called *The Rats*.

Year of the Rat

It was the year punk rock broke: 1974. It was also the year James Herbert published *The Rats*, which is pretty much the same thing. By the time Herbert died in 2013, he was the United Kingdom's most successful horror novelist, with 54 million books sold worldwide. He wrote ghost stories, alternate histories, and thrillers, but his first two books—*The Rats* and *The Fog* (1975)—are proto-punk ragers: nasty, mean, anti-establishment sleaze ripped straight from Herbert's id and redeemed by his complete and utter conviction to *go there*. Stephen King has noted that Herbert's books have a "raw urgency," and if by "raw" he means "totally flayed of skin" and if by "urgency" he means "gripping you by the collar and screaming in your face," then we agree.

The former is a blockhead of a book. What is it about? Rats. What do they do? Eat everyone. Martin Amis, reviewing for the *Observer*, wrote that the novel was "enough to make a rodent retch, undeniably, and enough to make any human pitch the book aside." But even back then no one cared what Martin Amis had to say, and the initial 100,000-copy print run sold out in a couple of weeks.

In the future, Herbert would design his own book covers, flouting conventions, insisting on white backgrounds (black was standard for horror) and shocking his publishers by combining silver and gold foil.

By chapter 3 the rats have eaten a puppy and ripped the flesh off a baby. There's stream of consciousness narration as people are eaten alive. "Rats! His mind screamed the words. Rats eating me alive! God, God help me." The only thing the rats don't eat is Harris, a man of action. A no-nonsense East London art teacher who comes complete with a girlfriend in need of constant rescue, Harris is practical and tough and suspicious of so-called experts. When the city of London hires exterminators, Harris scoffs.

The undersecretary of the Ministry of Health gasses the rats and they disappear. Problem solved? Not so fast, sneers Harris . . . and the rats come swarming back. They overrun a train and eat an assortment of Londoners. Only Harris proves inedible, saving his school by punching the rodents to death. Next up: ultrasonics. Harris thinks gas is for girls and ultrasonics are stupid. Instead he grabs an ax, drives over a living carpet of rats, and finds the gigantic two-headed rat boss. "Its body popped like a huge balloon filled with dark red blood." The End.

The man of action in Herbert's next book, *The Fog*, is John Holman, who's investigating a military chemical weapons site for the Department of the Environment when a fissure opens in the earth, sending a toxic gas spraying from its maw. It forms a cloud and drifts across England like a deadly fart, turning cows psychotic, making schoolboys castrate their gym teachers (Herbert hates gym teachers), causing pigeons to peck people to death, and making a pilot fly a loaded plane into the GPO Tower. In one of the book's most famous scenes, 148,820 people commit suicide by walking into the sea.

Proving that smaller was scarier, Herbert moved from hungry rats to insanity-inducing bacteria.

The gas turns out to be the work of a bacteria called a mycoplasma that has grown enormous, but Holman could give a flip. He's going to blow it the hell up. Scientists, cops, and government officials try to stop him, but inevitably they return red-faced. "Erm, it seems we might owe you an apology, Holman," they stammer. Damn straight, crybabies! London goes insane while Holman plays football with a severed head, drives a Devastation Vehicle over some religious fanatics, machine-guns a crowd of berserk bus drivers, saves the day with a bomb, then rescues his girlfriend and swears to bring down all the bastards in government. The End.

Herbert turned out two *Rats* sequels: *Lair* in 1979 and *Domain* in 1984, which don't quite stand up to the original (though the rats still eat a lot of gym teachers). It was *The Rats* (and to some extent *The Fog*) that set the template for everything that came after, for Herbert had revealed a great truth to aspiring horror novelists that would guide British horror books for the next twenty years: human beings are delicious, and England is full of them.

Man's Worst Friend

In the wake of *Jaws*, it didn't take a genius to figure out that the one way to make a killer shark scarier was to make it the family pet. But since most people don't let sharks sleep in their bed or take them out for walkies, dogs became the new sharks. *Cujo* (1981) is the book most associated with killer canines, but the subgenre was going strong by the time Stephen King published his ambitious novel about a good dog gone mad due to a bad bat with rabies.

The problem with killer-dog books is that most people like dogs, so as soon as a canine eats a kid, we find ourselves wondering what the kid did to provoke it. As a result, these novels are often real bummers. Robert Calder (a pen name for Jerrold Mundis) can't make us hate the lab animal on the run in *The Dogs* (1976), and in *The Long Dark Night* (1978; adapted for the screen as *The Pack*), callous summer vacationers pretty much get what's coming to them at the paws of the dogs they heartlessly abandon each year. Even homicidal Baxter the bull terrier in *Hell Hound* (see page 66) is the most likable character in Greenhall's book.

One way writers sought to make dogs scarier was to give them rabies. *Rabid* sees a pair of upper-class twits smuggle a French dog through British animal quarantine, unleashing a wave of death-dealing doggies on the U.K. All brown corduroy and tweed, the story's told in the deadpan tones of a BBC informational film, even as infected corgis turn on their owners and Jack Russell terriers rampage through the countryside, leaving half-eaten tramps in their wake.

But as robust as this trend was, dogs never became the new rats. That job was left to cats.

Angry puppies were England's worst nightmare, even in the future England of talking animals depicted in *The Haven.*

THE PACK
Fueled by an insatiable hunger, driven by a consuming madness, the pack ravaged the countryside, killing for sport—killing for food.
Possessed of an unnatural intelligence, skilled at stalking and attacking, they chased and devoured their human prey with the icy, snarling efficiency of the perfect killing machine.
Once they had been pets, now they were man's worst enemy—and their numbers were swelling.
BEWARE THEIR SLAVERING JAWS OF DEATH!
ISBN 0-8439-2532-9
THE PACK
WILLIAM ESSEX
NOWHERE TO RUN, NOWHERE TO HIDE.
THE PACK
WILLIAM ESSEX

BITTER WINTER, AND THE DOGS OF SUMMER HAVE GROWN HUNGRY… AND VICIOUS
THE LONG DARK NIGHT
formerly THE PACK
DAVID FISHER
A TRULY TERRIFYING MOVIE FROM WARNER BROS.

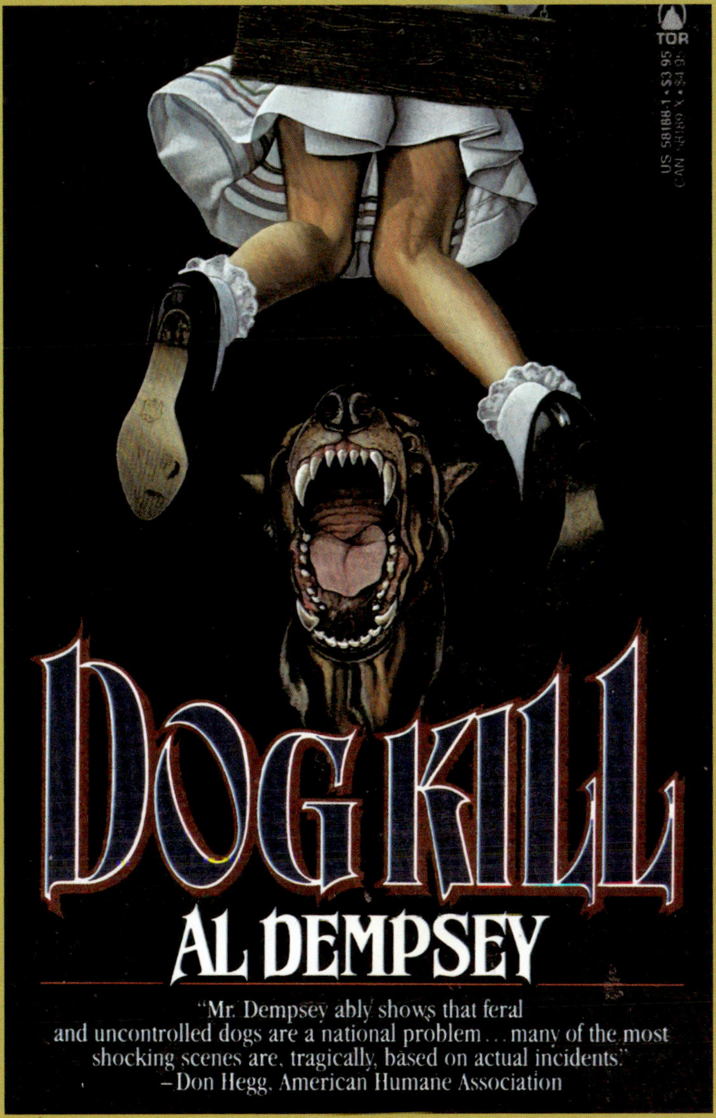
TOR
US 58188-1 $3.95
DOG KILL
AL DEMPSEY
"Mr. Dempsey ably shows that feral and uncontrolled dogs are a national problem… many of the most shocking scenes are, tragically, based on actual incidents."
–Don Hegg, American Humane Association

6398 $1.95
THE HAVEN
A NOVEL OF BLOOD CURDLING HORROR
BY G R. DIAMOND

SIGNET•451-AE1270•$2.75
THE KILLER WOLVES ARE COMING—A NOVEL OF GNAWING, HOWLING HORROR!
BLOOD SNARL
IVOR WATKINS

Eye of the Tiger

Imagine what it was like to be Nick Sharman. For three years he woke up every morning, checked the papers, and saw that no one had done it yet. He didn't want to do it. He kept waiting for someone else to do it, because it was so damn obvious. Then one morning, three years after James Herbert had unleashed his *Rats*, Sharman picked up his pen and unleashed . . . *The Cats*.

Just as we're predisposed to like dogs, most people consider cats far too lazy and irresponsible to engage in organized mayhem. Write a scene in which an army of cats descends on London, and most people will assume that at any moment they'll lose interest and start rolling around in a sunbeam or chasing laser pointers. Kitties are just too cute and fluffy to be scary, and scenes of their soft paws poking under doors induce giggles rather than gasps. When a radio announcer is buried alive in an avalanche of mewling kittens, the immediate reaction is not one of horror but a soul-deep "awwwww . . ."

In fact, it's the humans who look like the sadistic monsters in Cats Gone Wild books, saying things like, "So, the plan is to wait for the cats to show themselves and then go at them with flame throwers." When the felines are finally burned alive with napalm and the survivors are machine-gunned, it feels like something of an overreaction, especially when we all know that a helicopter dangling a bit of string could have led them out of town just as efficiently.

But cats have an inherent nobility that dogs and rats lack, which is probably why humans feel better when we bring them down to our buffoonish level by dressing them in reindeer antlers for holiday cards. Ha-ha! Look at the covers of *Night-Shriek* and *Satan's Pets*! The kitties are wearing wigs! Ha-ha-ha!

You're not laughing. What's the matter? Cat got your tongue? And your liver? And your face?

Before the internet, cats were sometimes considered less than cute.

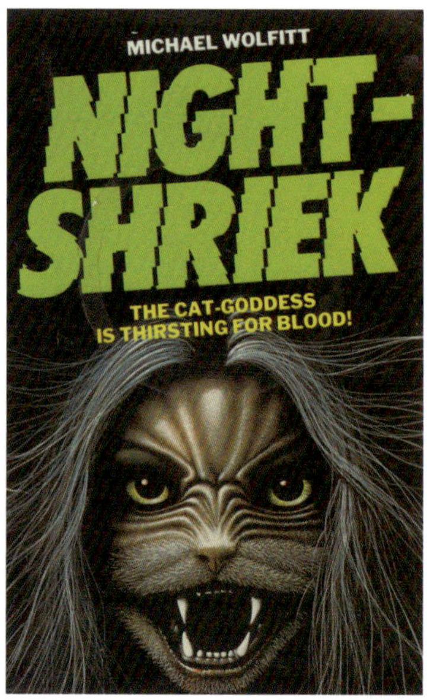

When Alan Ryan took his novel *Panther!* to Signet, he also brought a cover by his friend, artist Jill Bauman (see page 73). The publishers didn't like being told what to do, so they rejected the cover and commissioned new art by Tom Hallman. Published here for the first time is Bauman's unused cover (above), along with the image that was used in its place (right).

DAVID ANNE
THE FOLLY
By the author of Rabid-Day of the Mad Dogs

Today's Menu: You

There is not an animal that walks, crawls, swims, or flies that does not want humankind dead. Bears hate us, bats hate us, dogs and cats clearly hate us. Let's face it, humans are delicious. In the eyes of animals, we are walking pizzas, and the best thing is that we deliver ourselves.

In the four years after James Herbert's *The Rats*, every critter got a turn at the all-you-can-eat human-meat buffet. Authors reveled in an escalating arms race to find new creatures—bees, alligators, fire ants!—that could tear us apart like chicken wings. A mere year after his public-health-scare screed *Rabid*, David Anne thought he had a winner in *The Folly* (1978). What man could contain his screams when confronted with killer rabbits? And not just any rabbits—genetically engineered rat rabbits "from the spawning-ground of hell."

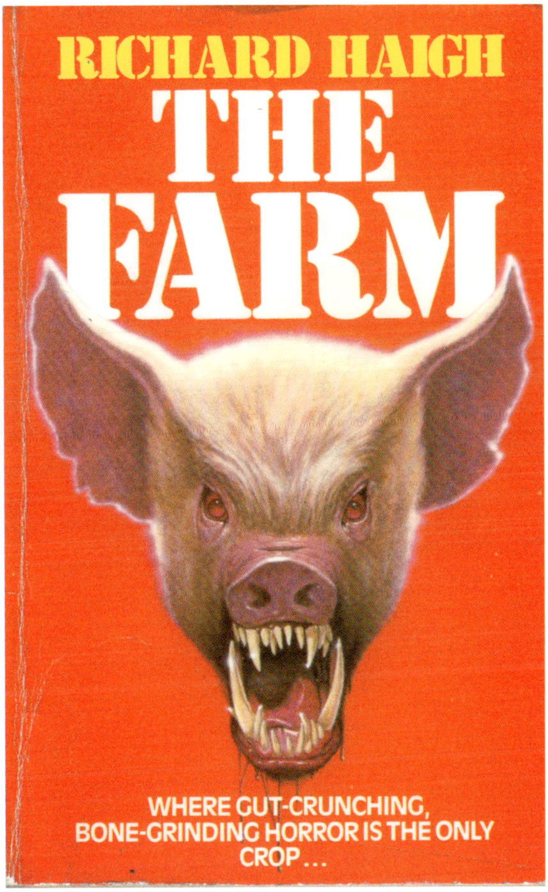

Apparently no species is too cute (*The Folly*), domesticated (*The Farm*, *Taurus*), or satisfied with its diet (*The Predators*) to want a piece of us.

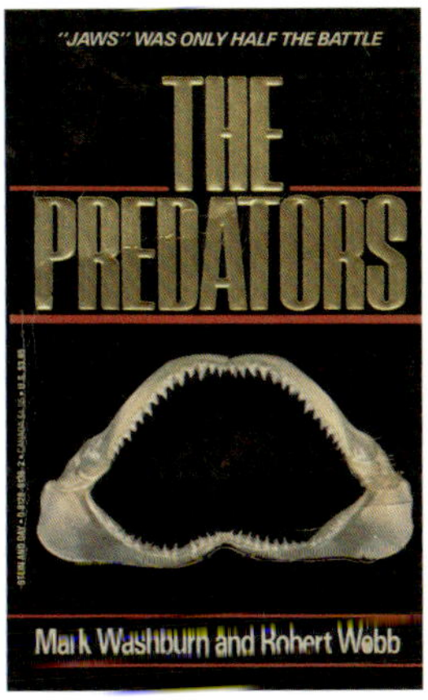

Those bunnies have nothing on Academy Award–winning screenwriter George Wells's sole novel, the scrotum-ripping *Taurus* (1982), about Mexican bulls retired from the bullfighting circuit who get stoned on agave roots and go on a crime spree across Mexico, murdering women with their enormous penises, killing men by goring them in the crotch, and generally demonstrating that bulls are "the most virile animal the world has ever known."

More stoned animals go wild as geese, pigs, goats, even cows get high on ketamine and unleash hell on Old McDonald's murder farm in *The Farm* (1984). The pigs proved popular and trotted off into the sequel, *The City* (1986). Animal-amok literature reached peak lunacy with Mark Washburn and Robert Webb's *The Predators*, in which a Kodiak bear and a great white shark battle each other on pay-per-view cable. Whichever one loses, the reader wins.

Seafood Gumbo

In the wake of *Jaws*, humanity was under siege from an all-you-can-eat seafood buffet of aquatic horror. Enraged tuna (*Fleshbait*, 1979), mutant lampreys (*Pestilence*, 1983), and even the lowly jellyfish (*Slime*, 1984) all worked together to make people the catch of the day. But the stars of this feeding frenzy turned out to be killer whales. As Arthur Herzog (author of bee-attack best seller *The Swarm*) reminds readers repeatedly in *Orca* (1977), killer whales are the only animals besides humans that kill for revenge.

Peter Tonkin builds a better *Jaws* with *Killer*, dropping the awkward Mafia and infidelity subplots from Peter Benchley's best seller and cutting right to the good stuff: five characters, stranded on an ice floe, at the mercy of a pod of killer whales, led by a crazed super-whale escaped from a military laboratory. It's a nonstop symphony of chaos as these angry pandas of the sea bite off blue whale tongues while botanists toss dynamite at herds of stampeding walruses. Arms are eaten, whales' brains are stabbed, and burst bodies sail through the air like exploded paper bags.

Next up: crabs. What could drive a crab to kill? Doesn't take much, as it turns out. They're the angriest residents in nature's death zoo. You barely have to look at one sideways before it's making menacing clickety-clicks.

Like some kind of crustacean Churchill, King Crab leads his minions out of the Irish Sea and onto Britain's holiday beaches in *Night*

Don't go *in* the water. Don't go *near* the water. You know what—move to a landlocked nation and stay there.

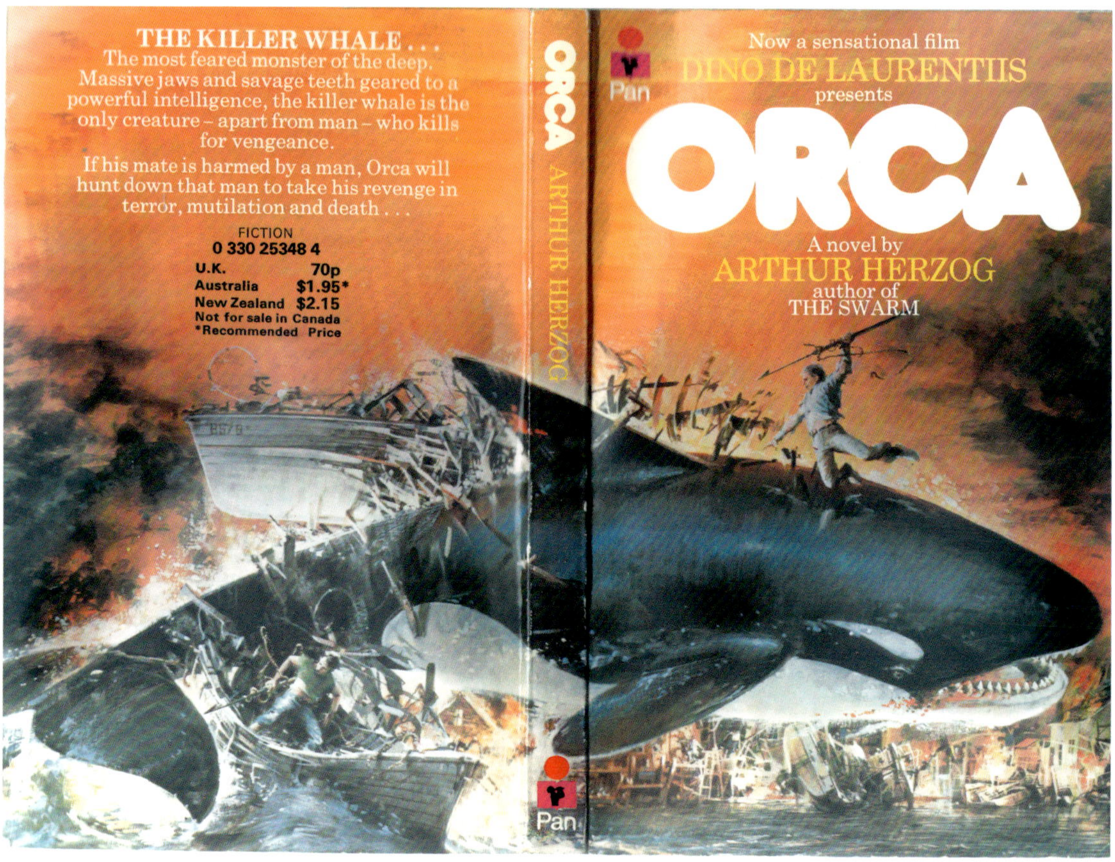

DAVID HOLMAN AND LARRY PRYCE
FLESHBAIT
SUDDENLY- -THE SEA BECOMES A FOCUS OF TERROR

Edward Jarvis
Pestilence
Don't go
near the water!
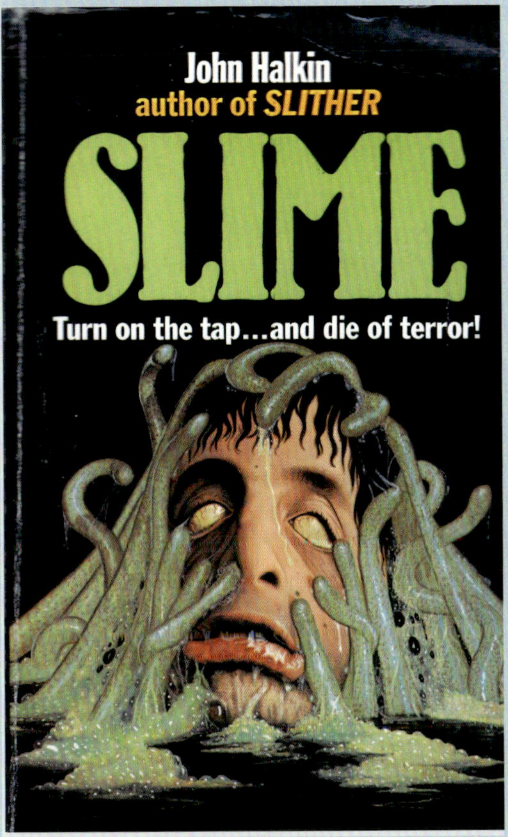
John Halkin
author of SLITHER
SLIME
Turn on the tap...and die of terror!

SIGNET•451-E9241•$2.50
FROM OUT OF THE DEEP CAME FREEZING
TERROR..."ADVENTURE, ROMANCE, BLOODY ACTION...
THE EXCITEMENT AND VIOLENT DRAMA OF JAWS!"
—LIBRARY JOURNAL
KILLER
A NOVEL BY
PETER TONKIN

of the Crabs (1976). It is an awesome sight. Crabs enjoy nothing more than a nice rampage, so for them it's an excellent bonus to discover that someone has brought their favorite food to the party: human guts. Don't mind if I do, say the crabs, although in their language it sounds more like clickety-click-click, as they start with the tramp platter.

As the crabs topple our bridges, it seems that humanity has no choice—mankind is on the menu. Yet King Crab has made one fatal miscalculation. He has eaten Professor Cliff Davenport's favorite nephew. Now it's personal.

Davenport is not only Britain's top marine biologist, he's also its loneliest. Only constant work can fill his long, solitary nights, and now he commits his stiff upper lip and his sad coping skills to avenge his nephew.

Davenport meets Pat, a young woman as lonely as he is, who brings his dusty old penis back to life after years in storage. Reinvigorated by her ministrations, Davenport remembers paraquat, the common weed killer found in every British garden shed that's so toxic it can cause Parkinson's disease. Davenport dives over King Crab's army in his helicopter, drenching them in this toxic soup, killing them where they scuttle. The few survivors retreat on a shame march back into the sea.

Still, these crustaceans are not crushed. In the next book they pop up in Australia, where they spring two surprises. First, they've developed a fire allergy since their last clash, and second, King Crab is actually Queen Crab. A last-minute crab boil saves the valiant Aussies, and the crabs return to Britain to demand what is rightfully theirs: London! Pushing inland, aided in part by animal rights activists who worship them as gods and tie human treats to bridges as snacks, theirs seems less a good-natured rampage and more a full-blown revolution.

Thanks to their previous poison shower, the crabs live up to their zodiac sign and develop cancer. They all die immediately, proving once again that no animal can withstand humankind's pollution.

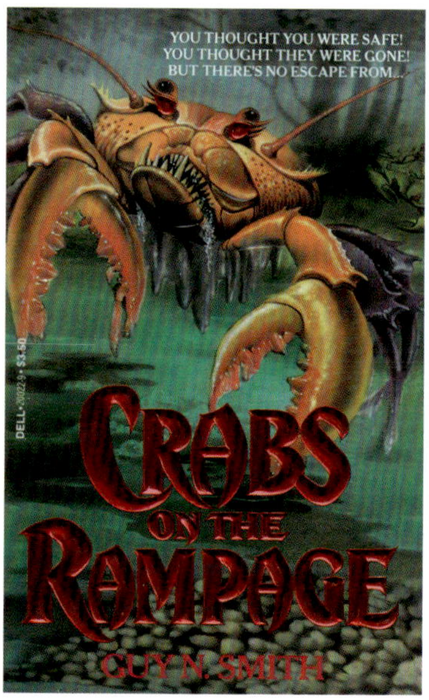

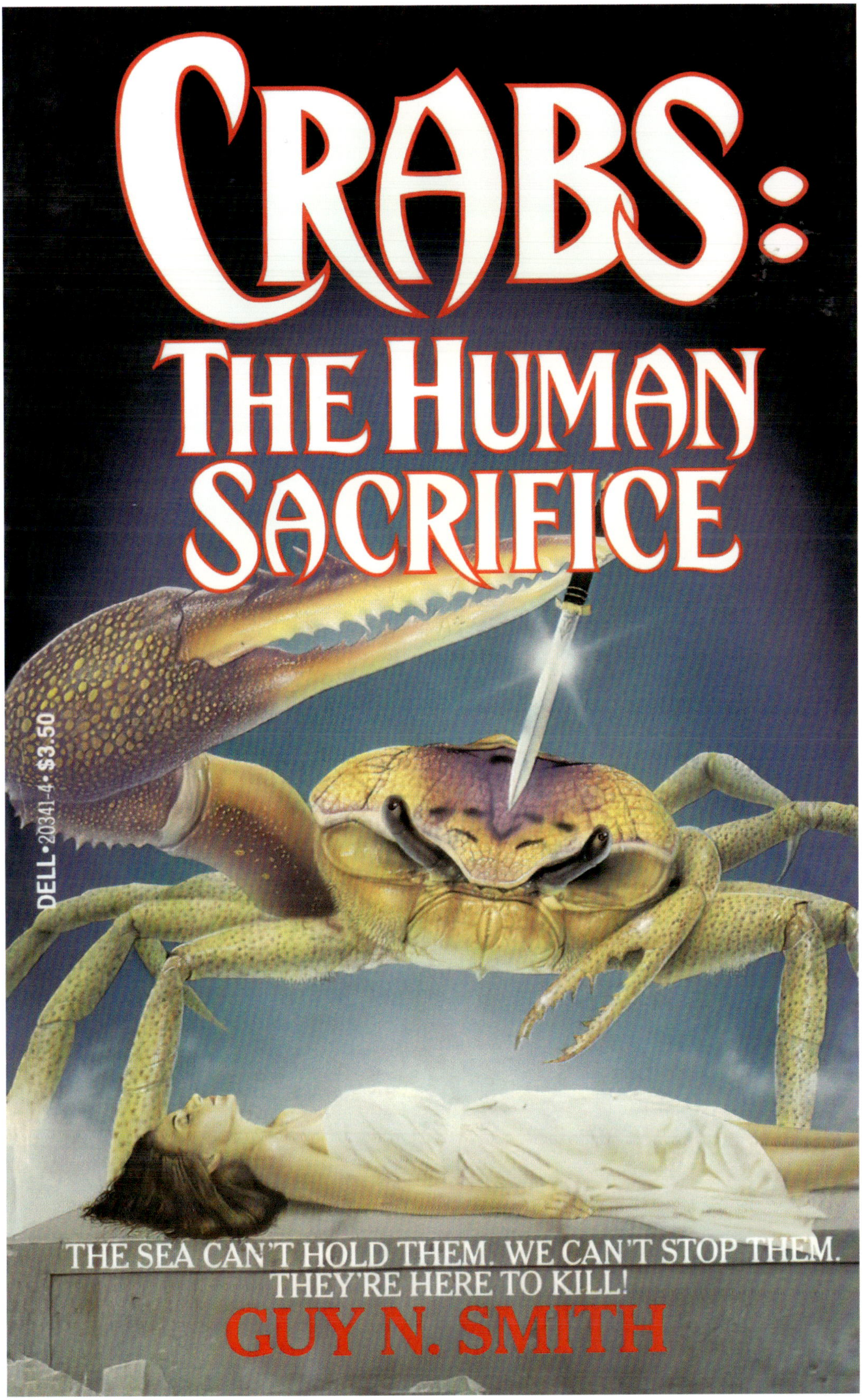
CRABS:
THE HUMAN SACRIFICE
DELL•20341-4•$3.50
THE SEA CAN'T HOLD THEM. WE CAN'T STOP THEM.
THEY'RE HERE TO KILL!
GUY N. SMITH

Death Comes Crawling

The smaller something is, the scarier it seems. Hence Michael Crichton's *The Andromeda Strain*, about a killer microbe, sold millions of copies, whereas no one has ever written a book called *Stomp*, about killer elephants. Insects nestle into that sweet spot: small enough to be disgusting, yet big enough to be dangerous. Even better, in their perpetual search for new critters to feast on human flesh, authors have 950,000 insect species to choose from. Whether in Peter Tremayne's *The Ants* (1979), Edward Jarvis's *Maggots* (1986), or Shaun Hutson's *Slugs* (1982), tiny beasties seem united in their hatred of humanity.

Starting with the inevitable prologue and always ending with the survival of a few hardy specimens (just in case sales justify a sequel), these books have much in common. They take place almost exclusively during the hottest day/week/month of the year after radiation/evolution/untested insecticide causes fauna to mutate. Insect-attack books are basically morality tales in which unscrupulous developers, ethics-free businessmen, and ineffectual local leaders find their scale-balancing comeuppances between chitinous mandibles.

The exception is Pierce Nace's wildly amoral *Eat Them Alive* (1977), in which Dyke Mellis tries to double-cross his criminal associates after a robbery. They foil his plan, castrate him, and leave him to die in the desert. Dyke recovers and is hiding in South America almost a decade later when an earthquake raises an island full of ten-foot-tall praying mantises off the coast. Immediately turning giant praying mantises into giant praying-mantis lemonade, Dyke trains them to kill at his command. He then makes his way to the home of each member of his old gang, letting his army of trained killer mantises eat them alive, usually starting with their genitals. In the end, someone with the same idea, only equipped with an army of even bigger praying mantises, lets them eat Dyke alive. There is no moral. God is dead and life is a bleak, dark tunnel lined with hungry insects.

Horror's biggest mystery: Who is Pierce Nace? The best guess is that she's Evelyn Pierce Nace, a 69-year-old Texan credited with authoring 40 paperbacks.

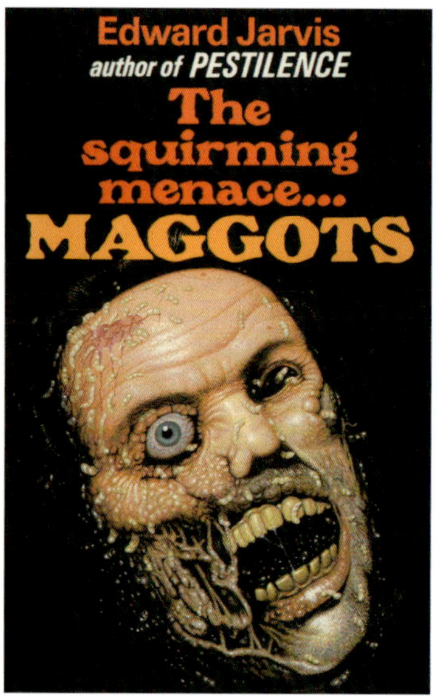

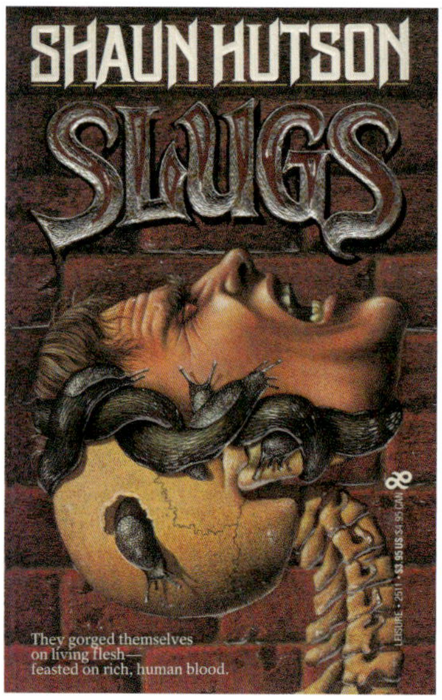

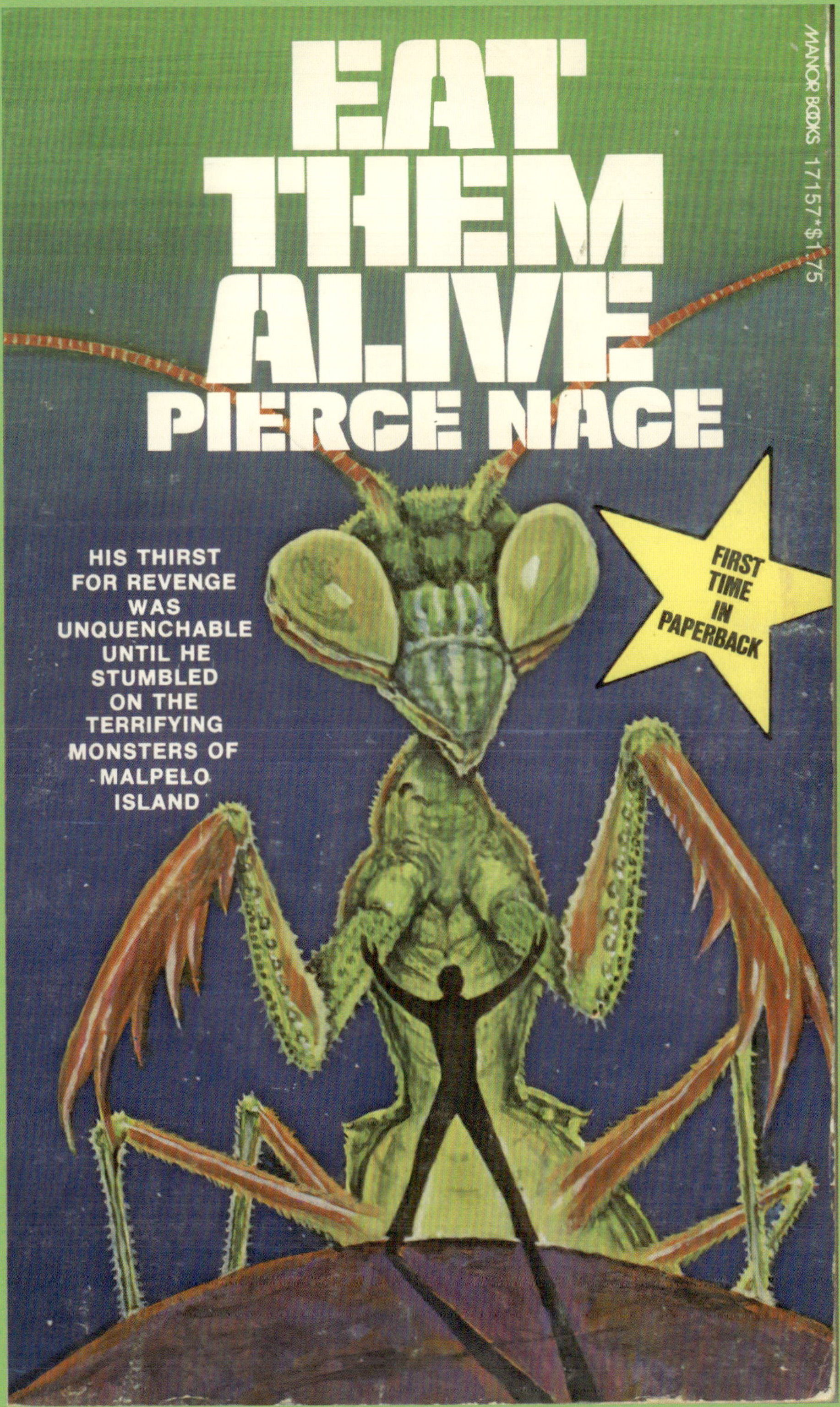
MANOR BOOKS 17157*$1.75
EAT THEM ALIVE
PIERCE NACE
HIS THIRST FOR REVENGE WAS UNQUENCHABLE UNTIL HE STUMBLED ON THE TERRIFYING MONSTERS OF MALPELO ISLAND
FIRST TIME IN PAPERBACK

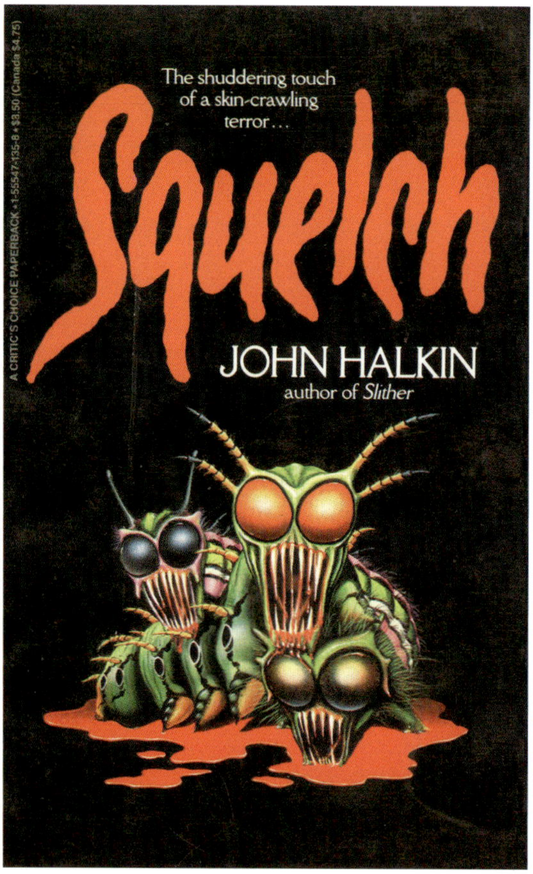

But insects don't just want to teach us how to be good by chewing off our faces—they also want to gobble our junk. Michael R. Linaker's scorpions (technically arachnids, but still likely to invade England, so basically insects) focus their attacks on women's breasts when they aren't spreading mayhem at the nearby circus. John Halkin's caterpillars in *Squelch* (1985) home in on a police constable's groin. And the seemingly benign moths of Mark Sonders's *Blight* (1981) are full of surprises, as one young mother discovers when she is swarmed to death:

"They could hurt her no more. They had done their worst. Or so she thought. An intense slice of pain, unlike any she had ever before experienced, made her body jerk upright into a sitting position as the moths attacked and conquered areas obscenely tender and private."

Moths are the Rocky Balboas of the killer-insect world. "They're moths, man. Just moths," someone observes. "They don't even have teeth." True, but, squeaking like bats, the moths unroll their savage proboscises and suck the blood out of humans, leaving baffled and dying characters in their wake. "Moths attack sweaters and fly around light bulbs. They don't devour humans." And yet they do, flying into ears and noses, down throats, and, unfortunately, up butts.

Strangely, the insect apocalypse seems to put everyone in the mood for love. In *Squelch*, after her sister has half her foot gnawed off by a hungry caterpillar, a young television director leaps into bed with her brother-in-law. In *Blood Worm* (1987; page 99), the main character's wife sleeps with an enormous number of men during the worm-and beetle apocalypse and then leaves a note for her husband saying she's a slut and, by the way, their daughter is missing. She immediately becomes an alcoholic hobo and is last seen stumbling around the ruins of London, which has been abandoned to the inevitable postapocalyptic motorcycle gangs.

These characters' inclination toward romance could be due to spending much of their time drunk in pubs. Always the first meeting place for farmers alarmed that their prize sheep have been eaten by something they've never encountered before, the pubs never seem to close, no matter how many slugs reduce the local citizenry to piles of grisly bones or how many snails drag their prey from bed and into their hell maws. Gin and whiskey are dispensed liberally all day long, and everyone seems to be playing a drinking game: receive a shock, take a drink.

It's also no surprise that in their inebriated state, humans often make terrible decisions—going outside in the dark to investigate why the dog suddenly stopped barking, or battling the caterpillar invasion by releasing thousands of five-foot-long lizards that eat the caterpillars and then quickly overrun the country themselves.

The weakness of killer-insect books is that bugs lack a compelling perspective on the world. Feral frogs, disgusting dictyoptera, gore-loving gastropods, angry arachnids, and lethal lizards (these are not insects, of course, but are still disgusting) have one-track minds: eat humans. Occasionally, an author will try to make us empathize with his insectoid invaders, leading to passages in which scorpions make "a grimace of rage" or spiders "howl with fury." However, most of us would be hard-pressed to tell the difference between a scorpion grimacing in rage and one giggling with glee.

Maybe that's why they hate us. We spend so much time swatting, slapping, spraying, and squeezing them to death that we never really take the time to get to know them as individuals.

Reptile, amphibian, arachnid—it doesn't matter. If they're gross and they want to invade England and eat people, they're insects.

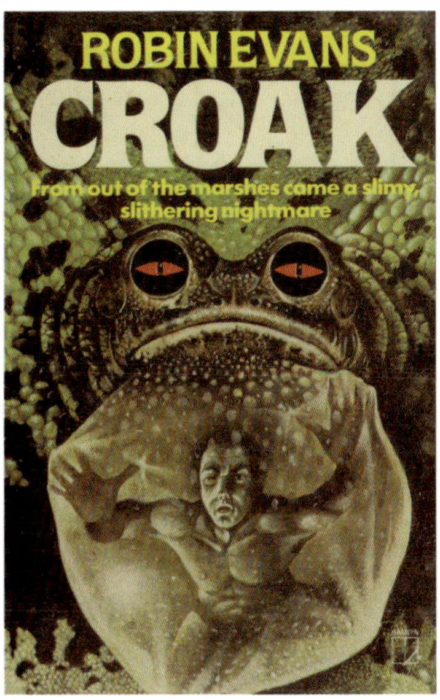

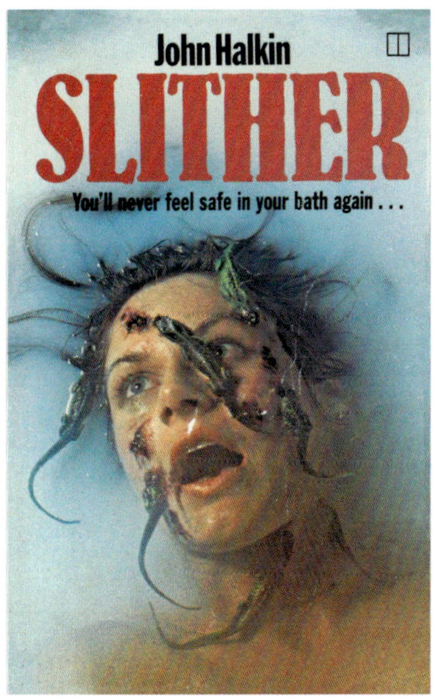

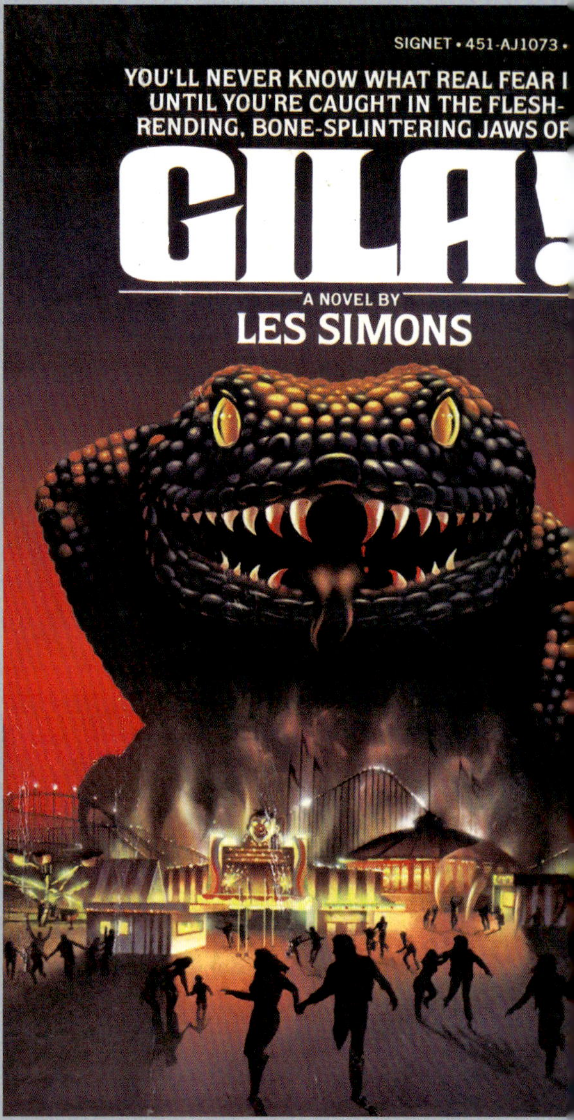

Gila monsters attacked New Mexico (*Gila!*), roaches infested Cape Cod (*The Nest*), and crocs swarmed New Guinea (*Creatures*), but everyone knew that all the really cool creatures were attacking the U.K. in *Blood Worm*, *Scorpion* and *Scorpion: Second Generation*, *Black Horde*, and *Parasite*.

Unpublished *Gila!* sketch courtesy of Tom Hallman.

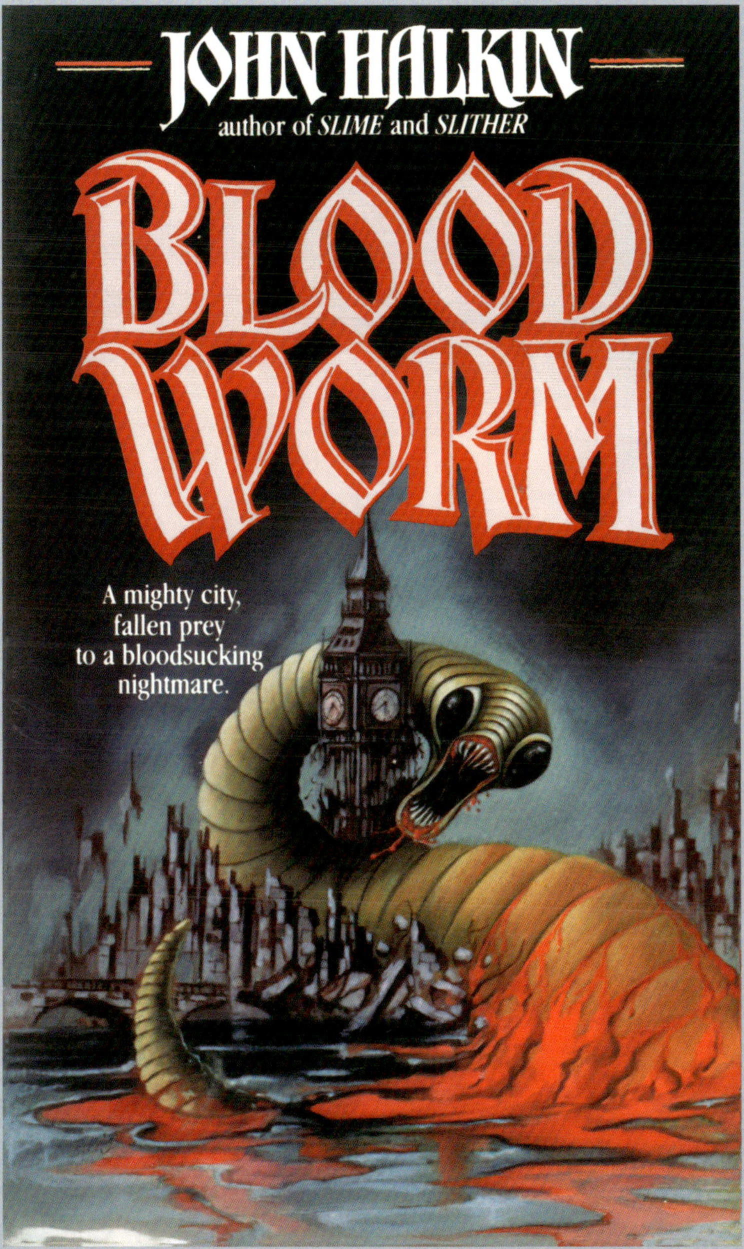
JOHN HALKIN
author of SLIME and SLITHER
BLOOD WORM
A mighty city, fallen prey to a bloodsucking nightmare.

THE NEST
IT WAS AN ORDINARY CAPE COD TOWN—UNTIL THE HUGE MUTANTS BEGAN TO LEAVE THEIR NEST
BY GREGORY A. DOUGLAS

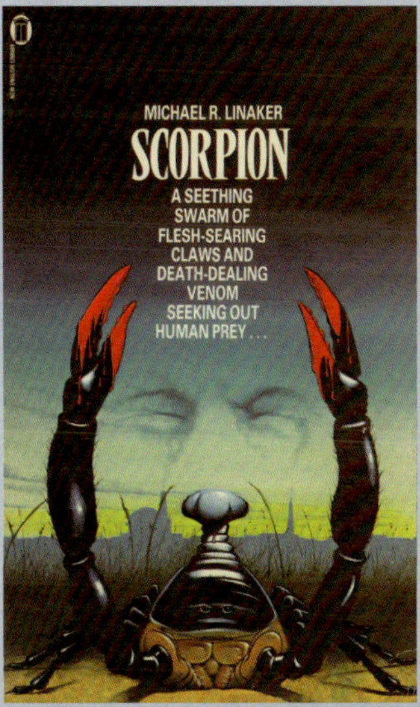
MICHAEL R. LINAKER
SCORPION
A SEETHING SWARM OF FLESH-SEARING CLAWS AND DEATH-DEALING VENOM SEEKING OUT HUMAN PREY . . .

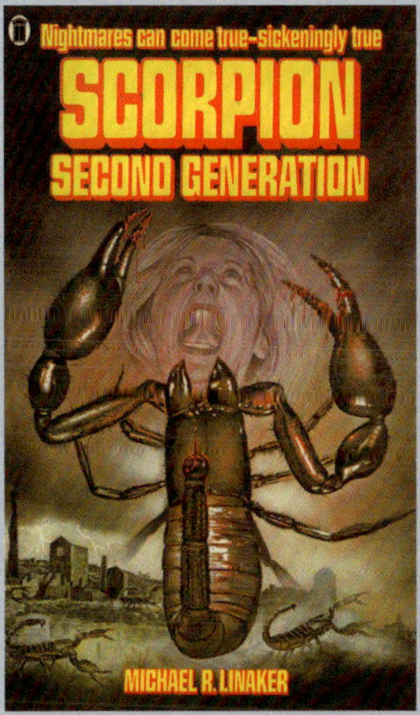
Nightmares can come true–sickeningly true
SCORPION
SECOND GENERATION
MICHAEL R. LINAKER

Salad of the Damned

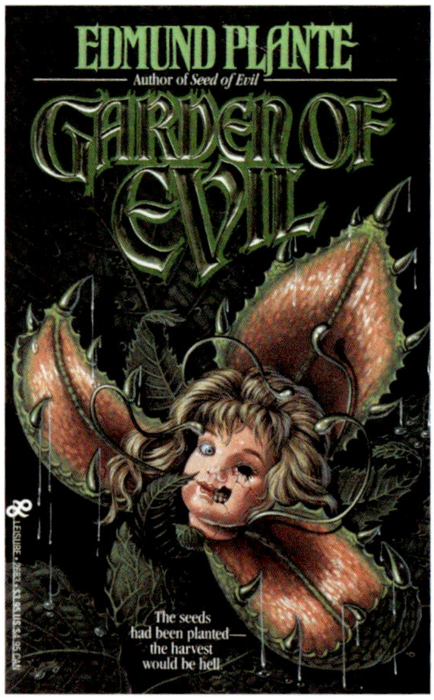

It's no surprise that swamps can be horrific (*Disembodied*, *Moonbog)*. But when flora go feral, not even gardens (*Garden of Evil, The Plants*), ponds *(Gwen, in Green*), or plantations (*Cherron*) are safe.

Here's more bad news: it's not just dogs and cats and insects and fish and birds and killer whales who hate humanity. Vegetables hate us, too. In a way, that hurts more. Old ladies putter about in their gardens, farmers lovingly tend their crops, and when we celebrate our most romantic occasions, we want our plant buddies with us, so we rip off their arms and bring them along. How could they not like us?

When John Wyndham's subjects turn their stinging vines on humanity in his 1951 novel *Day of the Triffids*, their betrayal was understandable. After all, they were Soviet plants, born with hatred in their sappy green hearts. But when plants mind-control us so that they can feed on our blood, it's hard not to be offended. After all, most of us don't eat plants if we can help it, and then it's mostly vegetarians who do the eating. If the plants want to murder *them*, something could probably be arranged.

When you can't take a simple swim in the pond without Venus flytraps turning you into a murderous zombie (*Gwen, in Green*; 1974), something really must be done. Diving into the literature, one quickly realizes that plants and humans have been enemies forever, or at least since Arthur Conan Doyle's 1880 short story "The American's Tale," about a killer Venus flytrap in Montana. Or consider the 1898 story "Purple Terror" or "The Man-Eating Tree" of 1899. Given the history, maybe it's too late for people and plants to live in harmony.

When considering the pivotal horror publications of the early '70s, like *The Exorcist* and *The Other*, maybe a book of real-world horror should be included: 1973's *The Secret Life of Plants*. In this popular work of nonfiction (which later became a documentary featuring music by Stevie Wonder), two hippies attach tiny polygraph machines to plants and discover that not only do they have rich emotional lives, but they are also telepathic. Probably. Plants also scream when pulled from the ground. Even worse, human sexuality causes them to recoil in disgust, and one plant was traumatized when it telepathically witnessed sexual intercourse. No wonder they want us dead.

Today, we think of ourselves as responsible stewards of this big blue ball called Earth, but literary evidence suggests we're just suckers. Given the chance, nature will turn on us in a heartbeat. This is one issue on which carnivores and vegetarians must stand united: we must eat nature, or nature will eat us.

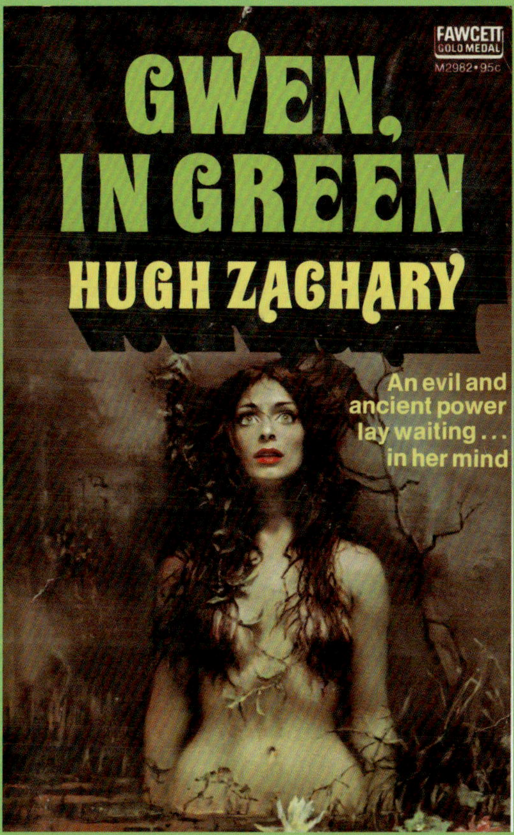
FAWCETT GOLD MEDAL
M2982•95c
GWEN, IN GREEN
HUGH ZACHARY
An evil and ancient power lay waiting . . . in her mind

A SUPERBLY CRAFTED NOVEL OF HORROR AND HIGH SUSPENSE
THE PLANTS
BY KENNETH McKENNEY

"HAUTALA'S NEW BOOK IS AN IMPRESSIVE NOVEL OF SUSPENSE AND DARK HORROR..."
—STEPHEN KING
MOONBOG
BY RICK HAUTALA
AUTHOR OF MOONDEATH

Cherron
BEWARE THE TORMENTED CHILD—
SHE HAS THE POWER OF EVIL
AND THE THIRST FOR REVENGE!
BY THE AUTHOR OF CALY
Sharon Combes

REAL NIGHT

CHAPTER FOUR

ESTATE
MARES

DELL • 2099 • 1.50

"BURNT OFFERINGS has no peer. Better than ROSEMARY'S BABY, THE OTHER and THE EXORCIST!" —Hartford Courant

BURNT OFFERINGS

The bestselling novel by

ROBERT MARASCO

Ah, the 1970s: High inflation! Rising unemployment! Oil crisis! Recession! School desegregation! White flight! High crime! Son of Sam! It was the decade when everything went to hell—and explains why the haunted-house novel reached critical mass. In *The Sentinel* (1974), a model moves into a brownstone . . . from hell. In *The Shining* (1977), an economically strapped family takes a last-chance job in a hotel . . . from hell. In *The House Next Door* (1978), nouveau-riche suburbanites build the contemporary home . . . from hell. But it all started with Robert Marasco's *Burnt Offerings* (1973), a chilling tale about a family who escapes the city to move into a summer rental . . . from hell.

Marasco was a high school English teacher, so his illusions about human nature had long ago been stomped to death. He originally wrote *Burnt Offerings* as a screenplay, and first intended it to be a black comedy, but as Marasco said in an interview: "It just came out black." Reviewers panned or patronized it, but the book caught on, sparking the wave of haunted-house novels later in the decade.

If social and political anxiety spawns zombies, then economic anxiety births haunted houses. Marasco created the now-common real estate nightmare scenario: a cash-strapped family (or individual) gets a deal on a place above their socioeconomic station. Hoping to start fresh, they go all-in, quickly realizing that their attempt to buy a better life at a discount is the worst decision they ever made. Now all they can do is run, screaming for their lives, abandoning their investment.

If there's any doubt that *Burnt Offerings* is all about the square footage, the first chapter is a long lament by Marian Rolfe, a housewife trapped in her family's stifling Queens apartment, desperate to escape the city. Her husband, Ben, agrees to look at a summer rental, which turns out to be a decrepit mansion at a bargain price. He takes it despite his better judgment. Deals like that don't come along every day.

Once they move into the old Allardyce place, the house reshapes the couple into their own worst nightmares. Marian cleans obsessively, hypnotized by the expensive uncared-for antiques. Dear, aging Aunt Elizabeth is sharing their vacation, and although she's a real live wire at first, she becomes frailer as the story progresses. Ben transforms into the kind of father he never wanted to be, practically raping his wife and nearly drowning his son while bullying him into "being a man." Their behavior gets worse, but every day the house looks better and better.

What Marian doesn't realize is that she's not the owner of this house—she's its slave. Summer is spent on her knees, waxing floors, dusting frames, repairing damage, letting her family die without batting an eye. To her, cleaning is an act of ownership, but the cruel truth is that the Allardyces had money and she doesn't and nothing will change that. She can live in their house, she can wax their floors, but she'll never belong.

Before Marasco, Shirley Jackson and Richard Matheson had written haunted-house books—*The Haunting of Hill House* (1959; see page 12) and *Hell House* (1971) are both genre classics, but neither had a thing to say about money. They were about psychic investigators going to abandoned mansions to figure out how they got so spooky. Marasco and his now-forgotten best seller focused on the real issue for most people with a haunted house: "Can I get my investment back?"

Marasco was the first American writer to bring anxieties about class, mortgages, and equity to the forefront of the haunted-house novel. Both Jay Anson's *The Amityville Horror* (1979) and Stephen King's *The Shining* (1977) follow his formula: cash-strapped family gets deal on new place and comes to regret it. When you're stuck with a haunted house, it doesn't matter how much you put into repairing the boiler or fixing the pool. At the end of the day, all you can do is run.

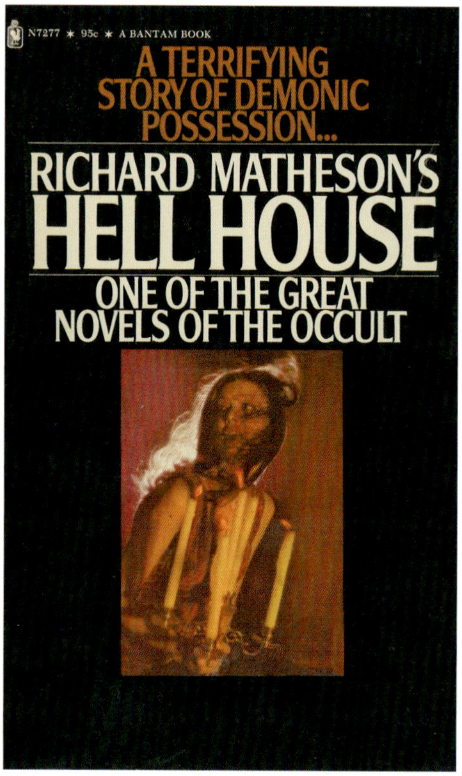

There Goes the Neighborhood

The '70s were a time of high interest rates and growing inflation. So, for Americans who'd finally scraped together enough to buy a house, the worst thing imaginable was an icy blast of wind and a satanic voice telling them to "Get out!" Families were moving from the cities to the suburbs and from the suburbs to the sticks, and new homes were popping up everywhere. A brand-new house was more than a place to hang your crucifix; it symbolized a new start, a new life, a new family.

But Americans have always been aware that their homes can be menaced by unseen forces. Perhaps those forces are the ghosts of people murdered there a hundred years before, or maybe it's toxic waste from a leaky landfill. Maybe demons are stealing your life force, or maybe it's radiation. Your kids might be sick because your house is built over a cemetery, or the radon in the basement. Large-scale environmental disasters like Love Canal, the near-meltdown at Three Mile Island, and a series of high-profile asbestos lawsuits made clear that invisible evil was hiding in your home. In fact, if the cause was Satan, you were lucky. At least the Lord of Darkness wasn't a carcinogen.

Despite Jackson's iconic *The Haunting of Hill House*, Matheson's go-for-broke *Hell House*, Anne Rivers Siddons's beautifully disturbing *The House Next Door*, and even Marasco's pioneering *Burnt Offerings*, the unfortunate fact remains that America's most iconic

Socialite Patricia Montandon hired a tarot reader for a party but forgot to get him a drink. Furious, he cursed her San Francisco apartment. *The Intruders* is her all-true account of the party snub . . . from hell.

haunted house is the title property from *The Amityville Horror.* Crass, commercial minded, grandiose, ridiculous, this carnival barker's idea of a haunted house is a shame-train of stupid.

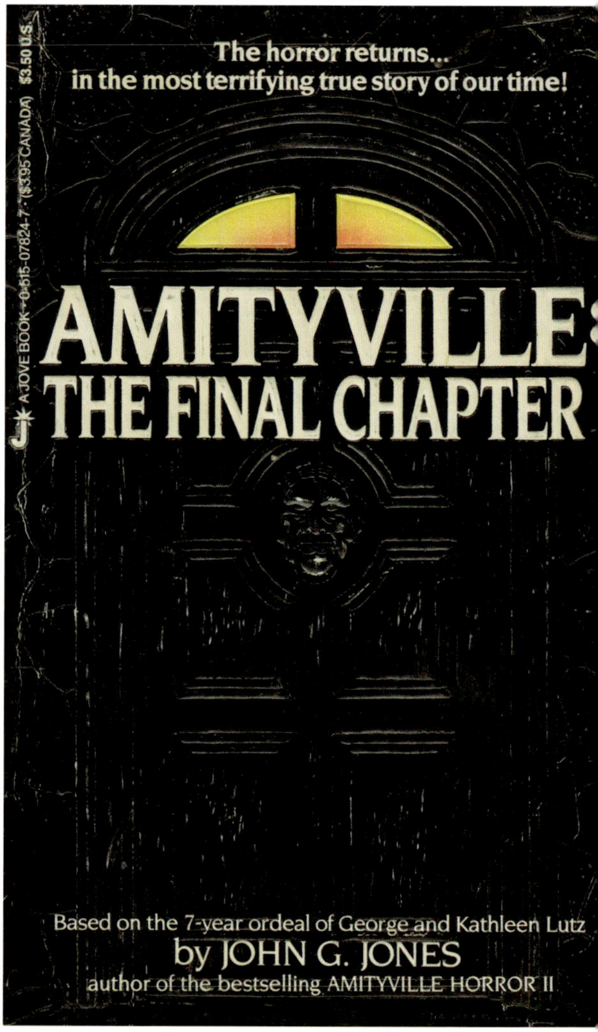

"George and Kathy Lutz moved into 112 Ocean Avenue on December 18. Twenty-eight days later, they fled in terror." So begins one of the most promiscuous horror franchises of all time, one that spawned at least six novels (all marketed as nonfiction), as well as books by pretty much everyone who ever crossed the property line.

Amityville's cottage-industry success stems from the fact that George Lutz stuck to his guns all his life, dishing out movie-ready claptrap from one side of his mouth while claiming it was all true from the other. Reportedly never happy with his share of the proceeds from the original best-selling book and movie, Lutz realized that he could still market his name. And so he did, desperately hoping to pad his bank account with sequel after sequel. After sequel.

Many people found the original story of demonic possession, goo flowing down walls, and mysterious voices shouting at priests hard to swallow. Those events pale in comparison to the sequels, with their devil pigs riding on the wings of 747s, attacks by fire bats, and evil forces compelling people to rent cars they don't even want. *The Amityville Horror II* (1982) was plenty ridiculous, with archangels working as lifeguards to rescue drowning Lutz children, but in the third installment the story went from a simple meal of possessed homes to an all-you-can-eat buffet of occult bullshit. *Amityville: The Final Chapter* (1985) follows the Lutzes as they ditch their kids and fly around the world on a studio-paid publicity tour, giving interviews to promote the movie. Keeping the franchise going, the Entity (the source of all evil from the first book) goes mobile, following the family everywhere. Fortunately, George Lutz is manly enough to punch and kick it into submission. "I knew this martial arts training would come in handy someday," he muses. *The Final Chapter* climaxes in a battle in which George puts the Abomination in a chokehold while his wife and kids form a human chain and channel love power into him. When the Entity finally taps out, the entire family, including Harry the Dog, kick and stomp its corpse into dust.

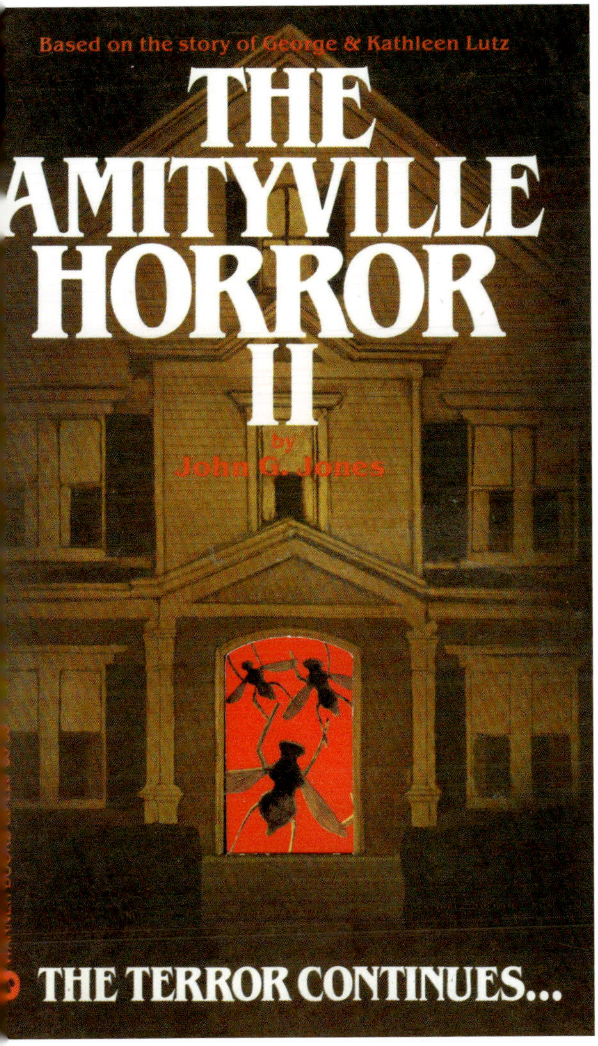

It's an inspirational story. "One day," author Ken Eulo said in an interview, "I read *The Amityville Horror* and I thought to myself, oh Christ, I could do this in my sleep." And so he wrote *The Brownstone* (1980), which spawned two sequels. He wasn't the only one. Even poor deceased Jay Anson, a jobbing writer brought on board to write the original *Amityville* book, wasn't allowed to rest in peace. His *666* (1981), effectively a smudged photocopy of *The Amityville Horror*, was published under his name a year after he died.

Sadly, the true story of 112 Ocean Avenue turns out to be worse than what's in the books. The crime that cursed the Amityville House wasn't the real-life murders of the DeFeo family. Nor was it that the land was supposedly home to John Ketcham, a warlock who escaped the Salem witch trials. Nor was it a violation of fabricated Shinnecock Indian Nation burial grounds. A 2013 documentary (*My Amityville Horror*) about Daniel Lutz, who was ten years old when his family moved in, puts a name to the Entity that haunted this house: George Lutz.

George was Kathy Connors's second husband, and he made it clear he would not invest his time and money in children who didn't belong to him. George demanded that Kathy's first husband surrender all parental rights; from then

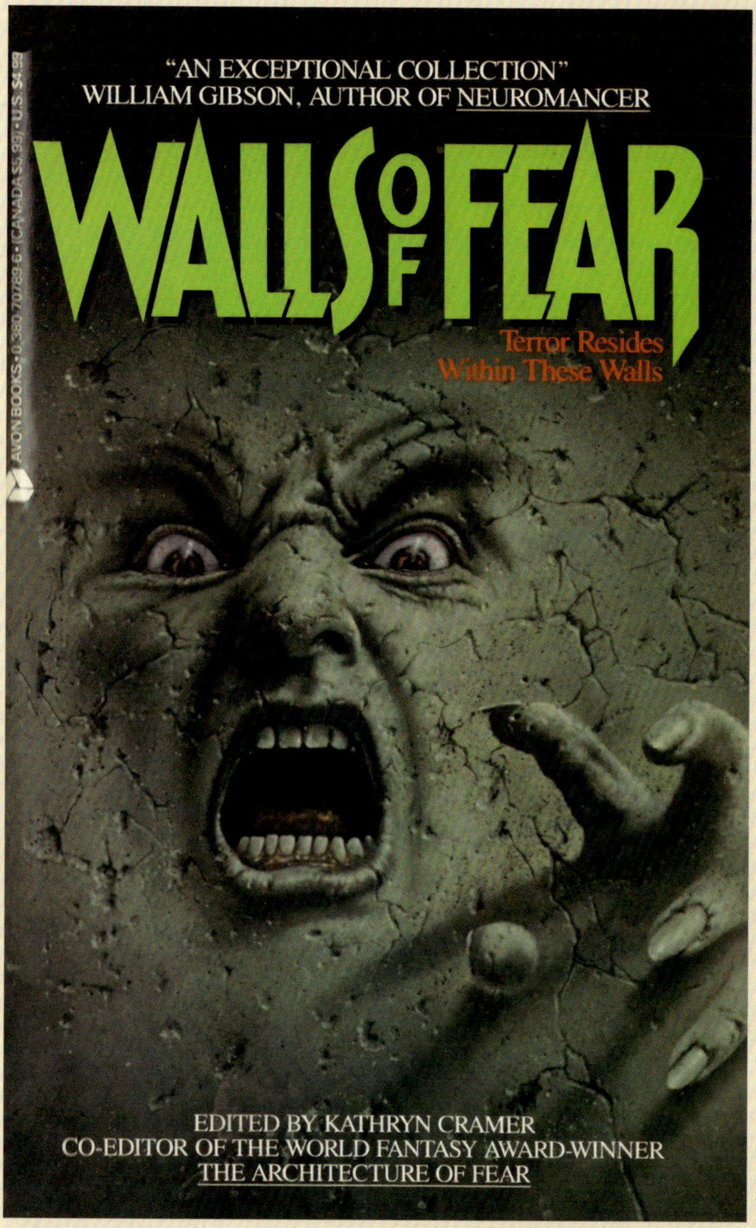

Don't sign the lease! *Witch House* was a 1945 occult detective novel spruced up for a seller's market with a new cover by fantasy illustrator Michael Herring. T. M. Wright's *The Woman Next Door* was an early standalone novel for the author that deliberately mixed hauntings, ghosts, and child abuse. *Walls of Fear* was a 1990 haunted house anthology, with a nightmarish cover by rock 'n' roll artist Jim Warren, edited by Kathryn Cramer, who also edited the 1987 haunted house anthology *The Architecture of Fear* (see page 107).

FICTION
POCKET
83126-7
$3.50
THE TERRIFYING NEW NOVEL FROM THE
AUTHOR OF THE 6 MILLION COPY BESTSELLER
THE AMITYVILLE HORROR
666
JAY ANSON

on, he insisted that Daniel and his two siblings call him either "sir" or "Mr. Lutz." As Daniel said in the documentary, "He's the biggest asshole you ever could meet."

Throughout the books, George and Kathy Lutz claim that the Entity changed their personalities and made them violently aggressive toward their children. But Daniel says that happened plenty of times before they moved in and plenty of times after they moved out. In fact, what happened after they fled was worse. While George and Kathy went on their year-long, round-the-world publicity tour for the movie, Daniel was ditched at a Catholic boarding school, where he claims the priests beat him and tried to exorcize his demons. He was eleven. By his account, those 28 days at 112 Ocean Avenue left him with physical and mental damage from which it took years to recover.

Maybe George, Kathy, and their lawyer concocted the haunting story over a bottle of wine, as the lawyer later claimed, but their children didn't. If every haunted house is built on the site of a terrible crime, the crime that *The Amityville Horror* rests on may be child abuse.

Small Town Trauma

You are a Vietnam veteran. You are 6 foot 4, 230 pounds of solid muscle. You can kill a man with your bare hands; you prefer not to. You are driving back to the small town where you grew up, somewhere in the South. Once there, you notice something strange: everyone in town is a sex pervert and a satanist. You reunite with your high school sweetheart. She is a zombie; it takes you a while to figure that out. You are attacked by a dark force. You sing hymns to keep it at bay. You kill a lot of satanists. You kill monsters. You kill some teenagers.

You are in a William W. Johnstone novel.

Johnstone wrote two hundred books, most of them Westerns and men's adventure stories. But with his five-part Devil series (1980–92) written for Zebra Books (*The Devil's Kiss*, *The Devil's Heart*, *The Devil's Touch*, *The Devil's Cat*, *The Devil's Laughter*), Johnstone became a horror novelist. And every one of his horror novels is insane. Characters act in ways that barely resemble human behavior. The carnage flies thick and cartoony, with popped-out eyeballs flying across a room, people's heads flattening when hit, cats gamboling in loops of human intestines. Johnstone loads his shotgun with tropes—incest monsters, zombie girlfriends, ghost werewolves, killer dolls—and blasts them at the reader again and again until nothing makes sense anymore.

If you're in a William W. Johnstone book, don't pet the kitties and don't play with the toys.

In *The Nursery* (1985), a small town in Louisiana has been taken over by the "Prince of Foulness, Lord of Darkness," and his friend "the Master on Earth of All Things Dark and Ugly and Evil and Profane." The cops have been bought off by Satan and are given to ending conversations with statements like, "I'd lick her ass just to see the little puckered hole. Bye, now." Satanic covens spread their message via heavy-metal music that teaches "self-mutilation, assault, suicide, drugs, murder, sex; anti-establishment and anti-social rebellion against parents, society, education, and law and order." Sometimes a firm spanking is enough to drive the Devil out of a teenager, but usually they have to be shot in the face. Dogs are good and often form armies to assist humans fighting Satan, whereas cats can go either way.

Toy Cemetery (1987) achieves maximum Johnstone. Vietnam vet Jay Clute returns to Victory, Missouri, where he grew up, with nine-year-old daughter Kelly in tow. Within hours of his arrival, Jay discovers that the two major local landmarks are (1) an enormous doll factory in the center of town run by an obese pedophile named Bruno Dixon, who films satanic kiddie porn in it, and (2) a high-security hospital/mental institution/underground research facility that houses the "products of incest," enormous man-monsters with apple-sized heads and superhuman strength. Tiny toys run amok, as does incest. Jay and his daughter almost hook up their first night, only to snap out of it when the crosses they're wearing clink together.

Reading this book is like driving through a dust storm while in a post-concussion haze: the harder you try to focus, the more everything slips away into an insanity vortex. A supermarket check-out girl's head explodes, but no one seems to mind. Possessed teenage boys follow Kelly through town, waggling their inappropriate boners until she fights them with karate and kills one with an ax. Everyone has a secret doll collection. A tiny French general leads a toy army.

Johnstone piles incident on incident, trope on trope, and if something isn't working he keeps on piling. When time itself needs to be brought to a screeching halt, Jay Clute just pulls out his gun and shoots a clock. Because clocks make time, right? In William W. Johnstone's world, why not?

Location, Location, Location

In 1964 the police shooting of a young black man kicked off the Harlem riots in New York City. In 1965 a dispute between a police officer and a young black man pulled over for drunk driving kicked off the Watts riots in Los Angeles. Those two incidents in turn kicked off white flight: middle- and upper-class white families fleeing the cities for the countryside, embracing a back-to-the-land lifestyle, buying farmhouses, and turning homey hamlets into planned communities.

Between 1970 and 1980, one million white people left New York City, and in the first four years of the '70s, six million Americans ditched the cities for the country. It was the first decade in 150 years that the rural population grew faster than the urban population. The horror novels from this time reveal that what was waiting for these homeowners was far worse than what they had fled. In a stroke of poor planning, apparently the majority of America's rural communities had been built on cursed land. Whether it's the site of an ancient murder (*The Owlsfane Horror*, 1981), a witch hanging (*Maynard's House*, 1980), or a Native American massacre (*The Curse*, 1989), America feels like a massive graveyard stretching from sea to shining sea.

Add in parts of the country rendered unfit for human habitation by invisible aliens who return every few hundred years to kill people with spontaneous orgasms that melt their brains (*The Searing*, 1980), sinister cults occupying abandoned mental hospitals (*The Turning*, 1978), or isolated beachheads where Satan is growing killer humanoids in church basements (*Effigies*, 1980), and you might as well stay in the city and get murdered by the sewer alligators. (Keep reading.)

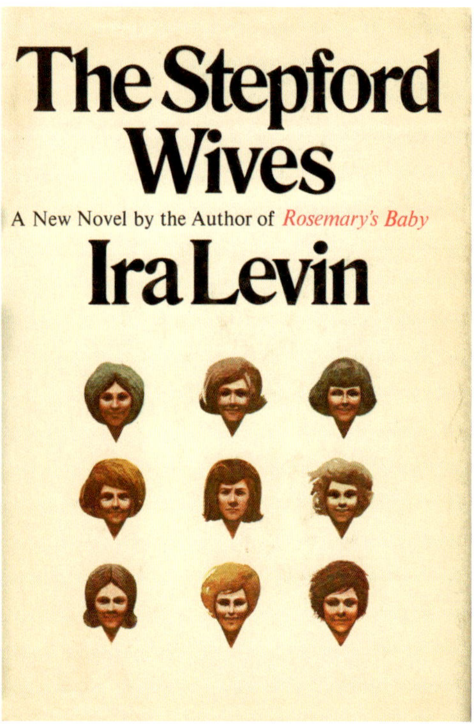

Depending on whom you asked, *The Stepford Wives* by Ira Levin (*Rosemary's Baby*) satirized either feminism or its backlash.

In a country dotted with mass-killing sites and derelict insane asylums, the sorts of small-town traumas one could encounter are limitless. In *The Stepford Wives* (1972), Ira Levin mocks the petrified patriarchy who fled the civil rights movement and feminism by retreating to elite Connecticut enclaves where they murder their unhappy wives and replace them with compliant fembots.

Not content to rest on the laurels of *The Other* (see page 19), Thomas Tryon wrote another classic, *Harvest Home* (1973), all about the dangers of romanticizing small-town life. Tryon had watched his colleagues abandon the city for the country, lecturing those they left behind about the clean air and good values of their new neighbors. The ex-urbanites buy failing

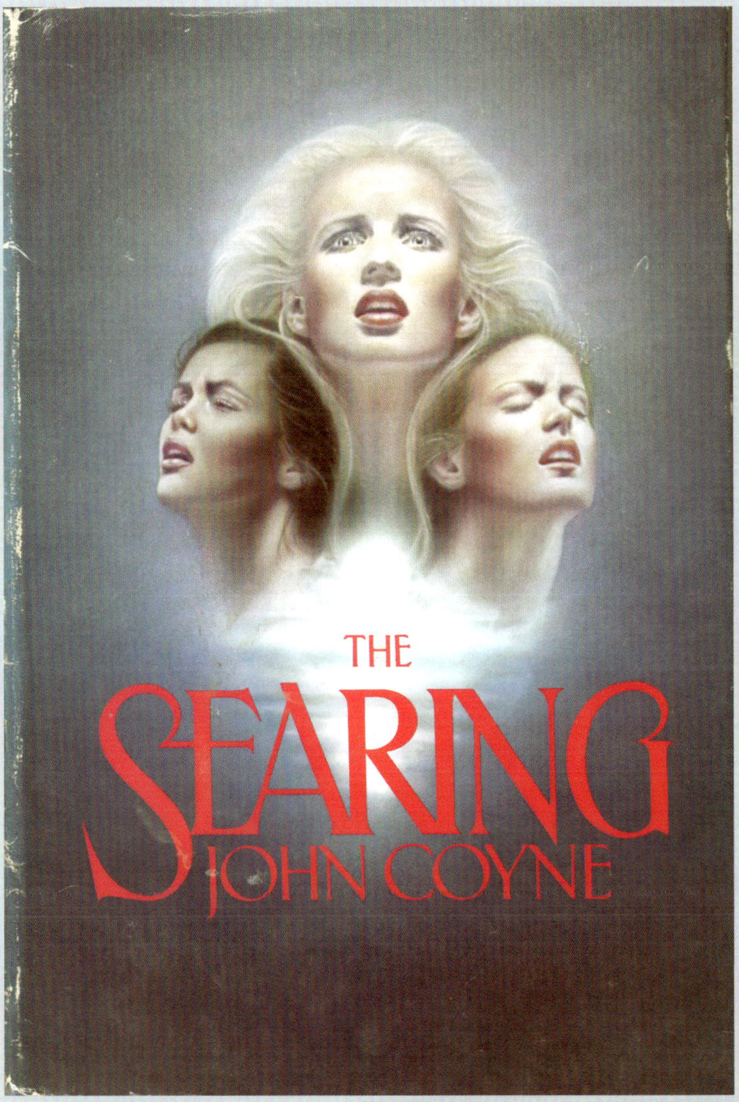

Wherever you go, there Satan is, be it Missouri (*The Curse*), upstate New York (*Effigies*, *The Turning*), or the D.C. suburbs (*The Searing*).

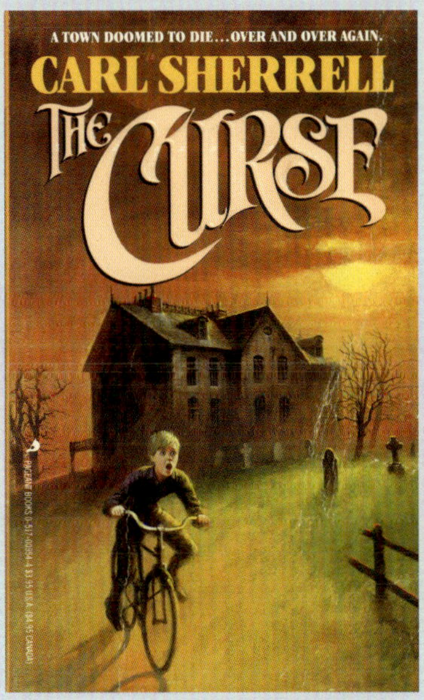

farms at rock-bottom prices and then fetishize what they've destroyed, scooping up farm tools at bankruptcy sales and nailing them to the walls of their brand-new kitchens. Tryon wondered if their new neighbors might not share the same values as these newcomers, if perhaps they were aligned with stronger, older, bloodier forces that the city folk had forgotten. So when his urban refugees land in the quaint village of Cornwall Coombe, they're totally unprepared for the bloody fertility rites the tiny town requires to ensure a good harvest.

Tryon, and the writers who followed in his footsteps, suggested that urban refugees patronized the flyover states at their peril. Joan Samson's *The Auctioneer* is a hard and flinty book about a small farming community decimated by the city dwellers who move in and start buying up all the wagon wheels and handmade quilts, then the town's small children, and finally its soul. *Maynard's House* is a snowy Maine ghost story about a Vietnam vet who moves to the countryside to heal his traumatized soul, only to find that the quiet country nights are more hellish than any tour of 'Nam, thanks to the spirit of a witch hanged there centuries before. Or maybe it's the PTSD that's loosening his grip on reality. Or maybe it doesn't matter because whatever the cause, the effect is the same: moving to the country is the worst decision he ever made.

Digging in Deeper

Jere Cunningham sums up small-town trauma in *The Abyss* (1984), his apocalyptic novel set in Tennessee coal country. The town of Bethel has shrunk to a dying cluster of cheap bars and trailer parks since all the old mines closed. But now investors are bringing in deep-drilling equipment to reopen an old shaft. Suddenly there are jobs, people are moving back, and the dream of manufacturing's return is alive again. A few ominous signs appear, but if you're loyal to Bethel, if you're the kind of person who belongs there, if you believe in America, then you're not about to question a good thing.

It turns out the shaft was shut down because the miners had accidentally drilled into hell, unleashing forces of darkness that were defeated thanks only to a freak cave-in. The mysterious investors want to drill down again, this time on purpose. Like a Springsteen song mashed up with *Dante's Inferno*, the mine reopens

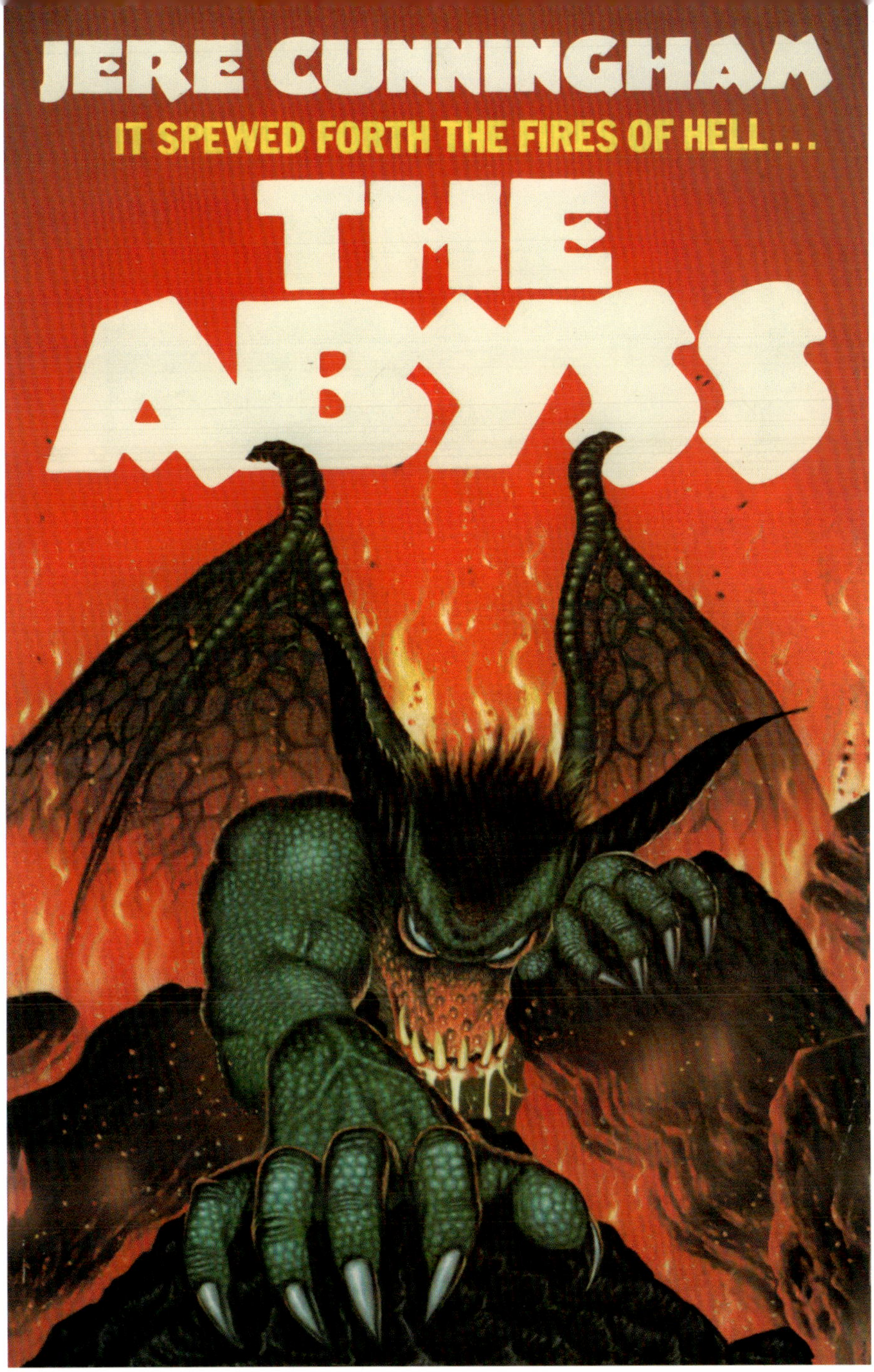

and the townsfolk receive a Bible's worth of plagues: their taps run with hot and cold blood, workers are zombified, and fast-growing thorns crack the foundations of homes. By the time it's raining hellfire, Cunningham has drilled home the idea that small towns are death traps and we're lucky to get out while we can. The only way manufacturing will return is through a deal with the devil.

Yet even as Satan rises up over the Appalachian Mountains, one character turns to another and shrugs. "Hoss," he says, "I never claimed to know what was normal in this world." Then he cracks open a beer and walks away. Small towns may be hell on earth, but they feel uniquely American in a way that big cities never will.

Welcome to Fear City

What were one million white middle-class New Yorkers fleeing in the '70s and '80s? Hell, apparently.

A 1968 sanitation strike left 48,000 tons of garbage rotting in the streets. Murder rates skyrocketed (the city's annual homicides reached an all-time high of 2,245 by 1990; these days they total around 352). Between 1965 and 1975, auto thefts doubled, rapes tripled, robberies increased tenfold. Hell wasn't the small town. It was the big city.

As the middle class fled, the tax base collapsed; by the mid-'70s, the Big Apple was within days of defaulting on a $150 million debt. So many city employees were laid off that twenty-six fire companies disbanded. Fifty firehouses were shuttered and the city went up in flames: in 1970, over 120,000 fires broke out, and arson investigations hit 13,000 per year.

The South Bronx was a moonscape of abandoned buildings and vacant lots. The East Village was crawling with junkies. The Upper West Side was a mugger's paradise. It was the perfect place for horror. In *A Manhattan Ghost Story* (1984), T. M. Wright imagines a city choked with ghosts, some of whom work in bordellos. Kit Reed's near-future *Fort Privilege* (1985) sees jaded New Yorkers holed up in a luxury building under siege from the scum outside. A newcomer watches people dragged from their cars during traffic jams and beaten to death for their wallets. "You're new to the city," a New Yorker says to the traumatized witness. "You're just not used to the pace."

It was hell aboveground and hell underground. A simple-minded mystic bites off young boys' penises in Spanish Harlem (*Rooftops*, 1981) while alligators roam the sewers (*Death Tour*, 1978). The real-life blackout of 1977 provides cover for half-human throwbacks to rampage up from the sewers in T. E. D. Klein's novella "Children of the Kingdom," and secret societies worship the subway-tunnel-dwelling Head Underneath in John Shirley's *Cellars* (1982).

Giant turtles and 50-pound goldfish flushed down toilets long ago live in harmony with *Death Tour*'s sewer gators.

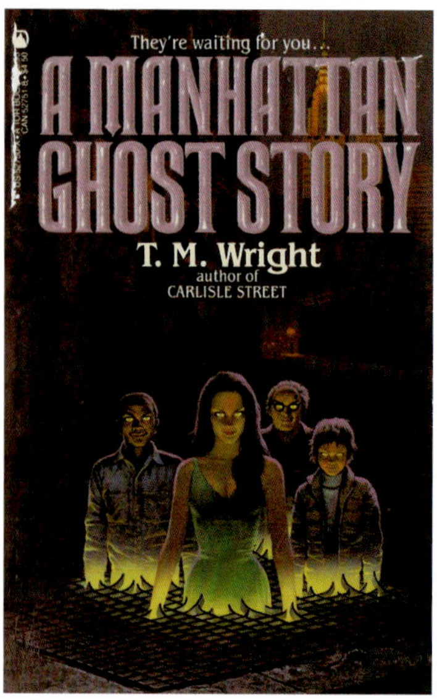

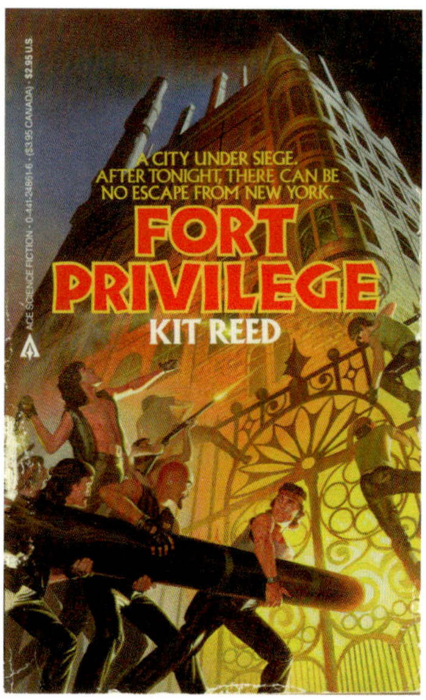

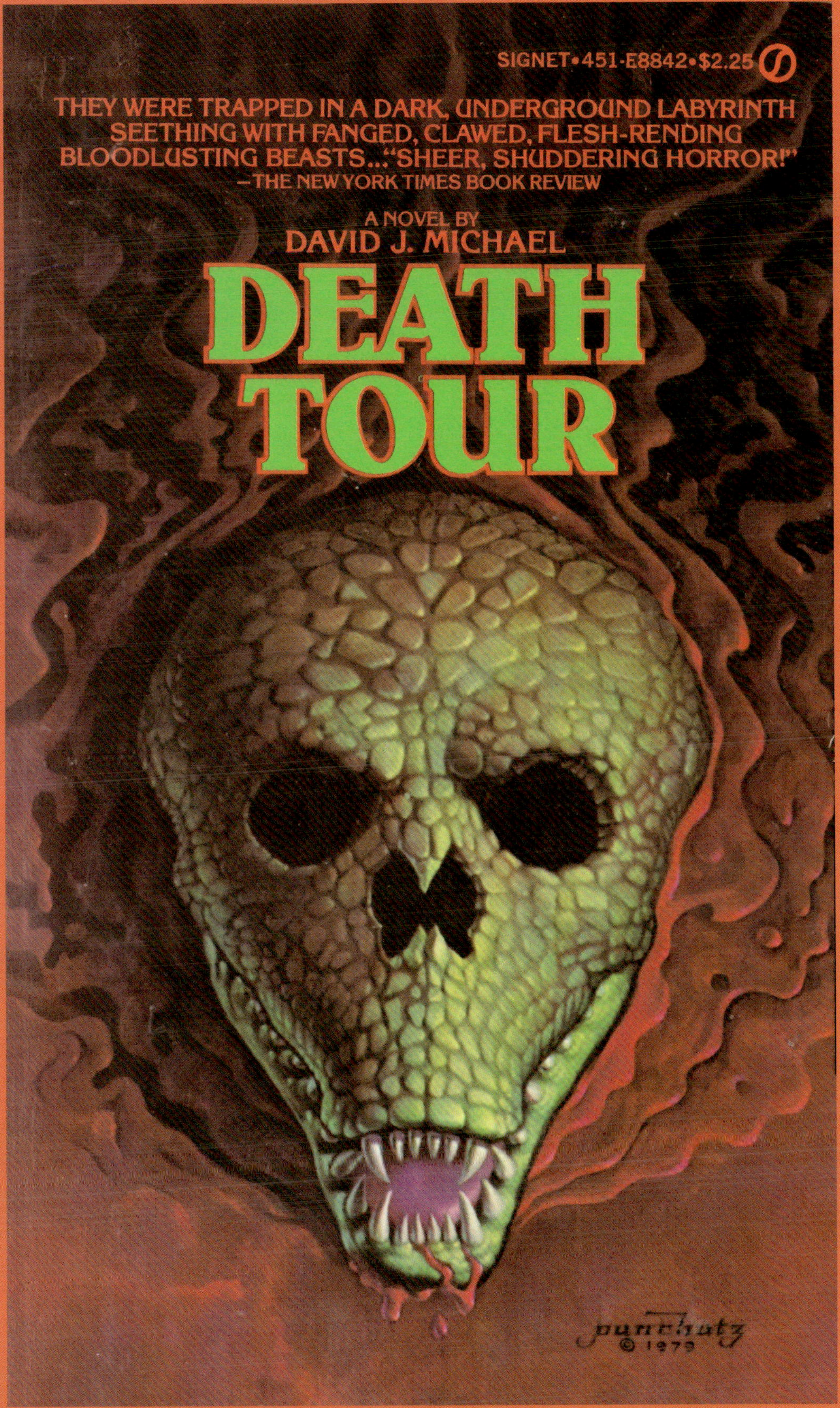
SIGNET • 451-E8842 • $2.25
THEY WERE TRAPPED IN A DARK, UNDERGROUND LABYRINTH
SEETHING WITH FANGED, CLAWED, FLESH-RENDING
BLOODLUSTING BEASTS..."SHEER, SHUDDERING HORROR!"
—THE NEW YORK TIMES BOOK REVIEW
A NOVEL BY
DAVID J. MICHAEL
DEATH
TOUR
punchatz
© 1979

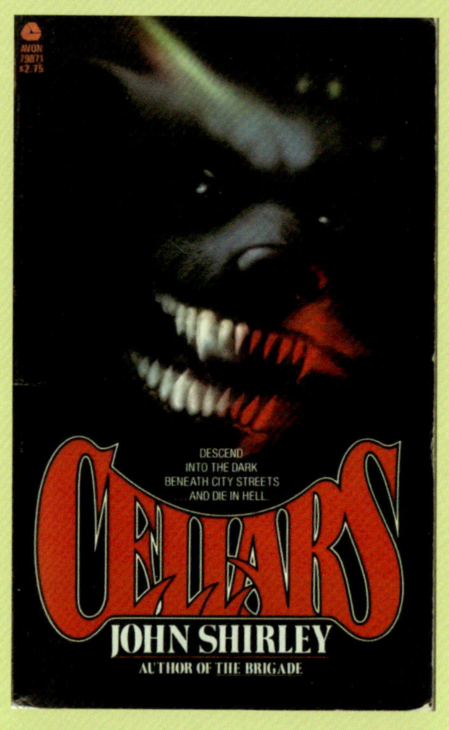

In horror fiction, the conveniences of city life come with significant drawbacks. The city might merge into other dimensions (*Night Train*), house an underground monster cult (*Cellars*), or attract dark magic (*Our Lady of Darkness*). You might run into those weird plant-children from Chapter 2 (*Children of the Island*), get on a train that channels demonic energy (*Ghost Train*), fall in with a bunch of physical fitness nuts (*The Glow*), or run afoul of the reprinted creeps in the *Urban Horrors* anthology.

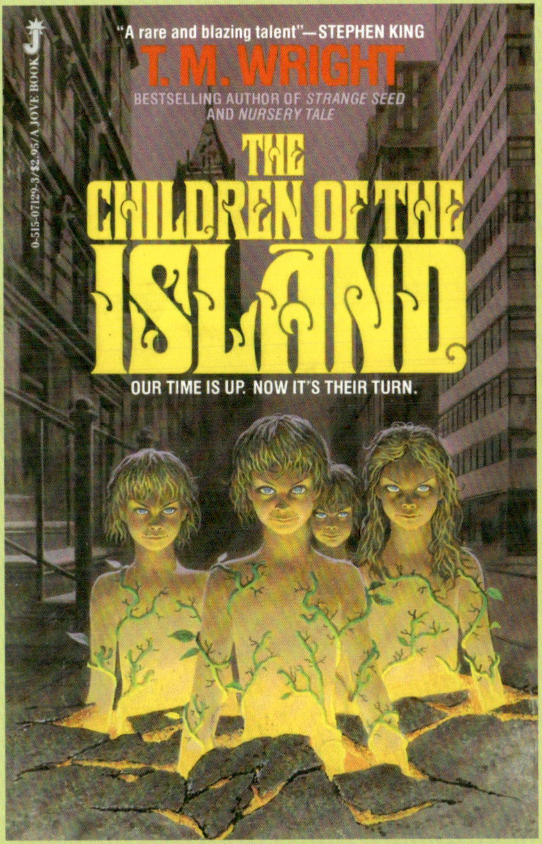
"A rare and blazing talent"—STEPHEN KING
T. M. WRIGHT
BESTSELLING AUTHOR OF STRANGE SEED AND NURSERY TALE
THE CHILDREN OF THE ISLAND
OUR TIME IS UP. NOW IT'S THEIR TURN.
A JOVE BOOK

"A FRESH, CHILLING VOICE . . . A WITCHES' BREW."
–United Press International
STEPHEN LAWS
GHOST TRAIN
"GHOST TRAIN HAS IT ALL, FANS . . . THIS ONE FAIRLY FLIES."
–New York Sunday News
US/52100-5 ★ $3.95
TOR HORROR

FAWCETT
THE GLOW
IT MAY MAKE YOU RUN FOR YOUR LIFE, OR NEVER DARE TO RUN AGAIN.
BROOKS STANWOOD

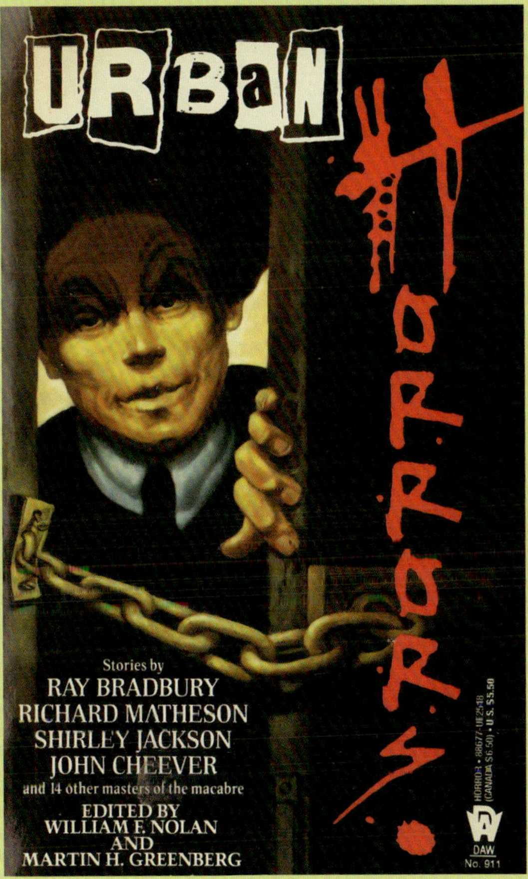
URBAN HORRORS
Stories by
RAY BRADBURY
RICHARD MATHESON
SHIRLEY JACKSON
JOHN CHEEVER
and 14 other masters of the macabre
EDITED BY
WILLIAM F. NOLAN
AND
MARTIN H. GREENBERG
(CANADA $6.50) • U.S. $5.50
DAW
No. 911

But if the supernatural was bad, real-world horrors were worse. Children were scared to go to bed because the landlord might torch the building. Again. A depopulated Brooklyn, slated for demolition, was a ghost town. College professors were mugged and murdered by thirteen-year-olds for subway tokens. There had to be a reason for the madness. In *Our Lady of Darkness* (1977), Fritz Leiber offers his theory of Megapolisomancy, a "new science of cities" formulated by his fictitious magician Thibaut de Castries. The streets and subway tunnels, water mains and gas pipes, steam tunnels and power cables formed lines of power that imbued cities with dark magic. Or, as a character in Thomas Monteleone's *Night Train* (1984) says, "In effect, the city may be coming to life, and if so, it's proving to be something quite malign."

In *Night Train* (see page 120), other dimensions are melting into ours, the main incursion point lying beneath the Lower East Side (also home to *Cellars'* Head Underneath). Albino dwarves, flesh-eating jellyfish, and a subterranean pterodactyl make appearances before the NYPD blasts them to hell with shotguns and concussion grenades. The monsters are defeated, but the city sleeps uneasily. As the book ends, one of the officers keeps an eye on crime stats. As long as they keep going down, people are safe. But if they start going up again, it means the city is stirring back to life. Only gentrification can keep the forces of darkness at bay.

The Crazy-Maker

Ramsey Campbell will show you terror in a plastic bag. Or a pedestrian underpass. Or a deserted council estate. Since the late '70s, he has written dozens of novels and hundreds of short stories, from erotic horror to the traditional ghost story. But in the '80s, he was the chief practitioner of Fritz Leiber's style of urban horror, luring readers into empty city streets and squalid basements and confronting them with the monsters that were born there.

Campbell's stories feel like week-old newspapers, swollen with water, black with mold, forgotten on the steps of the abandoned tenement. His titles scream like headlines: *The Face That Must Die*! *The Doll Who Ate His Mother*! *The*

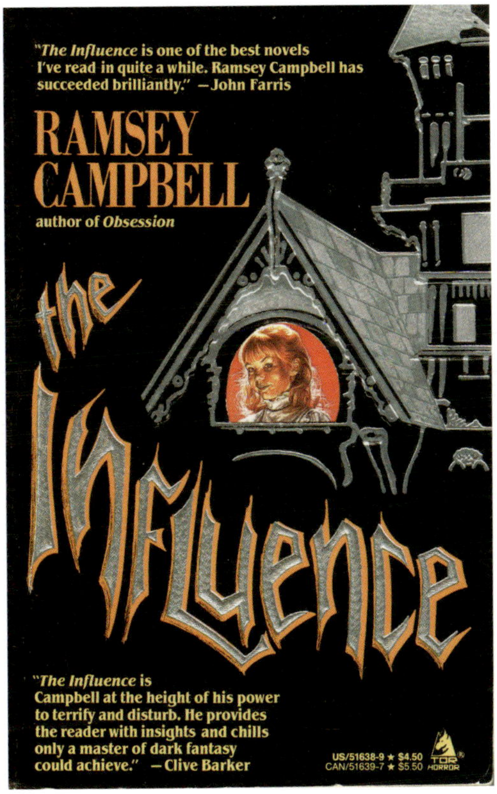

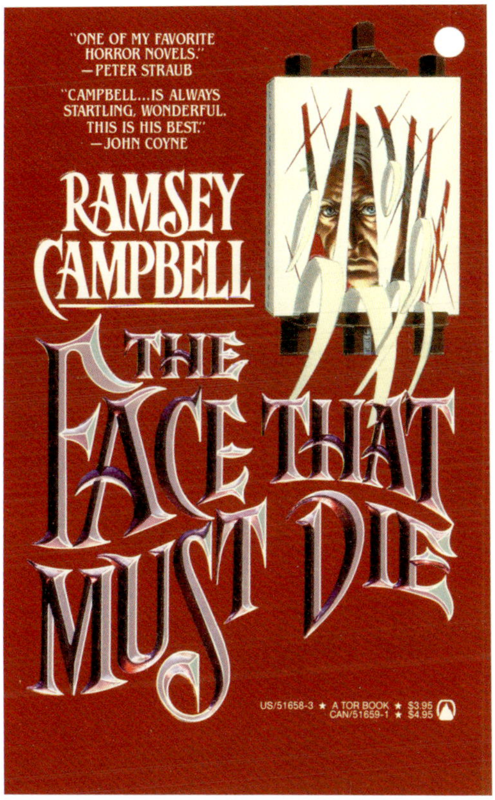

Ramsey Campbell's short stories cut deepest, but in the '80s he turned out his share of big, fat, Stephen King–sized novels that lurch between the supernatural (*The Influence*) and the psychological (*The Face That Must Die*).

Parasite! His Liverpool and London are necropolises of marginal people, hateful shut-ins, catatonic homeless, gutter-crawling journalists, their loneliness and isolation amplified by the urban hellscapes in which they're entombed.

Campbell writes the way schizophrenics think (he's said that for most of his life, his mother showed signs of schizophrenia). He doesn't want to describe actions; he wants to alter perceptions. His descriptions are full of visual miscues and the confusion of organic verbs with inorganic nouns. Living creatures behave like automatons, inanimate objects sprout and grow as if alive, personalities are overridden and replaced, the familiar is described in ways that make it seem alien and threatening.

Giving oneself over to Campbell's writing feels a bit like losing one's mind. Sounds are heightened, perceptions warped, and squalor becomes synonymous with horror. Reading his books, you begin to feel that your room needs to be scrubbed clean, that bugs are crawling over your skin, and that the city is driving you mad.

WEIRD

CHAPTER FIVE

SCIENCE

A NOVEL BY ROBIN COOK

COMA

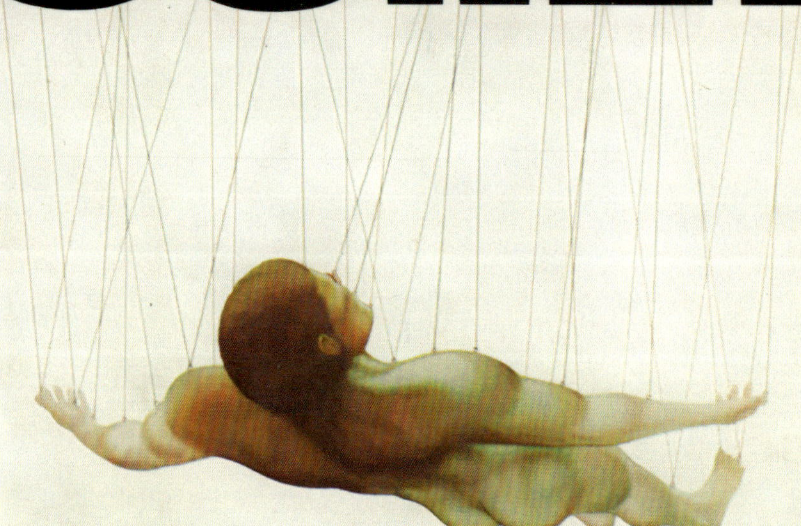

If there's one thing horror novels from the '70s and '80s can teach us, it's that doctors in hospitals are mostly interested in impregnating patients with Swedish clones (*Embryo* page 53), decapitating patients and using their heads to form a living computer (*Heads*, 1985), or harvesting putrid snot from the multiple anuses of alien worms with an insatiable appetite for human flesh (*Fatal Beauty*, 1990).

It all started with Robin Cook and his novels: *Fever*, *Outbreak*, *Mutation*, *Shock*, *Seizure* . . . terse nouns splashed across paperback racks. And just when you thought you had Cook pegged, he adds an adjective: *Fatal Cure*, *Acceptable Risk*, *Mortal Fear*, *Harmful Intent*. An ophthalmologist as well as an author, Cook has checked eyes and written best sellers with equal frequency. He's best known for *Coma* (1977), the source of the medical-thriller Nile. Written in 1977, the book spent thirteen weeks on the *New York Times* Best-Seller List and spawned a hit movie directed by Michael Crichton.

Its heroine, Susan Wheeler, is one of those beautiful, brilliant medical students who's constantly earning double takes from male colleagues or looking in the mirror and wondering if she's a doctor or a woman—and why can't she be both, dammit? On her first day as a trainee at Boston Memorial, she settles on "woman" and allows herself to flirt with an attractive patient on his way into a routine surgery. They make a date for coffee, but something goes wrong on the table and he goes into . . . a *COMA*!

Determined not to be stood up, Susan researches what happened to her date and discovers the hospital's dirty secret: they're selling internal organs to rich foreigners. There's a chase, a narrow escape, a betrayal by a trusted authority figure, a conspiracy revealed, and a final scene featuring a striking image of comatose chumps dangling from wires. There are also a lot of lectures on medicine and ethics delivered with the plodding rhythms of a man unaccustomed to interruption, a failing Cook shares with Crichton, that other M.D.-turned-author.

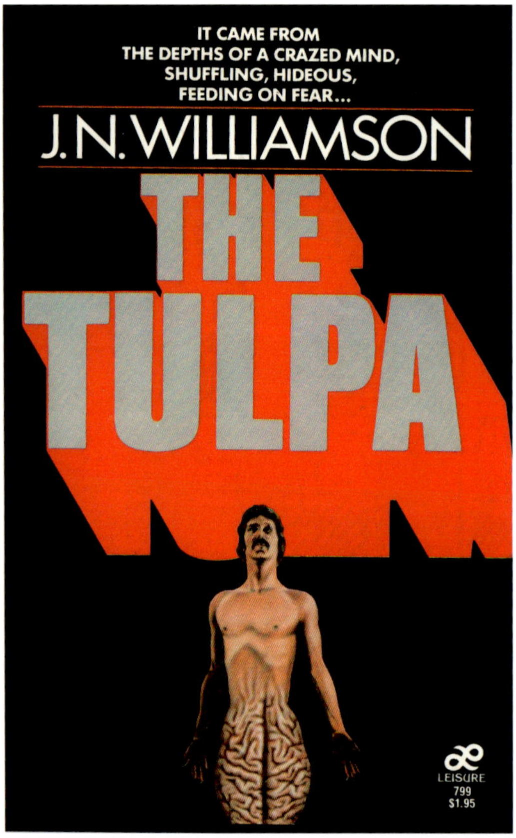
IT CAME FROM
THE DEPTHS OF A CRAZED MIND,
SHUFFLING, HIDEOUS,
FEEDING ON FEAR...
J.N. WILLIAMSON
THE
TULPA
LEISURE
799
$1.95

LIGHT
SOURCE
"A HIGH-VOLTAGE CHASE THRILLER!"
—PUBLISHERS WEEKLY
SIGNET • 451-AE3647 • (CANADA $5.50) • U.S. $4.50
A NOVEL BY
BARI WOOD
CO-AUTHOR OF
TWINS

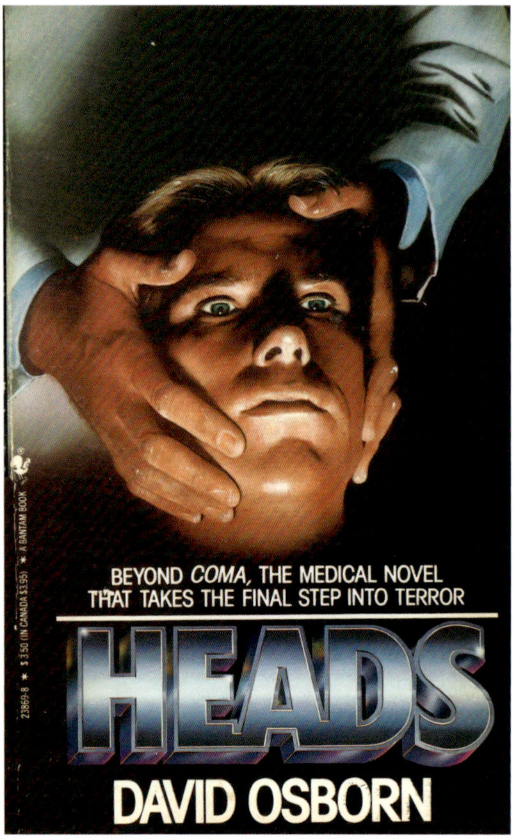
BEYOND COMA, THE MEDICAL NOVEL
THAT TAKES THE FINAL STEP INTO TERROR
HEADS
DAVID OSBORN
23869-8 ★ $3.50 (IN CANADA $3.95) ★ A BANTAM BOOK

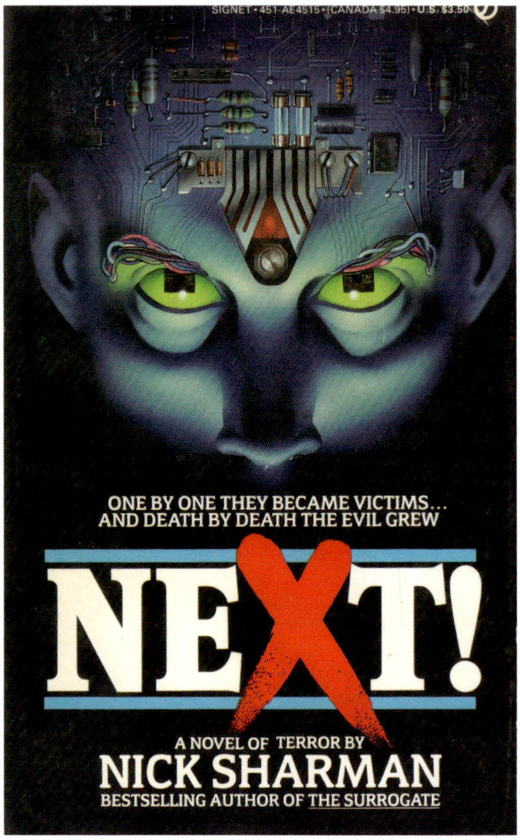
SIGNET • 451-AE4515 • (CANADA $4.95) • U.S. $3.50
ONE BY ONE THEY BECAME VICTIMS...
AND DEATH BY DEATH THE EVIL GREW
NEXT!
A NOVEL OF TERROR BY
NICK SHARMAN
BESTSELLING AUTHOR OF THE SURROGATE

Coma's success opened the floodgates for books like *The Minotaur Factor*, *The Theta Syndrome*, *The Orpheus Process*, and *The Compton Effect*. Suddenly, science was exciting—because scientists wanted you dead.

Indeed, science was no longer the domain of nerds wearing safety goggles; it was now the domain of action! Take, for example, the toxic effects of polychlorinated biphenyls (PCBs): boring when you read about them in academic studies on drinking water, but exciting when they achieve sentience, dissolve the skin off a trucker, and make him smash his hurtling rig into a speeding train (*Slime*).

Similarly, there's no time for dull academic debates about testing pharmaceuticals on animals when a lab monkey sheds its skin and becomes a tiny hell-skeleton wielding a hatchet and an erection, furiously trying to suck the blood from a housewife's leg. When that happens you don't need to consult a peer-reviewed journal—you just need to grab an electric knife and carve that sucker up. That's from Daniel Gower's *The Orpheus Process* (1992), a book whose totally metal chapter titles ("Breakfast of Crucifixions," "Deathwomb") and studly hero, Dr. Orville Leonard Helmond (who had "managed to love and lay quite a number of pretty women"), can't hide the fact that the good doc is a terrible scientist. He shoots monkeys with a .22, brings them back to life in his lab, and then either stabs them to death or takes them home to play with his kids. Depends on his mood.

One wonders if even stringent testing protocols could have prevented the tragedy in *Fatal Beauty*. The cosmetic Beautifique, whose ingredients mostly consist of telepathic worm snot harvested from alien slugs, is rushed to market without FDA approval. When placed on the flesh of nymphomaniacs, S&M freaks, or general weirdos, the compound either transforms them into giant castrating crabs, causes their breast implants to squeeze off the heads of police officers, or makes their skin melt. Results may vary.

Pursuing a degree in forbidden and dangerous science? There are plenty of specialties to consider, including parapsychology (*The Tulpa*), nuclear fusion (*Light Source*), surgery (*Heads*), computers (*Next!*), chemistry (*Slime*), and pharmaceutical sales (*Fatal Beauty*).

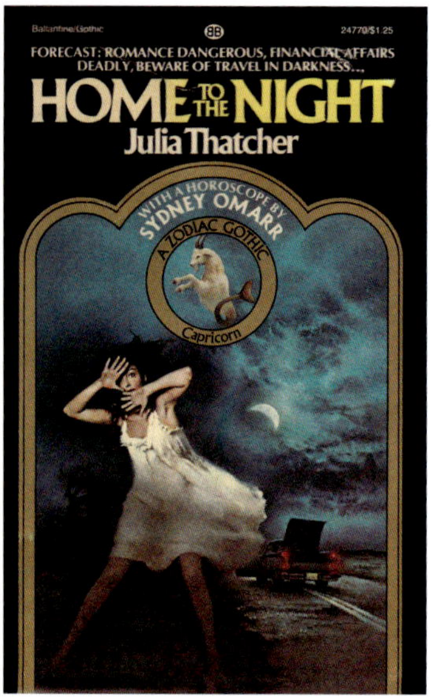

Launched in 1975, the Zodiac Gothic series (*top*) and the Birthstone Gothic books (*bottom*) barely lasted a year each, representing a final attempt by Ballantine to squeeze more cash out of the dying gothic-romance cow.

Starry Starry Nightmare

Most of the science that appeared in these books was pseudoscience, to put it charitably. After all, the '70s was the decade when finding a cure for cancer was abandoned in favor of finding the Loch Ness monster, searching for UFOs, researching ESP, and trying to establish a scientific basis for astrology. As we all know, the first three are valid areas of scientific inquiry; astrology is a bunch of bunk.

That didn't stop everyone from asking, "Hey baby, what's your sign?" In Linda Goodman's case, the answer was a dollar sign. The radio broadcaster and astrologer's 1968 book *Linda Goodman's Sun Signs* sold three million copies and became the first astrology book to hit the *New York Times* Best-Seller List. By 1978 astrology columns ran in 1,250 newspapers and 500 astrology books were in print.

Cashing in on this trend was Lyle Kenyon Engle's book mill, Book Creations. Based in Canaan, New York, Engel and his staff of twenty came up with a book concept, sold it to a publisher, and then hired a writer to churn out copy. If the series did well, they'd milk it dry (John Jakes's Kent Family Chronicles sold 35 million books). If not, they took it out behind the barn and shot it. Which is exactly what happened to Robert Lory's Horrorscope series, whose fifth volume, *Claws of the Crab*, was never published in America.

According to most astrology books, a Taurus is supposed to be stubborn. But according to Horrorscope, a Taurus is more likely to be abducted to a Greek island by a demented movie producer, locked in a labyrinth full of acid baths, and dismembered by a robot Minotaur. Aries, you're trapped inside a hollow volcano full of missing luxury yachts, where fiddling with strange piles of gold gets you burned to death by unquenchable green fire. Leo? You're a were-lion.

At least Ballantine made it through all twelve signs with their Zodiac Gothic series. Each installment began with popular newspaper astrologer Sydney Omarr doing the chart for the book's heroine. At the same time, Ballantine was publishing twelve Birthstone Gothics, under their Beagle imprint, in what was probably an attempt to prop up the flagging sales of gothic romances. As always, the fault lies not in our stars, but in our sales.

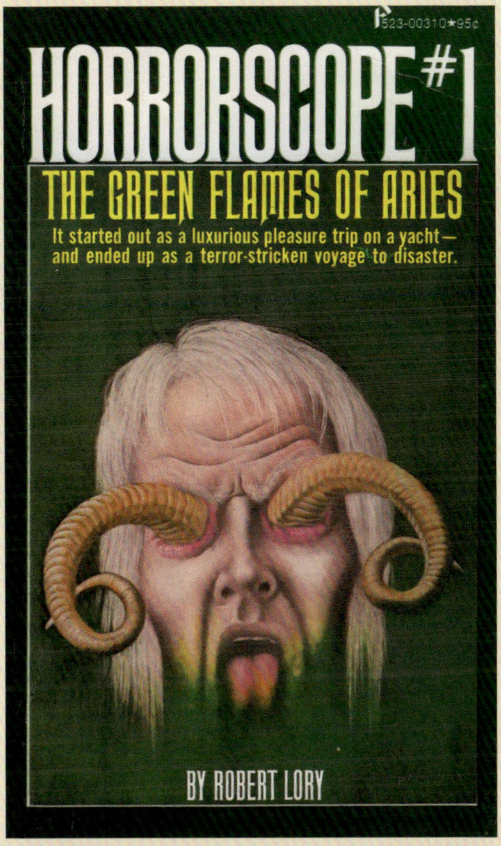
523-00310★95¢
HORRORSCOPE #1
THE GREEN FLAMES OF ARIES
It started out as a luxurious pleasure trip on a yacht—and ended up as a terror-stricken voyage to disaster.
BY ROBERT LORY

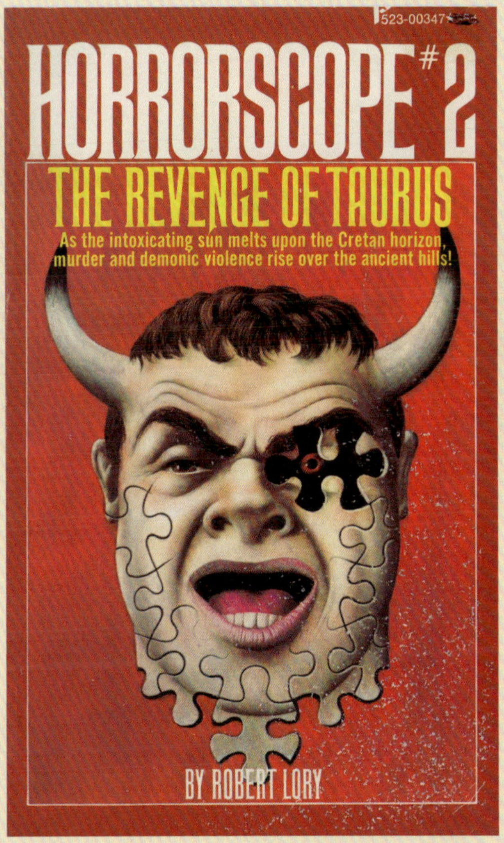
523-00347
HORRORSCOPE #2
THE REVENGE OF TAURUS
As the intoxicating sun melts upon the Cretan horizon, murder and demonic violence rise over the ancient hills!
BY ROBERT LORY

21-425★95¢
HORRORSCOPE #3
THE CURSE OF LEO
Calder Heath awakens in the jungle, covered with blood. The strange dream of terror has finally come true!
BY ROBERT LORY

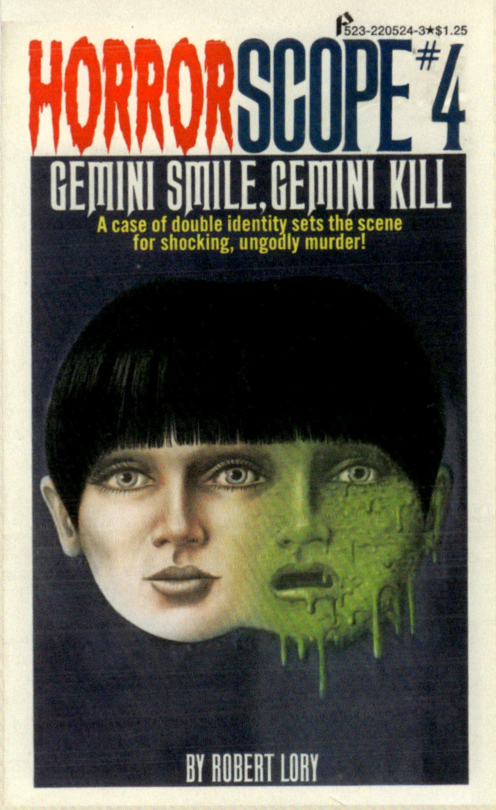
523-220524-3★$1.25
HORRORSCOPE #4
GEMINI SMILE, GEMINI KILL
A case of double identity sets the scene for shocking, ungodly murder!
BY ROBERT LORY

The eyes have it: ESP is usually invisible, so a piercing stare implies psychic talents for gifted (and not actually conjoined) kids (*The Fury*), a precognitive photographer (*The Nightmare Candidate*), a 19th-century hypnotist (*The Mesmerist*), and Nazi-bred psychic teens (*Psychic Spawn*).

It's All in the Mind

Astrology may be junk science, but horror readers know that hypnosis is A-1, grade-A science. Whether you wanted to know if your mother was raped by Dracula, whether you were raped by Satan, what sins you committed in your past life, what fantasies compel you to kill in your present one, whether you were possessed by a Vietnamese death demon or abducted by UFOs, in book after book, hypnosis was the answer.

It's one simple step from hypnosis (totally legit science everyone should use daily) to ESP (slightly iffier). That's not to say no legitimate ESP research was happening in the 1970s. In fact, both the Princeton Engineering Anomalies Research program and the U.S. government's Stargate Project logged intriguing but inconclusive results for years. But horror authors of the '70s weren't interested in "intriguing but inconclusive." They were interested in "totally horrifying."

The Scourge (1980) made the leap via a pharmaceutical company manufacturing a mind-control drug that "makes hypnosis look like a cheap conjuring trick." (As if it wasn't one already.) The results were impressive. At the story's climax, the CEO turns braindead intensive-care-unit patients into his own tiny zombie army.

In *Brain Watch* (1985), superpsychic powers are the result of splitting a doctor's noggin into a quadruple brain, unlocking his ability to project illusions, become superstrong, and control the pigment in his skin to ensure a really great tan. This sounds incredible, but apparently natural processes lie untapped inside our brains. As a doctor explains in *Psychic Spawn* (1987): "It's very simple, Mr. Stern. What's happened to you is that you have become psychic."

Unfortunately, as shown in *Mind War* (1980), these abilities can be perverted for evil, as the U.S.S.R. recruits a psychic strike team to telekinetically destroy the Golden Gate Bridge, then the Hoover Dam. Fortunately another holdover from '70s science comes to the rescue: the Prophecies of Nostradamus.

So now that we've covered astrology and ESP, what about UFOs? Fake science, or the best science?

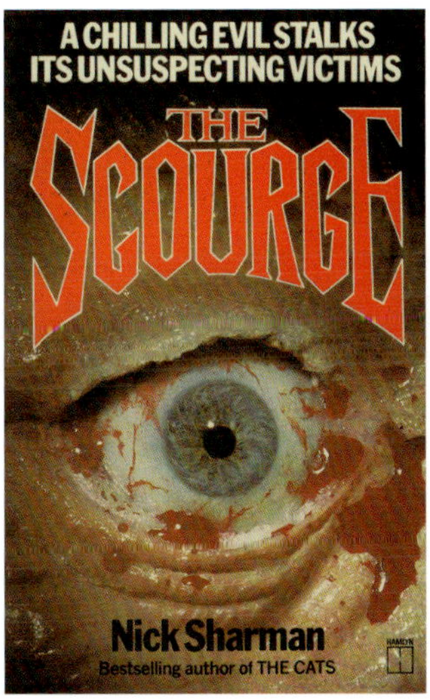

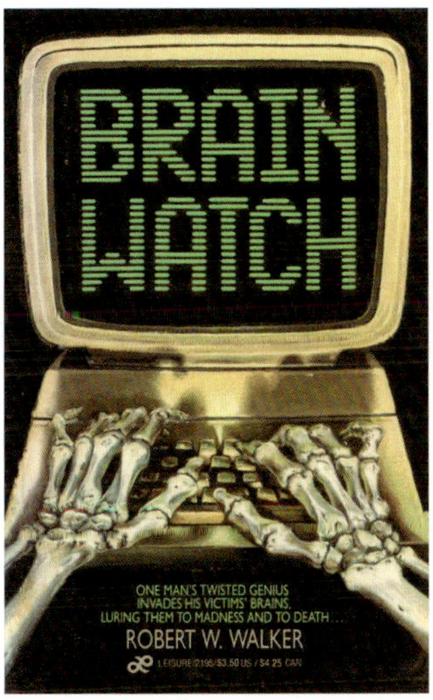

The Visitors Are Your Friends

In 1977, the launch of *Voyager* and the release of *Close Encounters of the Third Kind* kicked off a UFO wave. Carl Sagan's TV series *Cosmos* focused our attention on the skies, and every respected scientist came down on one of two sides: either aliens were coming to help us attain enlightenment or they wanted to eat us. Or kill us. Or kill us first and then eat us. There were conflicting theories.

Horror novelist Whitley Streiber (*Wolfen*, *The Hunger*, *The Night Church*) wasn't sure what the aliens wanted, but he managed to turn his own abduction story into a lucrative empire with books (*Communion*, 1987; *Majestic*, 1989), TV appearances, and eventually a subscription-based website. Strieber never proclaimed his extraterrestrials good or bad, but in Wetanson and Hoobler's *The Hunters* (1978) it's clear: the extraterrestrials will proclaim messages of universal peace and brotherhood to lower our guard, and then use the reanimated corpses of our loved ones to lure us into the open, where they'll shoot us and roast us over a campfire. They're probably neighbors with the aliens of *Earth Has Been Found* (1979), whose fart-propelled "xenos" abduct humans and impregnate them with eggs, from which parasites hatch and eat their way out.

Why would aliens travel all that way to eat us? Don't they have food on their home planets? Well, what if they're not aliens at all? Leave it to J. N. Williamson to reveal the truth. *Brotherkind* (1987) starts as your typical abduction story, with Sheila gangbanged on a UFO by a bunch of midget aliens who must use the power of their collective semen to overcome her DNA's natural resistance. Also, Bigfoot joins in because he was hitching a lift. Returning home, she finds hypnosis, and love, in the arms of parapsychologist Martin Ruben, but the two are menaced by Men in Black. Rubin unravels the conspiracy: alien Greys have teamed up with Bigfoot and the Men in Black and Mothman to seed humanity with alien/human babies. P.S., they're not aliens at

Ever since Eisenhower sold us out to the Greys in 1954, our planet has become a one-stop shopping solution for every jerk with a flying saucer.

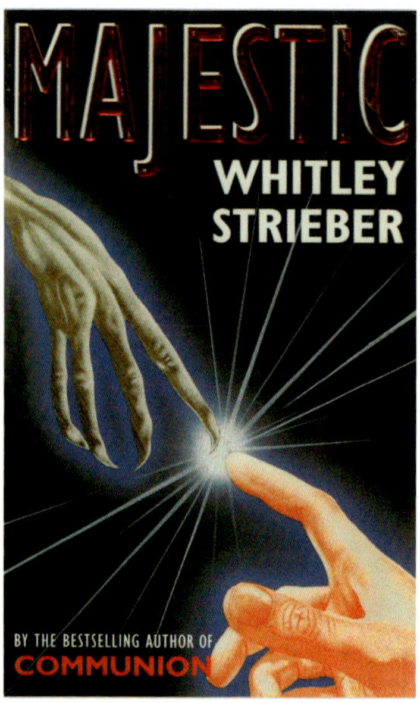

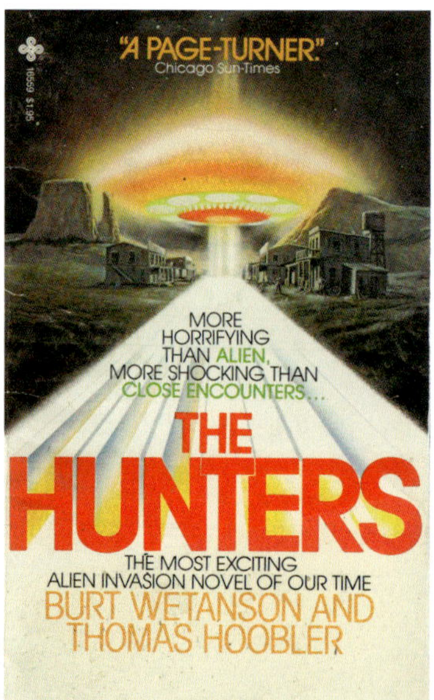

all, but part of a hidden race that we used to call fairies.

Fortunately, Martin is able to melt the Men in Black and the Greys with the power of the rock band KISS, specifically their hit "Firehouse," which he finds on an "acid rock" station. Then he simply refuses to believe in Bigfoot until his aggressive disbelief makes the ten-foot-tall manimal fall apart. Tragically, he cannot reach Sheila in time and her hybrid baby is abducted. The book ends with the author assuring us, as any good scientist would, that although the story we have just read is not true, it's also not *not* true either. Now that's science!

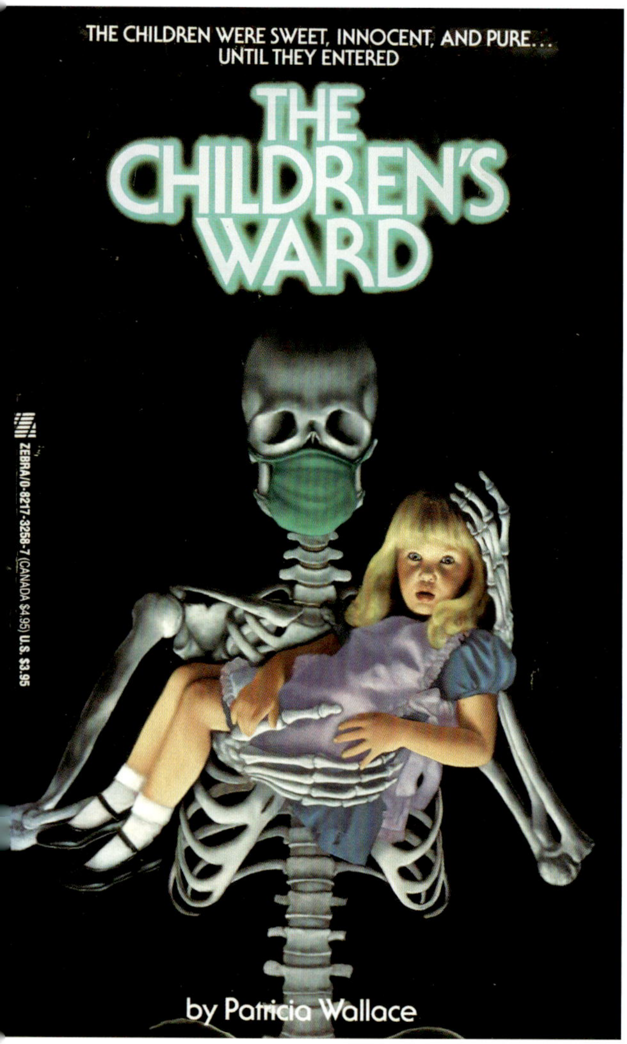

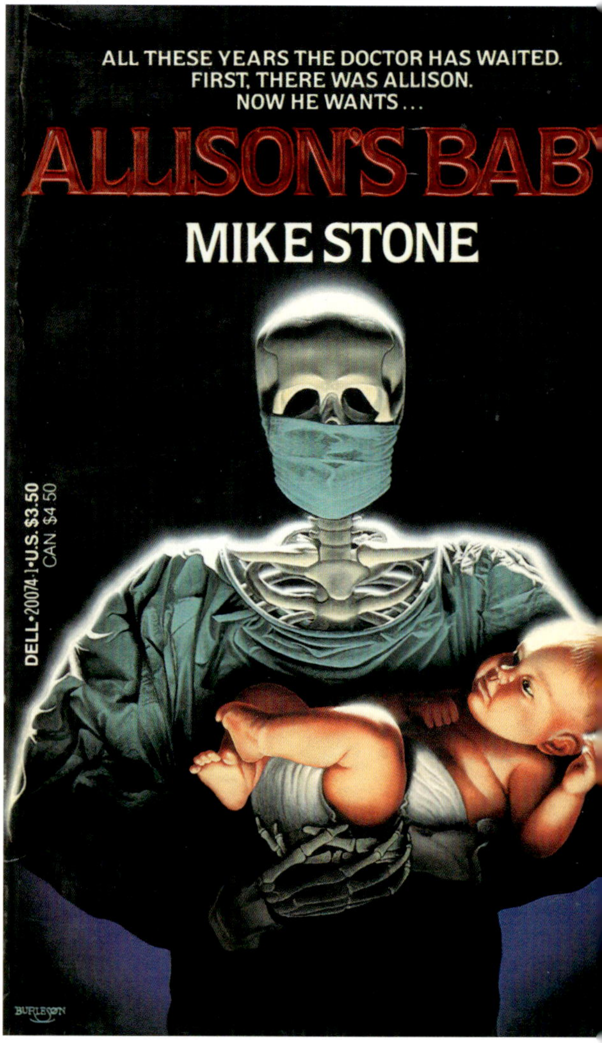

Skeleton Doctors Are the Worst Doctors

Skeletons are the worst. They lurk inside our skin, waiting to jump out and use our computers, dance obscenely in graveyards, and wield enormous scythes. But even worse than a skeleton is a skeleton doctor. To be honest, I'm not even sure their licenses to practice medicine are legal.

I have never discriminated against anyone based on the quantity of their skin, so it was educational to read *The Children's Ward* (1985) by Patricia Wallace and *Allison's Baby* (1988) by Mike Stone and realize that, yes, in fact all skeleton doctors are fabulously incompetent and should immediately be turned into xylophones. Wallace explores the issue of whether a cursed California hospital ward previously occupied by the criminally insane ought to house an experimental pediatric treatment program. (Conclusion: Probably not.)

On the isolated hospital's most isolated ward, four children are observed 24/7 by the head of the program, Dr. Quinn, who learns that all of their ailments, from brain tumors to paralysis to leprosy, are psychosomatic; the kids don't need surgery, they need hugs. But hugs are in short supply as a physical

Skeletons may have their faults, but you have to admire them for working hard enough to earn advance degrees in pediatrics, obstetrics, and nursing.

therapist's arm is yanked out of its socket, a custodian gets bisected by a power tool, a bad daddy shoots himself, and a ghost beats a mean mommy to death. Bad parents are getting punished, but by whom? It turns out that one of the kids is psychic, and the dark forces lurking in Ward D are amplifying her powers. We're never told what these dark forces are, but the sound of wind chimes is heard whenever they manifest, so I imagine they're spirits of long-dead Zen surfers.

Meanwhile *Allison's Baby* is, oddly enough, about Allison's doctor, Jason Fielding, M.D. He's researching memory, meaning that he takes hobos and the elderly, cuts out pieces of their brains, and sees if they remember anything afterward. Most don't, so he locks them up in a rapidly overflowing mental asylum. Why is Dr. Fielding conducting this stupid experiment? Because when he discovers what makes memory work, he's going to win the Nobel prize, and if he wins "the highest reward of his profession," he is certain to "finally prove to his father that he wasn't a failure." A noble goal, but Allison and her baby keep screwing it up.

What danger signs should patients watch for when selecting a skeleton doctor? Well, if the doctor refers to patients as "poor unlucky bastards," be careful. Also, doctors who turn abandoned mental institutions into their own private research facilities are probably up to no good. Especially when the entrance to said clinic is "an underground passageway behind the morgue." Most important, just remember that whenever a skeleton does science, innocent people wind up getting hurt.

The Party Decade

Horror paperback covers reflected their decade, full of big hair (*Hot Blood*), lurid neon color schemes (*Nocturnal*), shopping malls (*The Mall*), and the Cold War (*Black Magic*).

Welcome to the '80s, where life was a bitchin' ride in a sweet Porsche! Manufacturing was dead! We were a service and technology economy now! Everyone get rich! America is number one! Let's kill a commie for mommy and head for the mall!

Science may have been running amok in horror fiction, but in the real world it was making books more eye-catching. Greeting card technology was repurposed for the book business as Kluge embossers and Bobst stampers worked overtime to coat covers in foil, raised monsters, and die-cut windows showing swank stepback art. Coming soon: hologram covers! Strachan Henshaw printing presses ran hot, spitting out 450 new paperback titles each month and 200 new horror titles every year.

Paperbacks of the '70s had been shaped by grim, sober novels like *The Exorcist* and *Rosemary's Baby*. By contrast, horror fiction of the '80s was warped by the gaudy delights of Stephen King and V. C. Andrews. *The Dead Zone* (1979) became King's first book to debut on the *New York Times* Best-Seller List; by 1983 an estimated 40 million copies of King's books were in print. *The Exorcist* was for squares, and *Rosemary's Baby* smelled like grandma. If you wanted to do serious business, you needed an endorsement from King.

Anne Rice's 1976 *Interview with the Vampire* birthed a slew of sequels in the '80s, transforming Rice into a brand name and spawning an arterial gush of vampire novels. Besides King, Rice, and V. C. Andrews (more about Rice and Andrews next chapter), a second tier of writers turned out doorstop-sized books that quickly moved to bookstore racks in malls and airports everywhere. Ramsey Campbell, Peter Straub, John Saul, Dean Koontz, and John Farris bounced up and down the best-seller lists, earning much of their profit from paperback sales. Superagent Kirby McCauley and his Pimlico Agency represented all the big names in horror and sci-fi. McCauley had two pieces of advice for writers: write novels—the fatter the better—and sell paperback originals (hardcovers did a lot for authorial egos but little for sales). As everyone knows, an author is only as good as the last sales report.

Small horror imprints had flourished in the '70s, but in the '80s the big publishers gobbled them up. Penguin acquired Grosset & Dunlap and Playboy Press, setting off a trend that snowballed into an extinction-level event by decade's end. Once they had eaten the little guys, big publishers flooded the market with their own paperback original imprints, like Spectra, Onyx, Pinnacle, and Overlook.

The '70s saw horror get serious, but the '80s were party time. And the guest of honor at that party was *Time* magazine's 1982 "Man of the Year," fresh out of the lab and ready to rock and roll: the personal computer!

Dripping with dark obsessions and unholy desires!
POCKET
HORROR
66424-7
$3.95
Hot Blood
TALES OF PROVOCATIVE HORROR
Edited by JEFF GELB AND LONN FRIEND

HORROR
POCKET
43065-3
$3.50
WHEN HE STRIKES IN THE NIGHT,
HER DREAMS RESOUND
WITH MADNESS,
WITH THE SCREAMS OF
WOMEN DYING
NOCTURNAL
A NOVEL OF MIDNIGHT TERROR
KEN EULO
MILLION-COPY BESTSELLING AUTHOR OF THE BROWNSTONE

SUSPENSE
THE
AN AMERICAN DREAM
CAREENS INTO
BLOODY NIGHTMARE
MALL
STEVE KAHN
EXIT
42504-8 · $3.50 · POCKET

WHITLEY STRIEBER
BESTSELLING AUTHOR OF THE WOLFEN & THE HUNGER
Black Magic
THE ULTIMATE OCCULT WEAPON–IN THE HANDS OF THE
KGB

Horror Goes High Tech

The seeds of a computer revolution were planted in the '70s, when humanity was betrayed by the twin engines of government and commerce. Politicians lied about nuclear war, scientists lied about pollution, NASA lied about aliens. Private companies were poisoning the oceans with toxic waste and acid rain. But a technological counterculture was brewing in garages and spare bedrooms all over the country. Channels like the *Whole Earth Catalogue* and science-fiction movies seeded receptive minds with the idea that technology could be turned to more human needs.

Some writers overpromised, depicting computers as superheroes. Stephen Gresham, author of *The Shadow Man* (1986), believed that personal computers could generate hard-light holograms capable of running our errands, but then again Gresham also believed that pro wrestling was real, so he might have been a simpleton. In his book, eight-year-old Joey gets C.A.P. (Computer Assisted Playmate) when his pro-wrestler father, Jeb "The Dixie Strangler" Stuart, decides that his son is lonely

How will computers change everything? They might defend kids from witches (*The Shadow Man*), enable super-nerds to stalk and murder strangers (*The Hacker*), spawn software glitches that become actual insects (*Bugs*), or become addictions that control our minds (*Little Brother*). At least two of those predictions have come true!

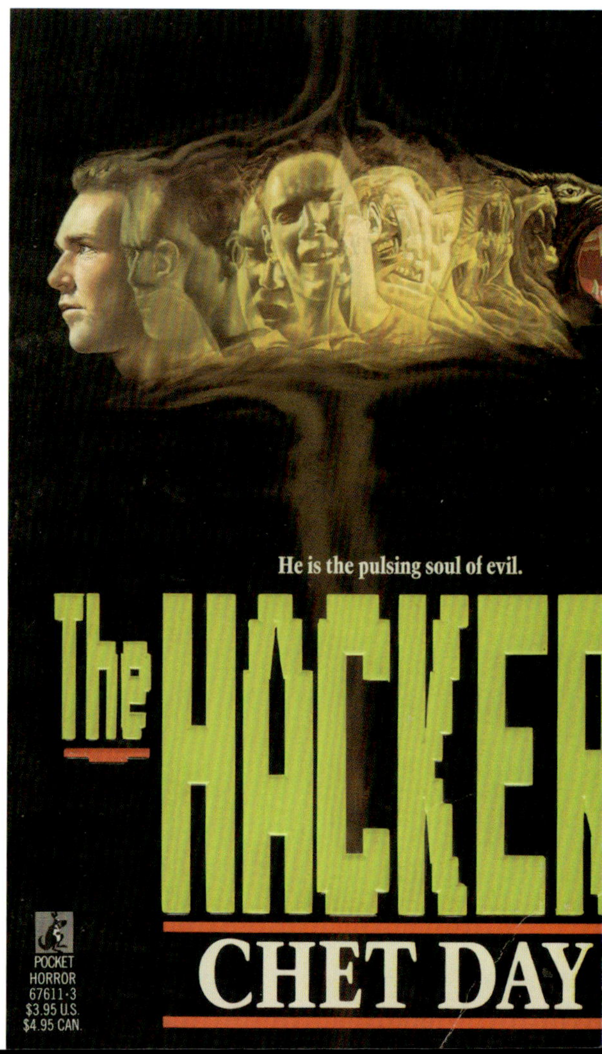

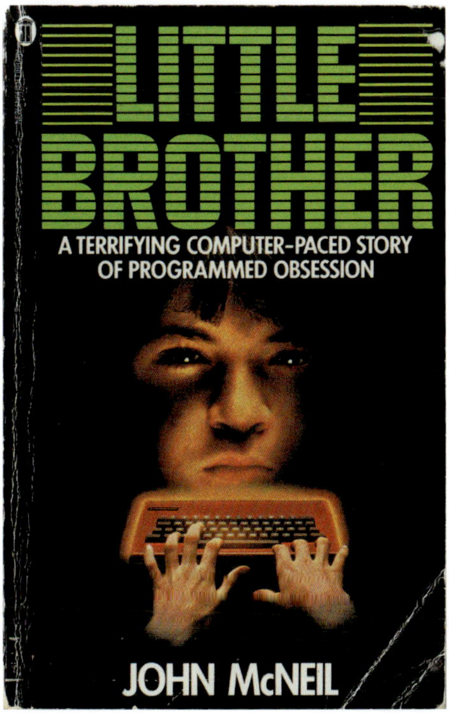

after his parents' divorce. Turns out that Jeb's ex-wife is a witch, and no matter how open-minded you are, you should never marry a witch.

Joey is C.A.P.'s "little friend," and when Mom summons the digital demon known only as the Shadow Man to kill her son, C.A.P. screams that "A PRELIMINARY SCAN SHOWS A HIGH RANKING DEMON OF SOME TYPE—A SHAPESHIFTER." Which is way more useful than "404: file not found." C.A.P. uses his "Timeshifter Beam" to trap Mom in the past, saving the day. But can C.A.P. help Joey win back his father's love? He wouldn't be a computer if he couldn't.

Back in the '80s we didn't know that one day all computers would be linked and turned into a giant delivery system for pornography and cat pictures, so networking seemed exciting. We learned our lessons only by trial and error. Trial: Why not let a fetus network its brain with the hospital mainframe? Error: Fetus becomes a big-headed psychic baby that wants to murder everyone (*The Unborn* 1980). Trial: Let's teach monkeys to control robots with their minds. Error: God intervenes and makes everyone either crazy or dead (*The Hacker* 1989). Yes, it's easy to sit here in the safety of the now and mock a bunch of paperback novelists for not accurately foreseeing the future, but they did get one thing right. All these books, no matter how silly, don't feel like much fun. An underlying pessimism runs through them, mostly because their suspicions about technology turned out to be true.

In *Little Brother* (1983), aliens land on Earth in 1908 and take over the Soviet Union. By 1983 they've infiltrated the American market with an iPad-esque toy called the Possum, which beams addictive subliminal messages into the brains of good American kids. When worried parents try to limit the ever-increasing screen time, the kids either commit suicide or attack Mom and Dad. In the end, the adults figure "What the hell?" and become addicted to Possum, too. Anyone who thinks this is baseless paranoia hasn't watched a parent texting while rocketing down a highway at 70 m.p.h. in the family van.

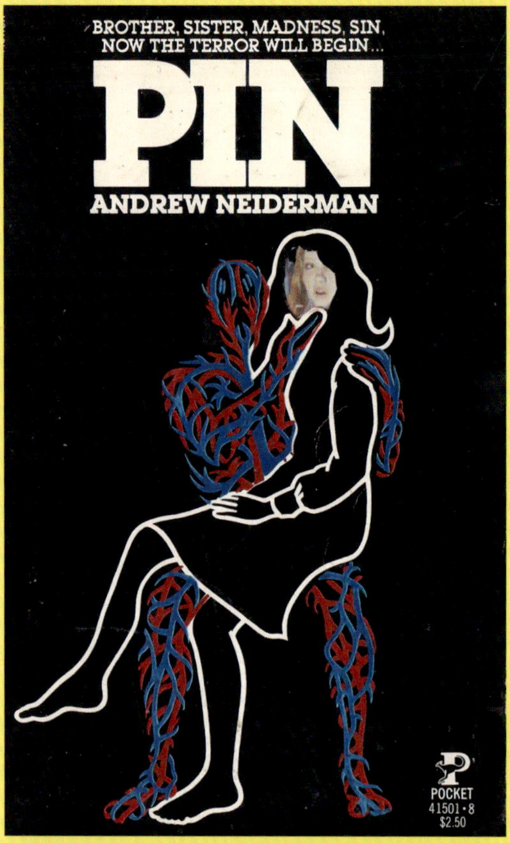
BROTHER, SISTER, MADNESS, SIN,
NOW THE TERROR WILL BEGIN...
PIN
ANDREW NEIDERMAN
POCKET
41501-8
$2.50

Man's Worst Fiend...
NIGHT HOWL
Andrew Neiderman
Author of Pin and Brainchild
60634-4·$3.50·HORROR·POCKET

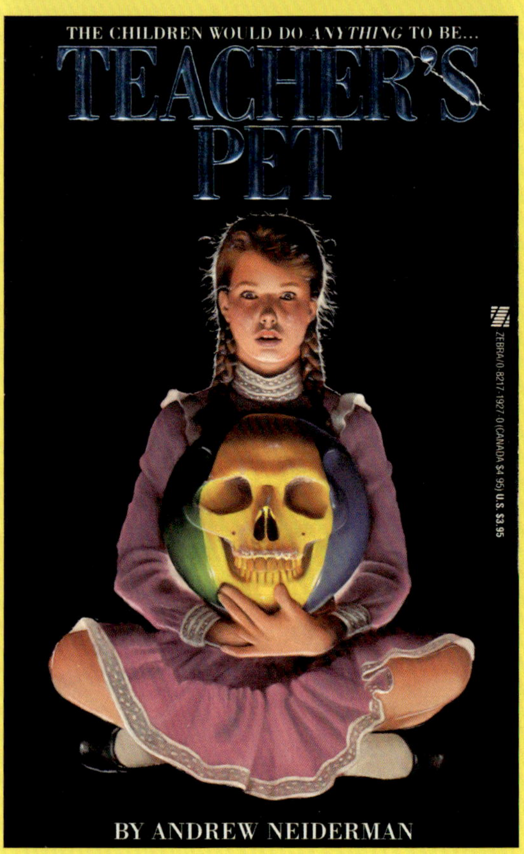
THE CHILDREN WOULD DO ANYTHING TO BE...
TEACHER'S PET
BY ANDREW NEIDERMAN

Andrew Neiderman Puts a PIN in It

Your children want to know where babies come from, so you:

a) give them a talk about the birds and the bees
b) buy them a book called *Your Changing Body*
c) show them a tasteful PBS documentary
d) use ventriloquism to make them think your transparent, life-size anatomical dummy is alive and capable of answering all their questions about human reproduction.

If you picked (D), then the storyline of *PIN* (1981) won't seem so strange. Leon and Ursula have lived together ever since their parents died in a car accident. The kids grew up thinking dad's anatomical model, PIN, was alive, and now Leon throws his voice unconsciously, keeping PIN talking. PIN eats with them, listens to Leon's weird poetry recitals, and when Leon and Ursula have incest sex, PIN likes to help. If you're a completely insane lunatic shut-in with ice water in your veins and screaming bats inside your skull, this would be paradise. And for Leon, it is.

Leon and Ursula are so hyperintelligent that they're basically insane, and that's Andrew Neiderman's specialty: characters who are too smart for their own good. In *Night Howl* (1986), it's a genetically mutated dog with a man-sized brain. In *Teacher's Pet* (1986), it's an afterschool tutor who turns the brightest kids into cold-blooded "rational" monsters. In *Brainchild* (1981), it's Lois Gilbert, high school senior, who turns her house into a behavioral psychology experiment that drives her entire family stark raving mad.

When Neiderman's not writing about mad scientists in training, he loves writing about families who put the "fun" in dysfunction. Maybe it's his way with toxic families that led to the other part of his career. While he's written forty-seven novels under his own name, he's written sixty-eight as V. C. Andrews, ghostwriting for the woman who raised gothic horror from its grave.

In Andrew Neiderman's books, every unhappy family is unhappy in its own neurotic, homicidal, totally psychotic, and sexually dysfunctional way.

GOT
ROM

CHAPTER SIX

HIC &
ANTIC

FICTION
V.C. Andrews
Flowers in the Attic
POCKET
43599-X
$3.50

Horror is a woman's genre, and it has been all the way back to the oldest horror novel still widely read today: *Frankenstein* by Mary Shelley, daughter of pioneering feminist author Mary Wollstonecraft. Ann Radcliffe's gothic novels (*The Mysteries of Udolpho*, *The Italian*) made her the highest-paid writer of the late eighteenth century. In the nineteenth century, Mary Elizabeth Braddon and Charlotte Riddell were book-writing machines, turning out sensation novels and ghost stories by the pound. Edith Wharton wrote ghost stories before becoming a novelist of manners, and Vernon Lee (real name Violet Paget) wrote elegant tales of the uncanny that rival anything by Henry James. Three of Daphne du Maurier's stories became Hitchcock films (*Jamaica Inn*, *Rebecca*, *The Birds*), and Shirley Jackson's singular horror novel *The Haunting of Hill House* made her one of the highest-regarded American writers of the twentieth century.

Even though two of the three great novels of the '70s horror boom featured female main characters (*Rosemary's Baby* and *The Exorcist*), V. C. Andrews was the first female brand-name horror writer, capable of selling millions of books simply because her name was on the cover. It's no accident that her style of horror was the one originally popularized by women: the gothic. Gothic horror was domestic horror in which affairs of the heart were as important as affairs of the flesh. Its subject matter was families, marriage, houses, children, insanity, and secrets.

The sexual revolution of the '60s encouraged a new frankness about sex, and movies like 1972's *Deep Throat* made the depiction of raw sex no big deal. When the Playboy Channel debuted on cable in 1982, it was greeted with a shrug. The culture was ready for a romantic backlash.

In the '80s, everyone was either in therapy or on talk shows talking about their terrible childhoods. Horror had returned to the shadowy bedrooms of the family home. It was up to Andrews to show us that families could house, and create, monsters.

Return of the Repressed

Like an unstoppable zombie, the literary career of V. C. Andrews cannot be destroyed. Put her in a wheelchair, throw her down the stairs, stick her in a coffin, it doesn't matter. Because every year since 1979 there has been a new book on the stands from V. C. Andrews. Some years there have been six.

Cleo Virginia Andrews was definitely not the frail, shut-in, gothic grandma that *People* portrayed her as in her very first interview in 1980. The magazine committed the cardinal sins of revealing her age (Andrews was in her late fifties when she published *Flowers in the Attic*) and photographing her wheelchair ("I refuse to allow pictures of me sitting in that thing," she later wrote), but she seemed most appalled by being portrayed as a victim. Andrews was nobody's victim.

At age 15, a fall down stairs at her high school exacerbated Andrews's back problems. A series of failed interventions left her spine unable to bend and confined her to a wheelchair. She had always wanted to be an actress; instead, her mother became her caretaker for the rest of her life (yet in all that time never managed to read a single one of her daughter's books). After her father died in 1957, Andrews supported the family by playing the stock market and becoming a commercial artist for magazines and department stores.

In 1972 she began to write, publishing stories with titles like "I Slept with My Uncle on My Wedding Night" in true-confession rags, but her fiction didn't sell until she confronted her fears. "I'm writing around all of the difficult things that my mother would disapprove of," she said in a 1985 interview. "So once I brushed her off my shoulder and got gutsy enough, I sold." She got her guts in 1979. The story of the Dollanganger children, locked away by their mother, poisoned by their grandmother, and falling in love with each other, became *Flowers in the Attic*. Agent Anita Diamant represented the paperback original and her assistant sold it for $7,500 to editor Ann Patty at Pocket Books. Patty's assessment of the writing was "it may be awful, but it is a style"—she was smart enough to see that it elicited a rabid reaction among female readers. Pushing for a big marketing campaign, Patty opted for the gender-neutral name V. C. Andrews (something the author didn't discover until she saw the cover), sending the book onto the *New York Times* Best-Seller List for fourteen weeks.

Diagnosed with breast cancer in 1986, Andrews hid her condition as long as she could; in December of that year, with 24 million copies of her seven novels in print, she passed away. Within days, Simon and Schuster's staff received a memo informing them that Andrews had left behind unpublished novels, as well as detailed notes and outlines for more, allowing them to publish books under her name for years to come, starting with a *Flowers in the Attic* prequel. Anita Diamant reached into her stable of writers and produced Andrew Neiderman, whose novel *PIN* (see pages 142–143) had found an eager reader in Andrews. To date, Neiderman has written over sixty-eight books as V. C. Andrews.

Whether it's the books she wrote herself or the ones ghostwritten in her name, Andrews's books are high gothic horror, with their shock treatments and split personalities (*My Sweet Audrina,* 1982), child selling (*Heaven*, 1985), and constant

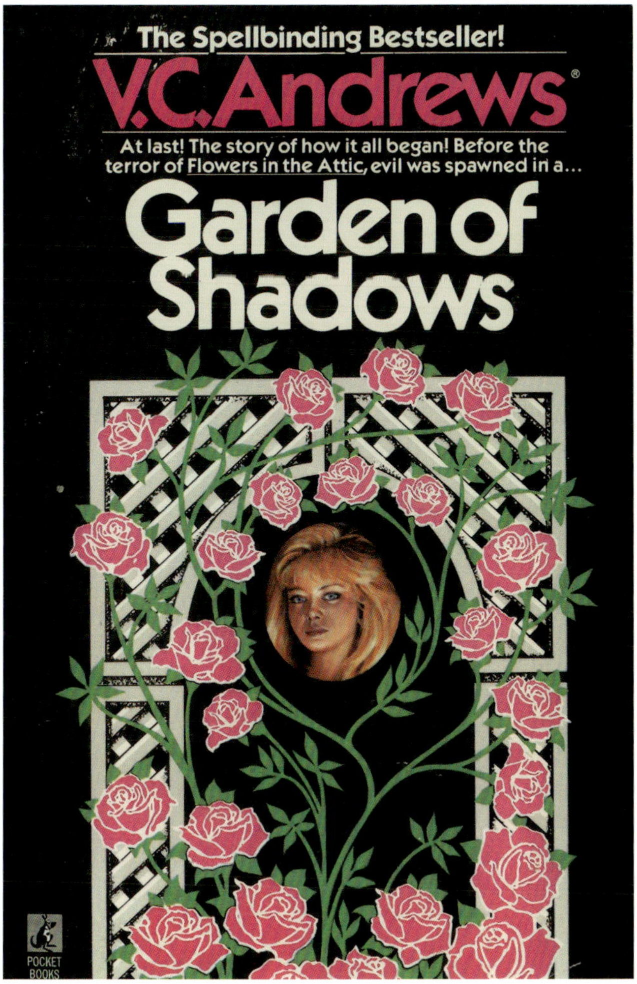

Editor Ann Patty rejected every cover treatment until art director Milton Charles designed what became the iconic V.C. Andrews cover: a die-cut opening revealing a character staring out morosely. It immediately launched a die-cut cover craze.

incest, child abuse, and cruel parents (pretty much all of them). Like Michael McDowell, another Southern author who made his name writing paperback originals, Andrews believed that families were forces of destruction. "There are so many cries out there in the night," she said in the same 1985 interview, conducted by Douglas E. Winter. "So much protective secrecy in families; and so many skeletons in the closets."

Andrews never phoned it in. She became her characters, crying when they cried, losing weight when they starved. "We all have primal fears of being helpless, trapped in a situation beyond our control," she said, talking about her disease; her books were about people breaking out of their prisons, finding freedom, becoming empowered. Later in that 1985 interview, Andrews was asked if her stories were autobiographical. "I don't want to write an autobiography," she said. "My life isn't finished yet."

A year later, she was dead. And yet she lived on. Andrews revived gothic horror by making fear less of a supernatural threat and more of a family affair. It would take another woman to introduce actual monsters to the new gothic. Anne Rice and her melodramatic vampires were ready to swoop in for the kill.

The Vampire Strikes Back

From their earliest appearances in literature, vampires have been jerks. Dracula was rude and smelly Eurotrash. Sheridan LeFanu's Carmilla was a terrible houseguest. And the less said about Varney the Vampire, the better. Then Anne Rice came along and completely overhauled their image. Sympathetic vampires had been given starring roles before, notably in Jane Gaskell's 1964 novel *The Shiny Narrow Grin*, about a going-nowhere girl who falls in love with a gloomy goth vampire, or savage and seductive Barnabas Collins in the rickety '60s soap opera *Dark Shadows*. But before Anne Rice took up their cause, vampire stories were told from the point of view of the people hunting them.

Rice gave vampires a voice. And then they wouldn't shut up. Narrated by an especially whiny Louis, *Interview with the Vampire* (1976) was greeted with critical disdain ("suckling eroticism" crowed the New *Republic*, "static . . . pompous . . . superficial" proclaimed the *New York Times*), which hit the author hard. Rice was writing her way out of a depression after her five-year-old daughter's death from leukemia, and she unconsciously put all her feelings of helplessness, regret, and guilt into the book. Louis was a passive victim because that's how Rice felt when she told his story.

Despite not finding a huge audience in hardcover, *Interview with the Vampire* quickly sold film and paperback rights. The sequel, *The Vampire Lestat* (1985), did even better in hardcover, selling around 75,000 copies. By the time the third book of the trilogy, *Queen of the Damned*, hit shelves in 1988, Rice had become so well known that the first printing alone was 405,000 copies.

As the series progressed and Rice's fortunes changed, so did her vampire's

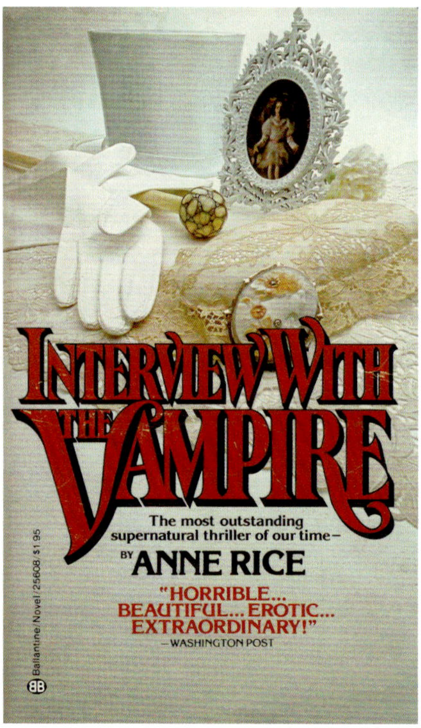

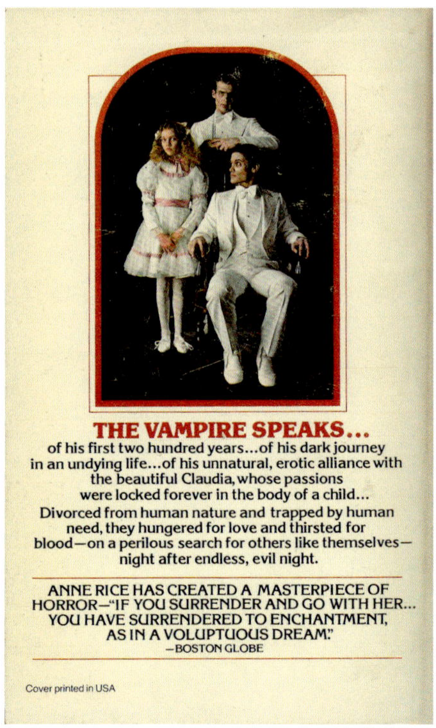

The front and back covers for the first paperback of *Interview with the Vampire* (*opposite*) felt modern, but the 1979 paperback saw H. Tom Hall, famous for his historical romance covers, go full gothic.

voice. Lestat wasn't a whiner. He was a rock star. Rice, who was born Howard Allen O'Brien and once described herself as a gay man trapped in a woman's body, said that with Lestat she was writing not about who she was, but who she wanted to be. This switch to a more proactive and fearless character not only matched where the author was in her life, but it was also a shrewd move that made the sequel a hit.

Rice's vampire trilogy is transparently autobiographical, allowing her to work through death, guilt, fear, and insecurity, emerging at the end as a fabulous superstar. Similarly, her vampires didn't bring stench and disease like their literary predecessors; they brought beauty and culture. They were romantic gods, and nothing as tacky as a cross or a stake through the heart could kill them. Only sunlight and fire were dramatic enough to take them down.

A Bloody Legacy

Anne Rice's vampires marked a significant transition for horror heroes. Before, the protagonists of horror fiction were blue-collar guys: Vietnam vets and salt of the earth types who staked first and asked questions later (if at all). Rice's vampires were cultured and elegant, powerful and refined, slim hipped and long haired and given to velvet cloaks.

And they loved to talk. Before Rice's books, vampires didn't have much to say beyond "slurp," but her stories are told from the undead's point of view, using the language of confessional magazines and talk therapy. Rice's vampires chat about their victimization, alienation, loneliness and suffering, because by talking through their feelings they can come to terms with them, and by coming to terms with them they can conquer them. These vampires cannot be monstrous or "other" because we hear their voices, and nothing that speaks to us about heart-break, or pretty clothes, can truly be alien.

But the difference between the minor success of *Interview with a Vampire* and the mega success of *Lestat* and *Queen* is hard to account for. Anne Rice didn't change how she wrote about vampires between 1976 and 1988; something bigger was going on in society. In *Dracula*, Renfield proclaimed, "The blood is the life!" By the time Rice published *Lestat*, the equation was blood = death.

Rarely has a disease engendered such fear and loathing as HIV. The term AIDS was first used in 1982, and by 1985 hundreds of parents would pull their children out of school based on rumors that an infected student might attend. Politicians proclaimed that children could "catch" the infection from a sneeze or a water fountain. Families abandoned the corpses of their dead sons in hospitals. The illness posited a future where human contact would be rare, bodily fluids poisonous.

Into the midst of this panic swooped Rice's vampires, sexy and shimmering. Swapping blood was all the high they craved, and they humanized the notion of the other. Everything our parents were telling us was wrong: these vampires

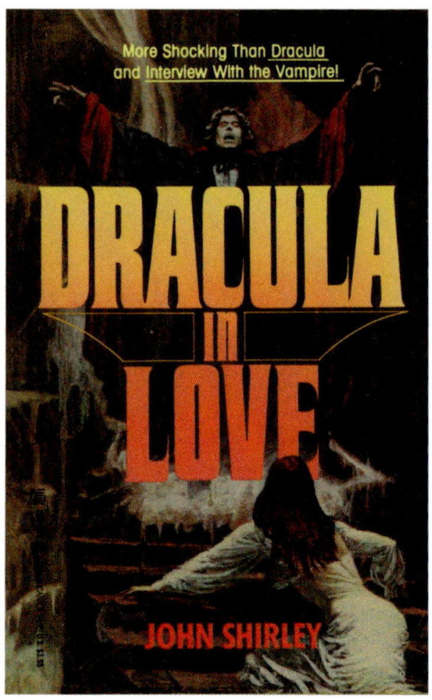

As vampires got chatty and romantic, even Dracula became a hero, both in John Shirley's first novel and in Fred Saberhagen's 10-volume series.

were scary but seductive, dangerous but delightful. Becoming one of them was described as receiving their "Dark Gift," and the transfusion made them not only permanently stoned, but, as Lestat said, "more fully what we are." You would become more fully yourself. And your real self was fabulous.

The old-fashioned Vietnam vet, plus *'Salem's Lot*, still couldn't create a formula capable of defeating emo vampires.

Alienated, lonely, brooding, gothic, glam, good dancers—Rice's vampires were everything we wanted to be. Other writers explored the possibilities, including Fred Saberhagen, who made the once-monstrous Dracula the hero of his novels. In John Shirley's *Dracula in Love* (1979) that old Transylvania hillbilly was an inhuman fiend wielding a prehensile penis with glowing eyes, but he could still be tamed. In true sensitive-male fashion, he only had to meet the right lady. Halfway through the book, he falls in love with a woman who saves his life. At the climax it's revealed that she is the living embodiment of Mother Earth and Dracula goes to her, crawling up inside her cavernous vagina while glowing like a 100-watt light bulb. Before Anne Rice, vampires killed humans. Now they got in touch with their sensitive sides while muffin-spelunking inside of them. They aren't predators, they are, literally, a part of us.

Vampires in modern horror fiction became a powerful metaphor for our attitudes toward outsiders and the AIDS epidemic—except for *Nightblood* (1990), which was for people who thought *'Salem's Lot* needed more machine guns. Its protagonist, Chris Stiles, is a Vietnam vet and the ultimate divorced dad, constantly disappearing at crucial moments, leaving his woman and adopted children in peril, then reappearing at the last second with his silenced Uzi to save the day. *Nightblood* is so hardcore, you grow hair on your palms as you read. And it ends the only way possible: by giving Stiles a leather trench coat and a katana and reassuring us that he will continue to kill vampires forever.

Anne Rice opened the bloodgates—er, floodgates—for everyone to take a stab at the vampire novel, and the variations were endless. There were Nazi vampires (*Darkness on the Ice*), rock star vampires named Timmy (*Vampire Junction*), splatterpunk vampires working out of Times Square strip joints (*Live Girls*), 19th-century riverboat gambler vampires (*Fevre Dream*), and always the standard-issue romantic vampire who lived eternally down through the ages.

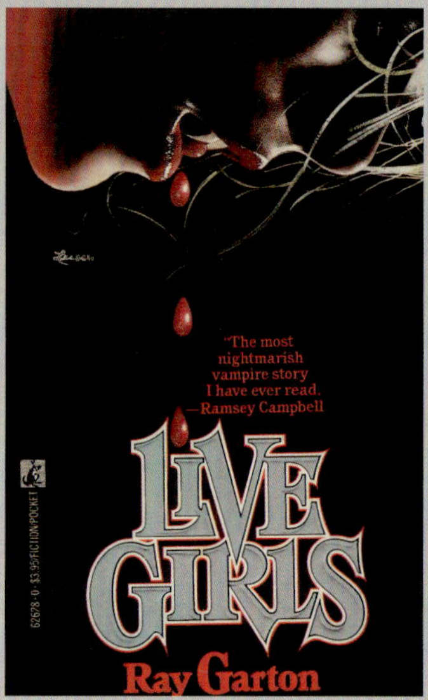

When your worst nightmare comes alive...
HOW DEAR THE DAWN
Marc Eliot
When the sun goes down, the horror begins.

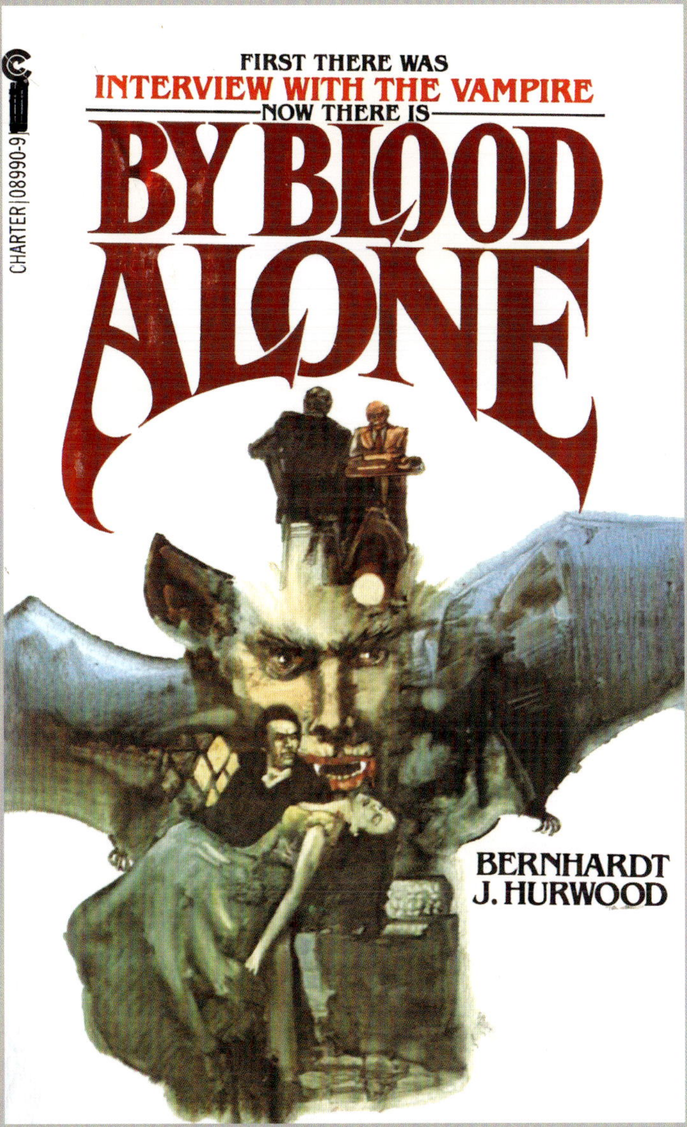
CHARTER 08990-9
FIRST THERE WAS
INTERVIEW WITH THE VAMPIRE
NOW THERE IS
BY BLOOD ALONE
BERNHARDT J. HURWOOD

The deepest evil from the past. The darkest horror of today.
VAMPIRE JUNCTION
S.P. SOMTOW
"The closest thing to a nightmare ever put on paper!" —Robert Bloch,

HE WAS A VAMPIRE, STALKING HIS PREY FOR THE NAZI CAUSE, BUT KILLING THEM FOR HIS OWN DESPERATE HUNGER...
DARKNESS ON THE ICE
LOIS TILTON

THE VAMPIRE TAPESTRY
"SCARY, ENTERTAINING, SUSPENSEFUL." —STEPHEN KING
SUZY McKEE CHARNAS

SIGNET
$1.95
A NOVEL OF EROTIC TERROR AND FORBIDDEN LOVE
HOTEL TRANSYLVANIA
CHELSEA QUINN YARBRO

Rise of the Blockbuster

There was nothing the '80s respected more than blockbuster success, and only brand names—V.C. Andrews, Anne Rice, Stephen King—would survive the decade. Blockbuster books permanently changed the publishing landscape, and it was all thanks to power tools.

The Thor Power Tool Co. case of 1979 radically changed how books were sold. This U.S. Supreme Court decision upheld the Internal Revenue Service's rule that companies could no longer "write down," or lower the value of, unsold inventory. Previously, publishers pulped about 45 percent of their annual inventory, but that still left them with warehouses full of midlist novels that had steady but unspectacular sales. The pressure to sell quickly was off because publishers could list the value of the unsold inventory far below the books' cover price. After the Thor decision, these books were valued at full cover price, eliminating the tax write-off. Suddenly, the day of the midlist novel was over. Paperbacks were given six weeks on the racks to find an audience, then it was off to the shredder.

A successful book now had to sell blockbuster numbers. And manufacturing blockbusters took a team, starting with the blurb writer, who created the breathlessly enthusiastic marketing copy for the back cover. Then the marketing department came up with flashy gimmicks to help each book stand out in a crowded field. Publishers gave out porcelain roses, perfume, and garters bearing the names of their latest romances.

But the most powerful promotional tool was the cover, presided over by the art directors, who were treated like kings. Art directors set the tone for cover artists, often drawing sketches of what they wanted to see. They made the big-picture decisions. The hardcover art for Peter Benchley's *Jaws* was a stylized shark with no teeth. For the iconic paperback (page 80), Bantam's art director Len Leone kept the basic layout, but hired Roger Kastel to paint an ultrarealistic, sharp-toothed shark instead. The paperback sold 6.2 million copies.

James Plumeri at NAL had a sophisticated sense of style, and his Stephen King covers were designed to intrigue readers with their quiet, centered images and plain black backgrounds. He left the title off the cover of *'Salem's Lot*, wanting readers to pick up the book and open it to see what it was called. Instead, bookstores shelved it backward, leading to a quick second printing with the title prominently displayed.

Milton Charles came up with iconic cover treatments for best sellers like *The World According to Garp* and Jacqueline Susann's *The Love Machine* before moving to Pocket, where he worked on *Flowers in the Attic*. Like all art directors, he was a problem solver, and the problem boiled down to how to turn a book browser into a book buyer.

In a 1977 interview, Charles declared himself "unenthusiastic about cover tricks" such as the use of foil and die-cut covers. But after the success of the V. C. Andrews books he became an advocate of foil covers, embossed covers, step-back art, and die-cut covers, because ultimately the point was to sell books. If foil caught the reader's attention, then foil it would be.

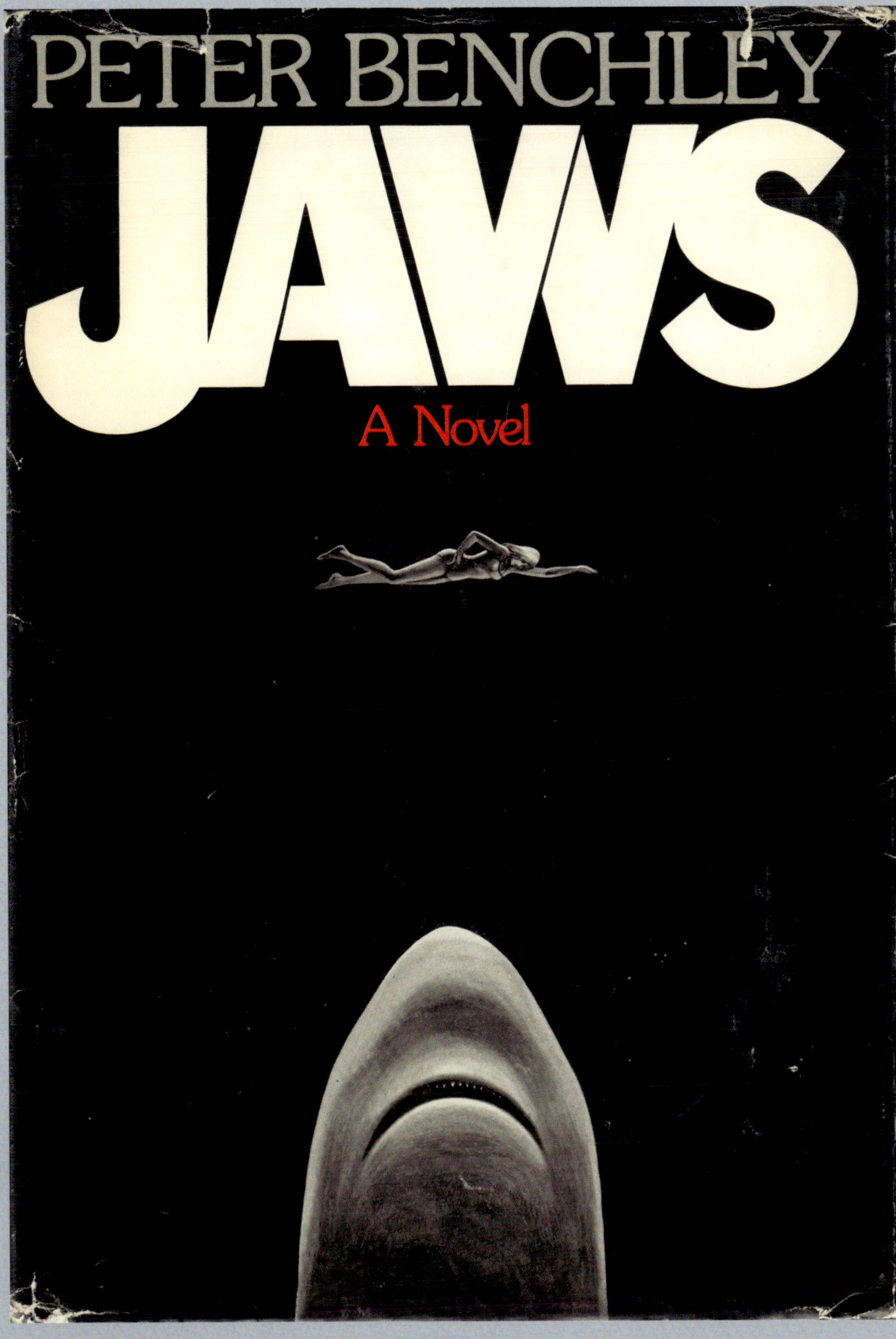
PETER BENCHLEY
JAWS
A Novel

Haunted and Haunting

Unlike the power wielded by art directors in the '70s and '80s publishing world, the cover artist's lot was not a happy one. Not only were their signatures cropped off covers, but they were rarely credited inside the book; their art was flipped, reused, and rephotographed. Publishers resisted crediting cover artists to avoid creating stars who could demand better terms. Cover artists were destined for obscurity.

Until recently, one of the most obscure was Jerzy Zielezinski, aka George Ziel. With more than three hundred covers to his name, Ziel was a machine, capable of turning out three paintings a month for romances, crime stories, and celebrity biographies. He was responsible for plenty of horror novels but was most famous for his distinctive gothics. From the '60s through the '70s, gothic romances were the bread and butter of publishers like Ace, Lancer, and Avon. The covers were formulaic in excelsis, inevitably featuring a woman running from a house with one lit window. Variations: maybe she was running from a chateau, fleeing a keep, or evacuating a shack.

Within these constraints, Ziel stood out. He painted more than forty covers for Paperback Library gothics alone, featuring intrepid brunettes and terrified blondes, lit by the silver light of the moon, their windblown hair dissolving into the ebony sky, their diaphanous gowns disappearing into mysterious mists, their wide eyes staring back over a shoulder at the dismal real estate they were escaping.

Born in Poland in 1914, Ziel was twenty-five years old when the Nazis invaded. He was a Polish Catholic married to a Jew, and he and his wife were sent to concentration camps. His wife was forced into labor in Germany, where she died in an Allied bombing raid, while Ziel was sent to Auschwitz, then Flossenbürg, and finally Dachau during the last days of the war. Beaten so badly that he went deaf in one ear, Ziel was fortunate to have his artistic abilities discovered by the camp doctor who treated him. Risking his job, the doctor smuggled paper and charcoal to Ziel, and as word of his talent spread, the guards started using him to illustrate their Christmas and birthday cards. Ziel also drew 24 stark, haunting sketches while interned in the camps. They were published in two books in Munich immediately after the war. Today a rare copy of *24 Drawings from the Concentration Camps in Germany* resides in the United States Holocaust Memorial Museum in Washington, D.C.

After the war, Ziel wound up in New York City, working as a waiter before finding jobs as a commercial artist. His first covers appeared around 1954. Because of his limited understanding of English, Ziel's second wife, Elsie, read him the manuscripts he was hired to paint. Eventually, the couple retired to Connecticut, where Elsie died in 1981. A few months later, in February 1982, George passed away at age sixty-seven. Art director and friend Rolf Erikson had drinks with Ziel on the last night of his life. "I really think he just gave up after Elsie died," he said. "He was tired and he made the decision he had lived long enough."

Artist George Ziel, who saw more than his share of real-life horrors, imbued his covers with an other-worldly, ethereal quality.

Lisa Falkenstern has more covers in this book than any other artist. A student of Milton Charles (see page 156), and, later, his wife, she relied on a creative process used by many cover illustrators of the time. After reading a manuscript, she'd submit three sketches for her painting to the publisher. When one was approved, she would rent a studio for a photo shoot, find props, book models, and take reference photos. For *Crib* (page 52) she used her infant niece. For the cover of Thomas Monteleone's *Night Train* (page 120) she shot photos on New York City's 7 train. For *PIN* (page 144), she worried about reproducing the human circulatory system on a man with no skin, so she studied anatomy books to get it right. The resulting painting was so complex, the art director took one look and said, "Make it simpler."

As the '80s progressed, Falkenstern lost interest in horror. "Everything was getting more and more gross and disturbing instead of funny and interesting," she said. Eventually, she started doing romance covers, which were still selling strong, even as horror sales tanked.

Cover sketch for *The Nestling* by Milton Charles.

Pause and Reflect

Be they demons from hell or crabs from the sea, skeleton doctors or sensitive vampires, we've seen who and what bring the horror to these paperbacks. But what about the hapless man or woman who must suddenly cope with a telepathic baby or a haunted bungalow? We always learn about them in the old reliable mirror scene, a horror novel staple that's as inevitable as death and prologues. It's easy to put together a profile of the average horror protagonist. Because in every book, at some point, a character will gaze into a mirror and assess his or her looks for the reader.

First, the *horror man*. He is big but not muscular and usually comes with a deep tan, although he is in fact Anglo-Saxon. He might be Irish or Italian, and in a few weird cases even Greek, but his skin is dark because he works outside doing hard, honest labor, not because of his ethnic heritage.

The horror man is made of chisels. His profile is chiseled, his nose is chiseled, his forehead is chiseled. Sometimes even his powerful shoulders are chiseled. The only things that are not chiseled are his eyes. Those are piercing, but also surprisingly soft, and they light up when he smiles. In fact, as serious as the horror man appears, the best way for him to show his feelings is through soul-deep, passionate lovemaking, which he uses to reaffirm his commitment to marriage, or to show that he is the kind of man a woman can feel safe with.

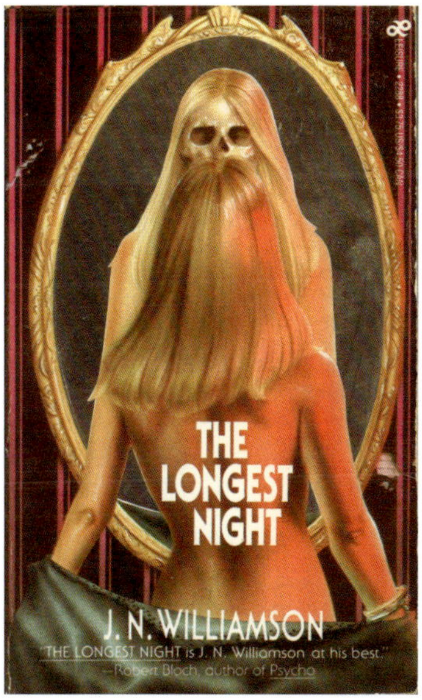

Horror fiction protagonists often pause to stare into a mirror; they don't always like what they see.

The *horror woman* has a willowy, athletic figure with dynamite legs. Contrary to expectations, she is often flat-chested (with notable exceptions). She comes in two flavors: either dreamy and artistic, in which case she is given to precognitive dreams, shivers, and a sense that this place is pervaded by an indefinable evil; or practical and hardheaded, ready to sacrifice herself by performing an ancient ritual to save the world or racing into danger to save either her beloved man or child. The most expressive parts of her body are her nipples. They noticeably harden, when she is aroused, surprised, confused, or meeting new people. They are practically prehensile tentacles, capable of lengthening, thickening, unfurling, budding, flaring, and swelling. If she's nice, she's blonde, or maybe brunette. If she likes sex too much, her hair is red. Her eyes are almost always green, occasionally gray.

Surprisingly, the horror woman is usually employed. If she is married, she owns a fashionable boutique. If she is single, she is a gifted artist or ambitious reporter looking for her big break. (It is worth noting that if the horror man is a reporter, he is always a washed-up alcoholic looking for a second chance.) No matter what the job, she is obsessed with proving herself to her male colleagues, which often leads to throwing herself into dangerous situations from which she can only be rescued by the horror man.

Southern Deluge

Horror would eventually turn into thrillers, and gothics would become romances, but another offshoot of the gothic revival remained stubbornly itself: the Southern gothic. Michael McDowell was an Alabama native whom Stephen King once called "the finest writer of paperback originals in America," and his *Blackwater* series is the *One Hundred Years of Solitude* of the genre. He'd be considered one of the great lights of Southern literature if his books dealt with things other than woman-eating hogs, men marrying amphibians, and vengeance-seeking lesbian wrestlers wearing opium-laced golden fingernails.

McDowell started his career with *The Amulet* (1979), his own 100-page screenplay that he adapted into a 200-page novel after no one would buy it. Avon eventually acquired the book and encouraged McDowell to make it longer. In this story of a disfigured soldier recuperating under the baleful gaze of his malignant mother in the tiny town of Pine Cone, Alabama, we follow a cursed necklace as it sows destruction. It's not the carnage, rendered in apocalyptic understatement, that is so engaging but the language and social mores of the inhabitants. The story captures midcentury small-town living as few books do. Everyone in Pine Cone lives a life bounded by trivial jealousies, petty rivalries, unwritten rules, and microscopic grudges they nurse all their lives. Everyone knows how to behave (this is the black part of town, this is the white; this is the kind of thing we say in church, this is the kind of thing we keep to ourselves). But the titular amulet weakens those barriers and coaxes feelings to the surface like pus. Pine Cone is poisoned before the amulet arrives, not because it's built on an Indian burial mound, but because it's another dying American town.

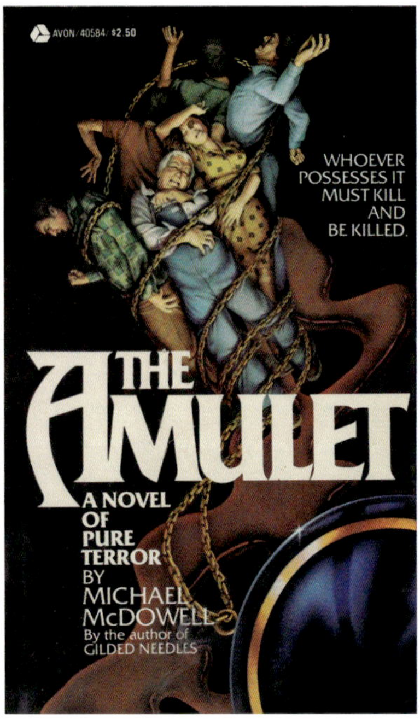

McDowell's first novel started as a screenplay; later he'd write the *Beetlejuice* script for Tim Burton.

McDowell's six-book *Blackwater* series was published one title per month between January and June 1983, and it was his farewell to the horror genre. Beginning with the flooding of Perdido, Alabama, it follows the fortunes of the Caskey clan beginning with Oscar Caskey's marriage to Elinor, a mysterious redheaded woman he rescues from the flood, who turns out to be a finned and gilled river monster assuming human form.

The series follows their marriage, and their family, from 1919 to 1960, as new generations are born and older generations pass away. The horror feels more like magical realism, and McDowell balances scenes of genuine human kindness and grace against scenes of a rapist having his arms chewed off by a mutant teenager. McDowell is as enthusiastic about his horror as he is about delicately depicting social hierarchies. He knows that two rival bridge clubs can war with each other for decades. He knows what it feels like to get old. But more than anything, these six books are about women and the power they wield behind the scenes.

McDowell's equally accomplished *The Elementals* (1981) is about another Southern family, this one haunted by ghosts that dwell in the sand around the family's Victorian beach house. But it's the *Blackwater* series that feels like a major accomplishment. Beginning with two people—one white and one black, one rich and one poor—paddling slowly through a flooded town, and ending the same way almost fifty years later, the series is a heartbreaker. As is the fact that today it's completely forgotten. Then again, McDowell might have wanted it that way. He once said it was a mistake to try to write for the ages. And yet somehow he did, even when writing disposable paperback originals.

The Elementals is shorter than the *Blackwater* series, but both explore the horror that lurks behind all those Southern manners.

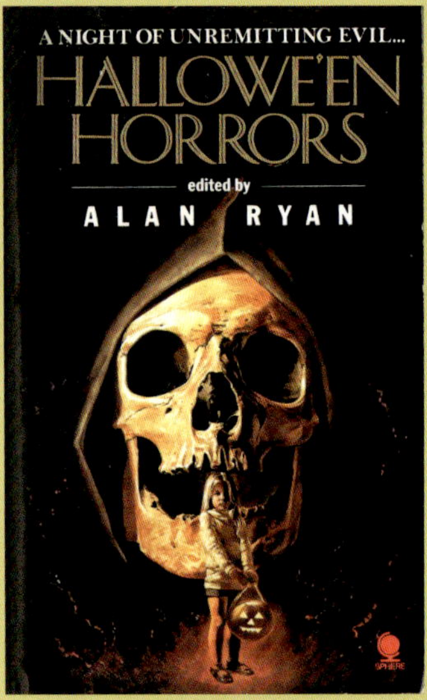

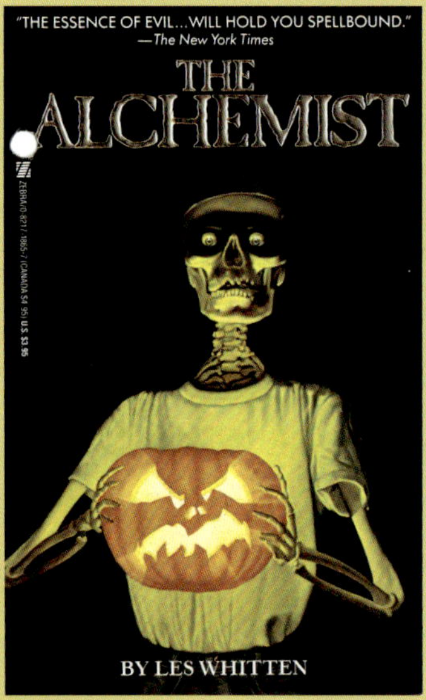

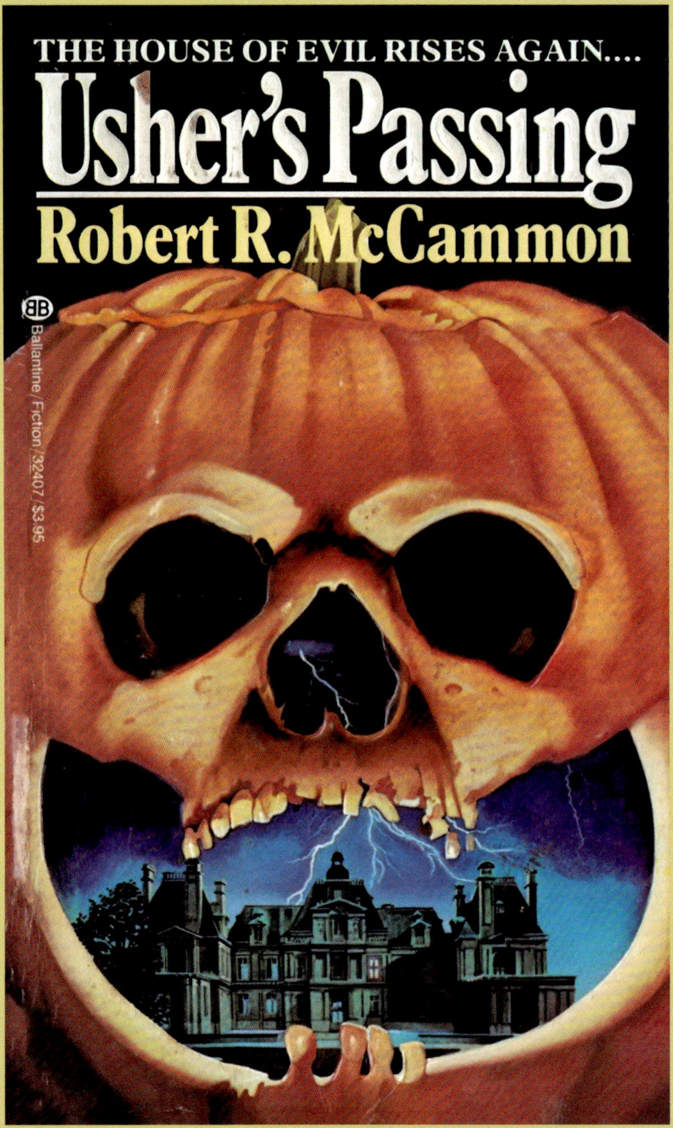

What could be more gothic than Halloween? Ray Bradbury was the Norman Rockwell of horror, turning the eve of All Saints' Day into an all-American holiday awash in pumpkin patches and scarecrows. But Halloween imagery is hard to find on horror covers, with only a few gnarly pumpkins to remind us of the reason for the season.

BB
Ballantine Books Science Fiction 75¢ 01637

RAY BRADBURY
THE OCTOBER COUNTRY

"THE UNCROWNED KING OF THE SCIENCE FICTION WRITERS"
THE NEW YORK TIMES

The vampire protagonist of *Black Ambrosia* wasn't cursed. She was just born that way.

Marginalized Monsters

Elizabeth Engstrom feels like an Anne Rice who cares about normal people. Deeply rooted in the details of hard-scrabble lives, her language is heady and romantic, occasionally dissolving into a dreamy haze. But she never loses sight of, or interest in, the needs of her half-humanoid, underground incest monsters: they eat, sleep, and go to the bathroom. Where Rice is mostly interested in magical people, Engstrom's writing is most uncomfortably alive in its unflinching depictions of the drab, humdrum existences of people living on the bottom rungs of the economic ladder. Her cast of barflies, drifters, hitchhikers, and those who prey on them feels right out of James M. Cain's hardboiled noir novels. *Black Ambrosia* (1986) contrasts most obviously with Rice's work. Here, Engstrom's vampire, Angelina Watson, is totally traditional—she doesn't like crucifixes, can turn into fog, controls mens' minds, sleeps in a coffin, sucks the blood of lovers and is not a metaphor for AIDS.

Angelina bums around the country, resisting her blood hunger not because she's noble, but because the more she feeds, the sooner she'll be discovered by an ex-lover who's determined to destroy her. Engstrom's attention to mundane details—of traveling from town to town, the dangers of hitchhiking, and the crummy blue-collar underbelly of '80s-era America—worms its way under your skin. You can practically feel the hard-packed frozen dirt beneath Angelina's heels as she walks down the trash-choked shoulders of desolate highways.

Hot off an advertising career in Hawaii, Engstrom ditched corporate copywriting to take a fiction workshop with Theodore Sturgeon. Out of that workshop came her first novella, *When Darkness Loves Us* (1985), as twisted and sharp as a corkscrew jammed in your ear. Sally Ann Hixson is sixteen, newly married, relishing her first taste of sex, and pregnant. One afternoon she ventures down a long-abandoned set of stairs on her farm and finds herself locked in an underground tunnel. Frustrated, she follows the unexplored tunnels deeper, figuring they have to come out somewhere.

Wrong.

Cut to eight years later. Sally Ann lives in total darkness, eating slugs, with her son sleeping by her side. Determined for him to meet his father (whom the boy

The hardcover version of *When Darkness Loves Us* (*left*) references the title novella with its cover image, while the paperback cover (*right*) invokes the companion story, *Beauty Is*.

doesn't believe in—he also doesn't believe in sight), she claws her way to the surface and discovers it hasn't been eight years, it's been twenty. Her husband remarried and has four kids, and before long Sally Ann, feeling like an intruder, returns underground, taking her husband's four-year-old daughter with her. What follows is an escalating series of revenge schemes that become deeply horrifying.

On the opposite end of the spectrum is *Beauty Is*, the story of Martha, a developmentally disabled adult born without a nose. The story unfolds simultaneously in the past, telling the story of Martha's mother, a faith healer, and the present, as Martha bumbles into a group of drunks who take advantage of her (based on a real incident Engstrom observed). The book evolves into a beautiful mediation on love, appearance, romance, and devotion.

What makes Engstrom's stories so memorable is that she speaks from the point of view of her monsters but never becomes their cheerleader, as Rice does. Instead, she captures the voices of women on the margins, pushed aside, hungry for the lives they've been denied, beating on the glass to get in. It's their voices that linger.

INHUM

CHAPTER SEVEN

ANOIDS

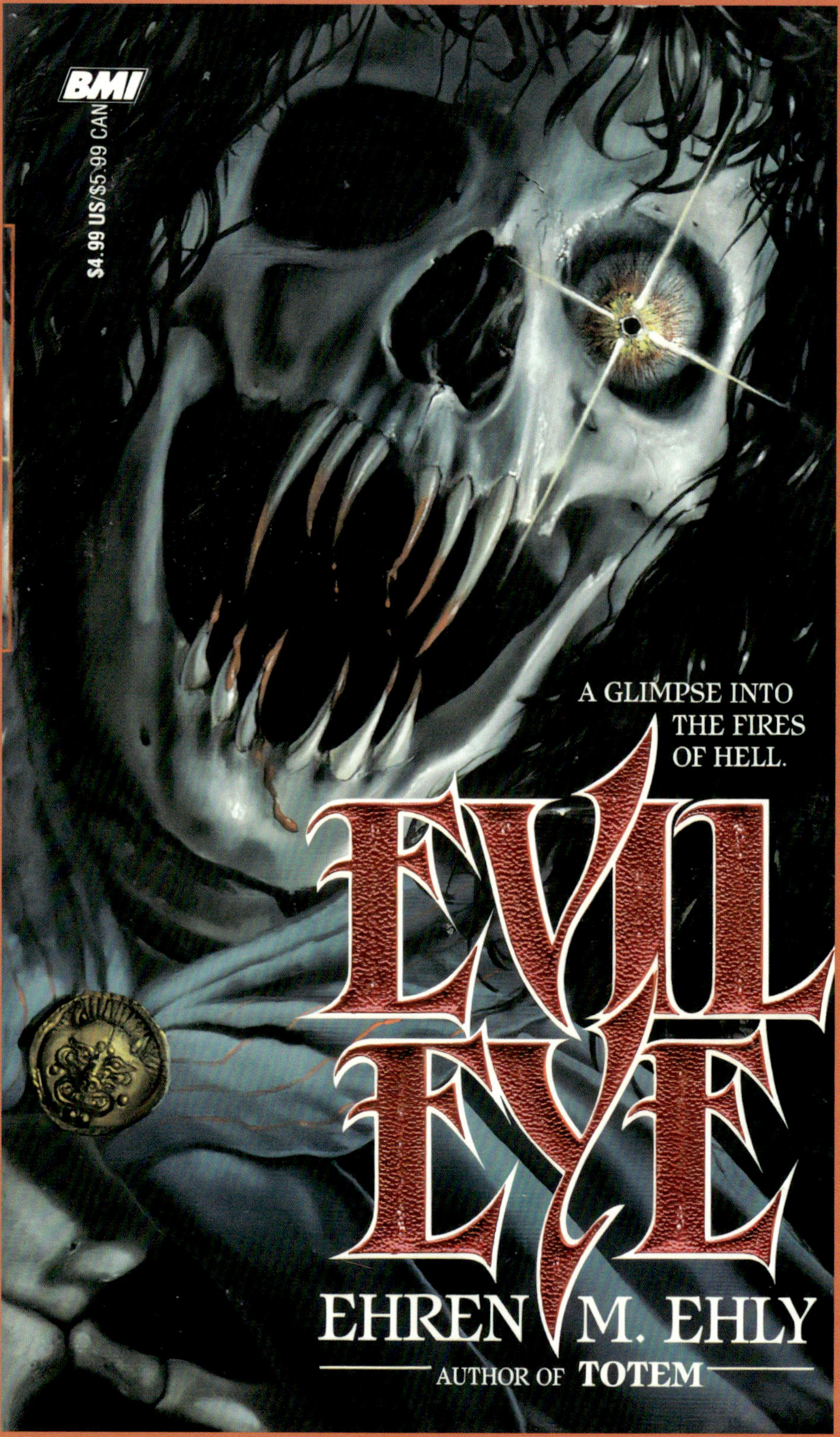
BMI
$4.99 US/$5.99 CAN
A GLIMPSE INTO
THE FIRES
OF HELL.
EVIL
EYE
EHREN M. EHLY
AUTHOR OF TOTEM

Inhumanoids may look normal at first, but they're one skin-peel away from giving you nightmares.

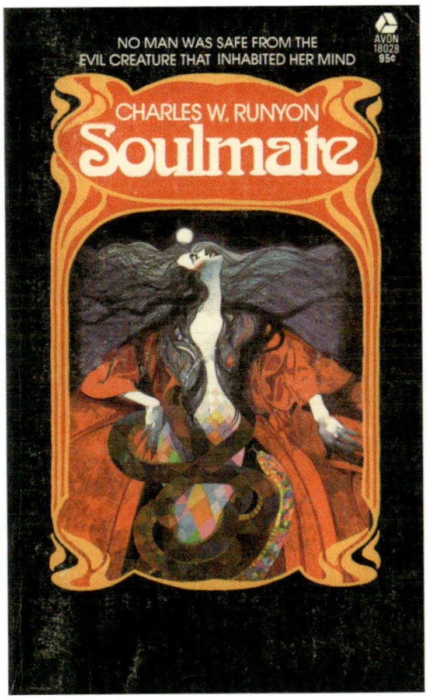

There are two kinds of creature in this world: Americans and inhumanoids. Whether it's alien super-predators possessing little girls, hyperaccelerating them through puberty, and sending them out to kill with sex (*Soulmate,* 1974), or Yetis riding icebergs to California so they can decapitate our Miss Snow Queen 1977 (*Snowman*, 1978), it's simply a fact: foreign monsters want to get into our country and mess up our stuff. And they all have three things in common: they smell bad ("fetid" is the name of their cologne), they're dirty (ruining carpets everywhere with dripping pus, goo, slime, and ectoplasm), and they have terrible manners.

It's the lack of politeness that really rankles. In Frank Spiering's *Berserker* (1981), no one in New York City even notices a 12-foot-tall Nordic giant in a horned helmet wielding a battle-ax as long as he confines himself to decapitating homeless people. But then he tears off a ballerina's leg and eats two precious children, and, well, that's just rude. And though we all feel sympathy for the yeti who hates snow in *Snowman*, how many ski instructors will we to allow him to decapitate before we hire a bunch of hunters and Vietnam vets to go after him with crossbows armed with tiny nuclear arrowheads? Answer: Three.

The real problem isn't keeping inhumanoids out of America, it's keeping Americans out of other countries. Because every time an American goes abroad, a monster hitches a ride on the return trip. "It had been impossible to foresee that Bradford's search for the Snowman would terminate in this devastating spectacle," writes Norman Bogner in his book's prologue, obviously from the point of view of someone who does not understand that traveling to Tibet pretty much guarantees death for nine out of ten Americans. "Ten sherpa porters and nine men in his party were already dead," reads the next paragraph, "hacked to death, their dismembered bodies consumed by a beast with an insatiable hunger for human flesh," a turn of events that anyone who's traveled abroad could easily predict.

In *The Shinglo* (1989), Scott Pillar fights in the Vietnam War and brings home a head full of trauma that doesn't just ruin his life, it also shatters his family and destroys large swaths of Cleveland. As he says under hypnosis when asked what he does for a living, "I tear things apart . . . bit by bit I'm going to tear this whole fucking country right down to the ground." Not to get too symbolic, but Oliver Stone won an Oscar for making a movie with that exact premise.

International travel may broaden your horizons, but you'll wind up bringing home a flesh-eating Viking, a demonically possessed army buddy, or just a really bad infection.

Where were the classic monsters—the vampires, the wolfmen, the zombies—while all this was going on? Vampires were getting sexy courtesy of Anne Rice, and, to be honest, no one much cared about werewolves . . . although Robert McCammon's *The Wolf's Hour* (1989) featured a British secret agent who was also a werewolf going behind enemy lines to kill Nazis. That storyline was echoed in reverse by *Blood on the Ice*, a take on World War II's "Weather Wars" during which Nazi and Allied forces conducted military operations over weather-reporting stations in the North Atlantic. This historical event was made almost interesting by the addition of an SS officer who happens to be a vampire. As for zombies, despite their inescapable popularity today, they weren't doing much in '70s and '80s horror novels. Surprising, given that those years were something of a golden age for movie zombies courtesy of George Romero (*Dawn of the Dead*, *Day of the Dead*), Dan O'Bannon (*Return of the Living Dead*), and Lucio Fulci (*Zombie*, *City of the Living Dead*). Mummies, however, were another story . . .

Berserker gave us the mummified corpse of an ancient Viking on the loose in modern-day Manhattan, but it took Egyptian-born Ehren M. Ehly to bring a mummy to the big city. Born Moreen Le Fleming and named Miss Egypt in 1949, Ehly lived in Cairo and married a U.S. marine guarding the American embassy. She and her mother fled the Black Saturday riots in 1952 and wound up in London, trapped in immigration limbo. Ehly reached the United States courtesy of the game show *Truth or Consequences* (her husband was asked to judge a

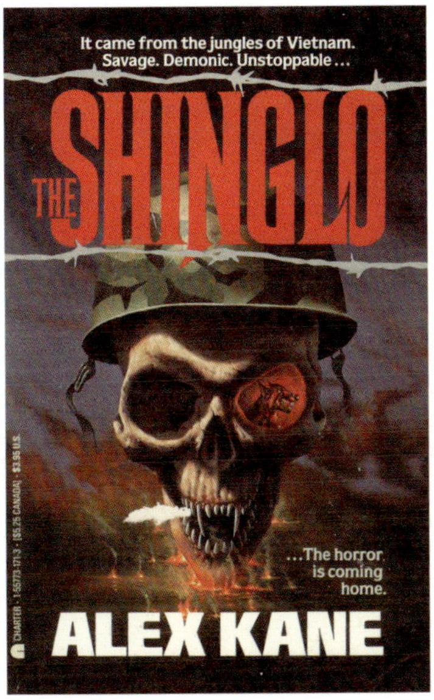

King Tut's golden face was a familiar museum exhibit.

beauty contest on the show, and Ehly popped out of an oversized can of condensed milk).

After an injury forced her to retire from her department-store salesperson job, Ehly took writing classes at a community college. Influenced by Dean Koontz and Stephen King, she abandoned plans to write romance novels and sold four horror novels in quick succession to Leisure. Her first was *Obelisk*, a charming fish-out-of-water scenario featuring an undead cannibalistic Egyptian high priest causing chaos in Manhattan.

Millions of Americans visited the touring *Treasures of Tutankhamun* museum exhibition at the end of the '70s, so Egypt was in the air. Ehly capitalized on the trend, starting *Obelisk* in Cairo, where Steve Harrison and a cultural attaché rob a pharaoh's tomb. Steve is stabbed with an artifact and becomes a were-Egyptian: by the light of the full moon he turns into the ancient priest Menket. Retracing Ehly's real-life path to the United States, Steve vomits blood on a British Airways flight to London and then heads to New York City, where he meets up with his long-suffering girlfriend, Sara Fenster. Instantly she knows something's wrong because Steve goes nuts over the Egyptian obelisk in Central Park and starts decorating it with severed penises and hobo guts, like a tourist.

Steve tries to tell Sara his problems, but she doesn't want to hear how he murdered two people and ate a dog. All that happened over there, in the Middle East. He's home now. Unfortunately, Steve's problems will take more than denial and a prescription to solve. We know, before Sara does, that Steve's fetid breath means he may as well turn in his U.S. passport. As one guard at the Metropolitan Museum of Art says to another when Steve runs past, "Funny thing about foreigners. They smell different. I mean, this one really stank, you know?" Steve demonstrates his true foreignness when he sets fire to the Met's Egyptian wing (no respect for our cultural institutions), eats all the orangutans in the Central Park Zoo (no respect for our monkeys), and impregnates Sara with his half-undead Egyptian baby. In the end, he stabs a cop and then slashes his own throat in front of the obelisk as the baby rustles ominously in Sara's womb.

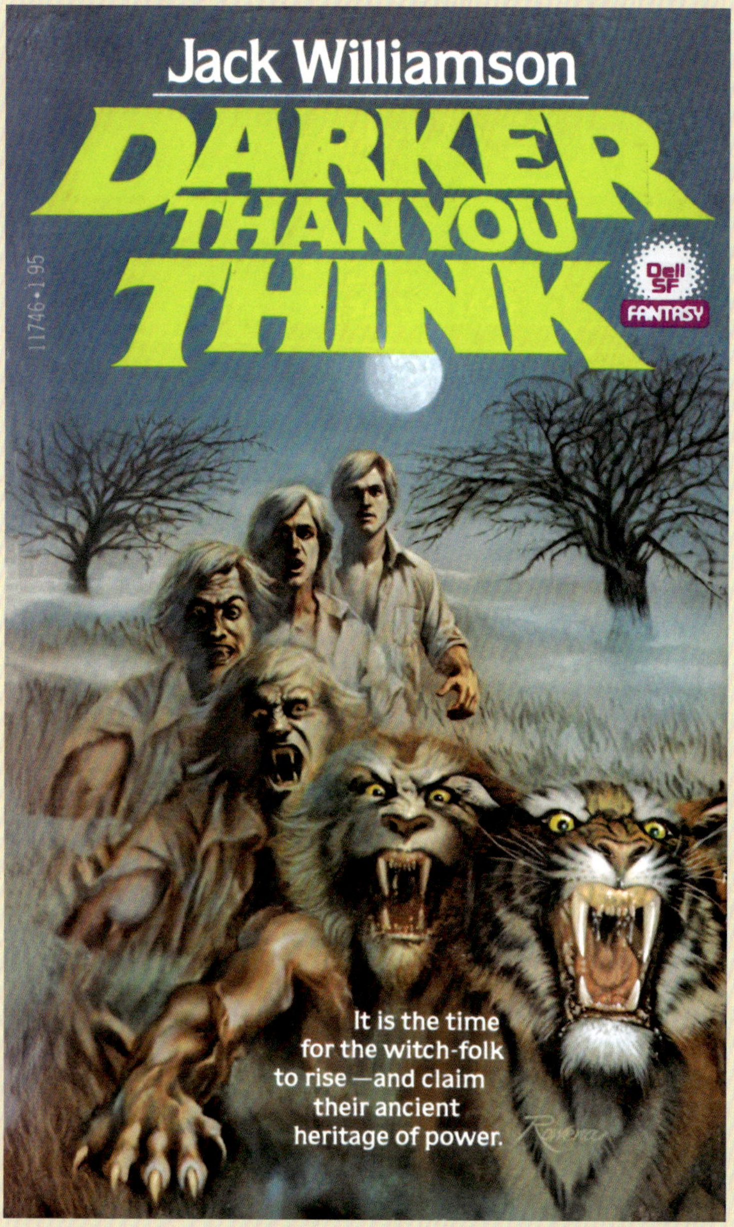

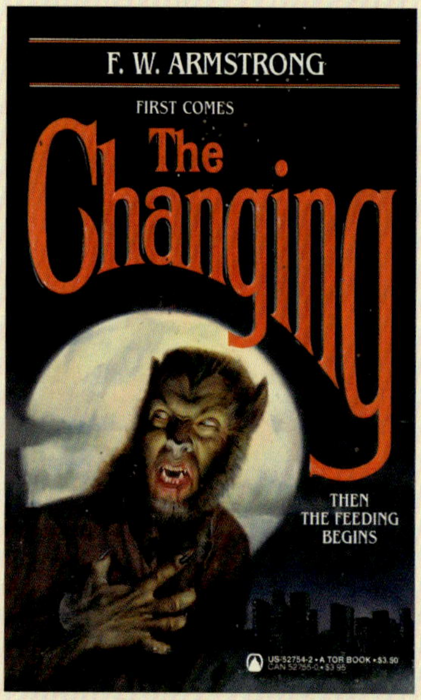

Along with updated vampires (pages 150–155) mummies (previous page), and werewolves (*The Changing*), the great rainbow of inhumanoids includes all-purpose shape shifters (*Darker Than You Think*), aswangs (*The Bamboo Demons*), Middle Eastern shape-shifting djinn (*The Djinn*) and the Eluthi, a 6,000-year-old super-race (*Birthpyre*).

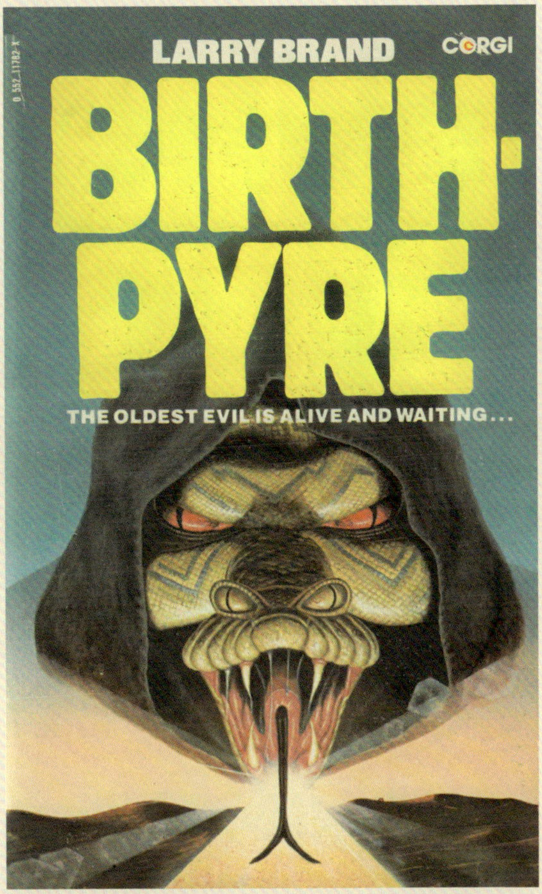
LARRY BRAND
CORGI
BIRTH-
PYRE
THE OLDEST EVIL IS ALIVE AND WAITING . . .

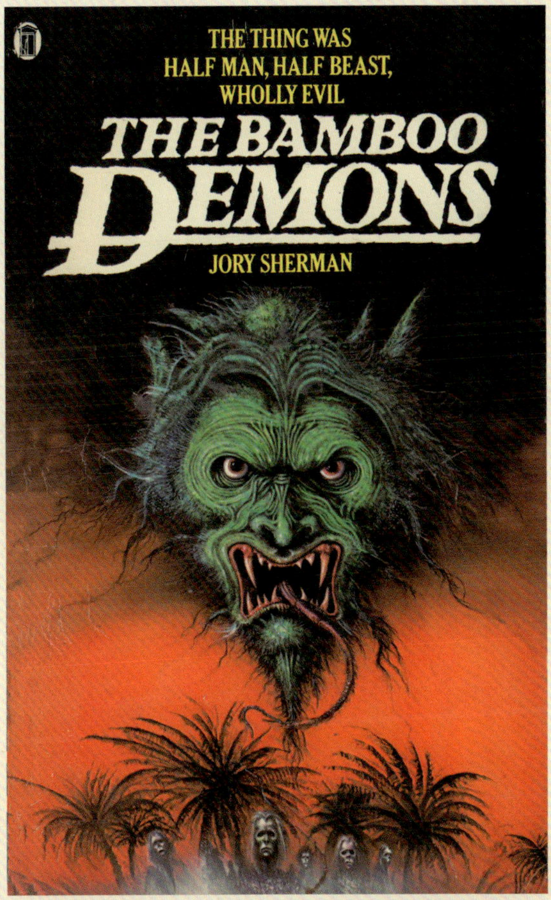
THE THING WAS
HALF MAN, HALF BEAST,
WHOLLY EVIL
THE BAMBOO
DEMONS
JORY SHERMAN

PINNACLE BOOKS 40-061★$1.75
There was
THE OMEN-
Then came
'SALEM'S LOT-
And now there is
The djinn
GRAHAM MASTERTON
author of The Manitou

Horror Goes Native

Despite the drippy, be-tentacled, foul-smelling foreign monsters that slimed into America from overseas, riding over in the museum shipments, rucksacks, cocaine deliveries, and wombs of its citizens, the worst monsters came from our own shores. Let's face it, the Amityville Horror house wasn't built on an old Korean deli. It was built on an Indian burial mound.

In 1975 a Scotsman named Graham Masterton published his first novel, a short book called *The Manitou*, about a young lady suffering from a slight swelling on the back of her neck. Turns out it isn't just a swelling: Karen's neck is pregnant! With Misquamacus, a 300-year-old Native American medicine man who's out for revenge against the Dutch who wiped out his tribe. Misquamacus is the most evil and powerful medicine man in pretty much forever. He's such a pain in the neck (sorry) that he returns in a sequel with a whole convention of medicine men to inaugurate a new holiday, which guarantees "24 hours of chaos and butchery and torture, the day when the Indian people have their revenge for hundreds of years of treachery and slaughter and rape, all in one huge massacre." Maybe we could call it Reverse Columbus Day?

The massive success of *The Manitou* (more on its author on pages 182–183) alerted horror writers to the threat posed by not just inhumanoids overseas, but those under our very feet. We had wiped out the Native Americans, but maybe we didn't get them all, especially the super-angry ones? Besides, American Indian–sourced inhumanoids were our very own homegrown monsters ripe for exploitation. It was a horror gold rush, unleashing a diversity seminar's worth of tribal monsters and spirits to deliver mass mayhem in mass-market paperbacks.

The best-selling *Crooked Tree* (1980) features a blurb from the *New York Times* claiming that it's "an intense, meticulously researched thriller that handles Native American beliefs with both suspense and dignity." That may be stretching the definition of dignity, although, like many of these books, author Robert C. Wilson takes great pains to point out that the spirit of his evil medicine man—who possesses a woman and turns her into a were-bear that eats campers and stores their tongues in an attractive leather pouch—is not from

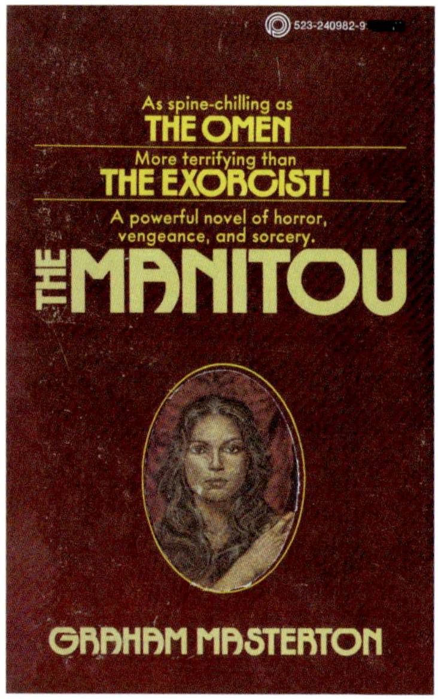

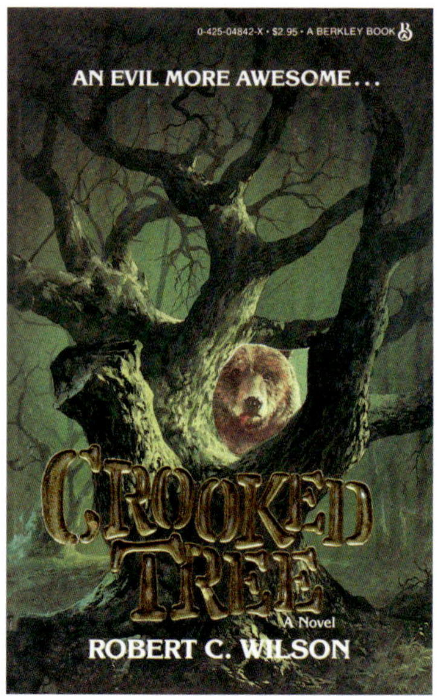

As if indigenous cultures weren't stereotyped enough in mainstream fiction, they became fertile ground for inhumanoidism.

any tribe we know but from a far older tribe, far more ancient than any that exists today. The same origin story appears in *Totem* (1989), with its evil spirit-walker who causes contractors violating its ancient burial grounds to impale themselves on surveyors' stakes. Likewise for the tiny monsters of *Shadoweyes* (1984; page 181). Most of these books begin when ancient native tombs are disrupted, burial baskets are punted off cliffs, or mummified corpses are decapitated. Soon after, white people are having bad dreams and feel compelled to seek out someone who knows "the old ways."

Native American monsters are portrayed as fetid as overseas inhumanoids, but more often than not they use possessed everyday animals to do their dirty work: insane chipmunks, coyotes with "dead eyes" walking on hind legs, grizzly bears with castration on their minds, killer elk, hordes of rattlesnakes, or even, as in *The Devil's Breath* (1982), a flock of birds that tries to drown white people in their droppings. Because the mass murder of indigenous Americans is this country's original sin, these stories are marinated in extra-strength cynicism, complete with conspiracies cooked up by mayors, newspaper reporters, law enforcement officers, and land developers who want to keep stealing artifacts, building condos on hallowed land, and generally being culturally insensitive, all with total impunity.

It's tempting to see hidden depths in these books; however, no one in these stories does much self-analysis and the authors rarely, if ever, engage with the dubious morality of, after wiping out the original Native Americans, now wiping out the few traces of their ghosts, however bloodthirsty, that remain. *Skeleton Dancer* (1989) is one of the few to engage with bigger issues, such as, "Why would skeletons want to take our son?" Good question.

The aforementioned skeletons are naked, gay, and undead; as usual, they're also unaffiliated with any known tribe, instead calling themselves the Brave Men-Boys. Acquiring eternal life by sucking the blood (or sperm—the author is hazy on this point) out of their male sacrifices, they come back to life when their leader, cleverly called the Leader, is awakened by twin brothers with ESP, just like he and his twin used to have. In fact, the Leader is a nice skeleton Indian—he wants to bring the twins into his immortal tribe so they can live forever and never be separated, unlike he and his brother. He also plans to resurrect the rest of his Brave Men-Boy tribe to murder all the white people, so you can see he exists in a sort of gray area. In this book, however, the white men do not acknowledge gray areas, and they murder all the skeleton Indians with a SWAT team. The last paragraph reveals that not all the Brave Men-Boys are dead; some are sleeping in an underground cavern, waiting for more psychic twins to reawaken them. It's an apocalypse paused, which was a hallmark of the subgenre.

The '70s and '80s were a time of growing unease about apocalyptic global destruction, and no one spoke the language of annihilation better than H. P. Lovecraft. He was the first horror writer to discuss the end of the world in a nonreligious context, spawning a brand of horror that posited the extermination of the human race in purely secular terms. It's no mistake that *The Manitou*'s Misquamacus is not trying to kill humanity on his own, but instead plans to summon Lovecraft's Great Old Ones to do the job for him.

For decades, readers had been weaned on a steady diet of Armageddon, whether it was the environmental collapse predicted in Rachel Carson's 1962 best seller *Silent Spring* or the end times in 1970's best seller *The Late Great Planet Earth*. The greatest threat to humanity in the '80s was nuclear war, of course, which hung over the planet like the sword of Damocles. Men's adventure paperbacks of the era were full of tough warriors striding through postnuclear wastelands, leading a resistance against the invading Soviet army (*C.A.D.S.*, 1985), fighting horrible mutants (*Phoenix*, 1987), or battling an oppressive American government (the thirty-four-volume *Ashes* series, starting in 1983). But, oddly, the closest thing we get to nuclear apocalypse in horror paperbacks are Native American curses.

Capable of massive destruction, dreaming peacefully beneath the earth's surface until they're disturbed, these curses are depicted as forces that modern man cannot control and that he unleashes at his peril. At the end of *Chumash*, when the Malibu coastline is destroyed by an Indian curse, 30,000 people wind up dead and a massive "blast zone," unsafe for human occupation, is established. It resembles nothing so much as the irradiated wasteland left in the wake of a dirty bomb.

The endings of these books often occur in some kind of underground tomb or chamber where the forces of aboriginal destruction are contained, but never destroyed, usually at great sacrifice on the part of the Anglo heroes. And so, like underground silos containing weapons of mass destruction, Native American curses are sealed away to lie dormant for now, resting uneasily in the darkness, capable of awakening at any moment and destroying us all.

What do vengeful native spirits want? Maybe some company (*Skeleton Dancers*), maybe an apocalypse (*Chumash*).

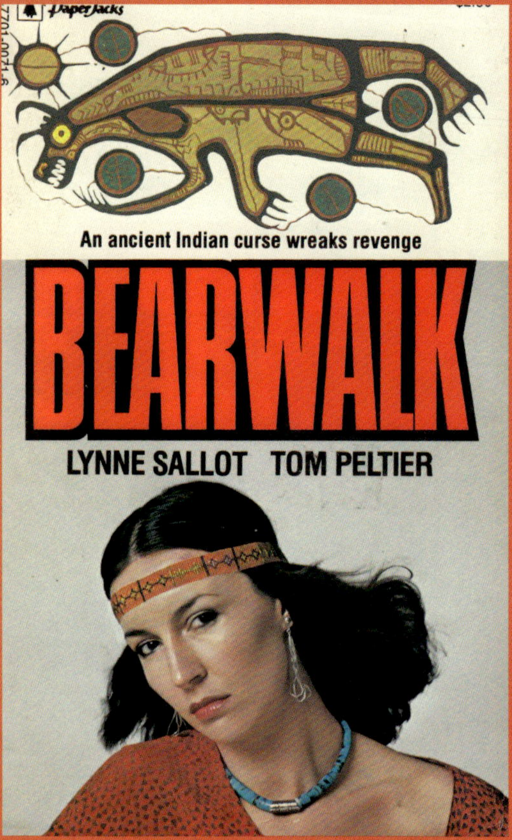
PaperJacks
An ancient Indian curse wreaks revenge
BEARWALK
LYNNE SALLOT TOM PELTIER

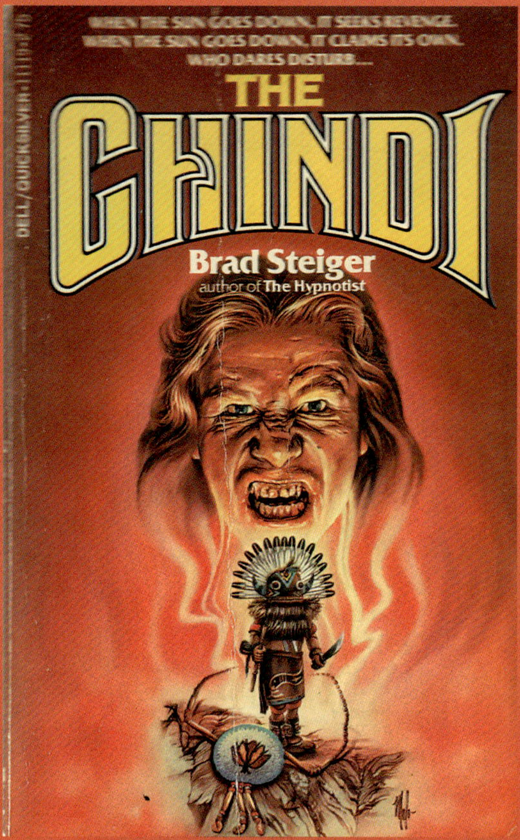
WHEN THE SUN GOES DOWN, IT SEEKS REVENGE.
WHEN THE SUN GOES DOWN, IT CLAIMS ITS OWN.
WHO DARES DISTURB...
THE
CHINDI
Brad Steiger
author of The Hypnotist
DELL/QUICKSILVER

16947 $2.95
THE
SHAMAN
FRANK COFFEY
"FANS OF HORROR FICTION WILL FIND THE FAST PACE, THE SHOCKS AND THE THRILLS THEY'RE LOOKING FOR IN THE SHAMAN."
Dean R. Koontz, author of Whispers

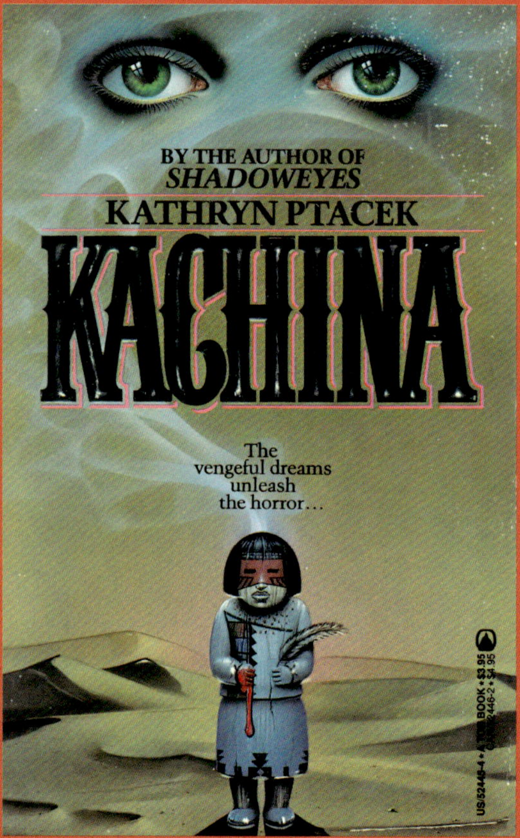
BY THE AUTHOR OF
SHADOWEYES
KATHRYN PTACEK
KACHINA
The
vengeful dreams
unleash
the horror...

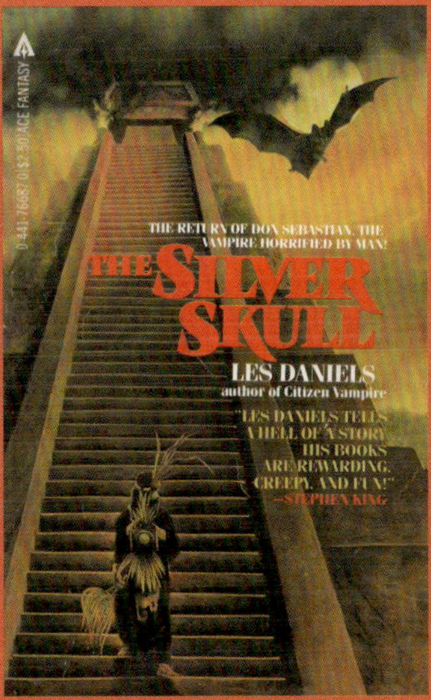

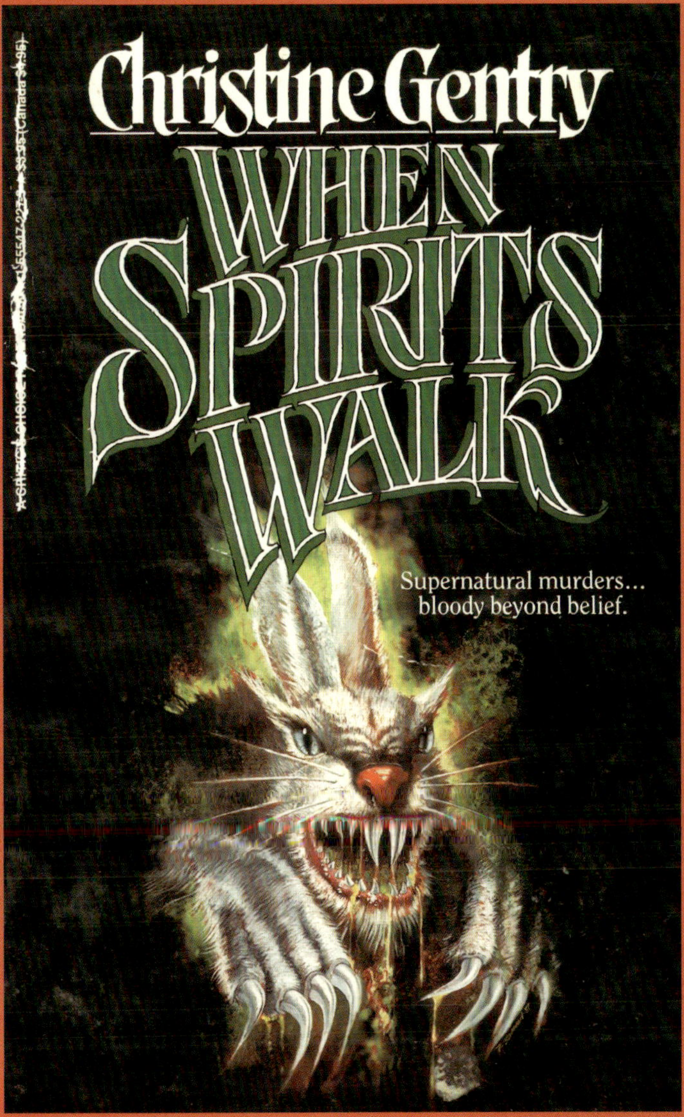

Stories of North America's homegrown inhumanoids offer madness-inducing hallucinations (*Bearwalk*), shapeshifting spirits (*The Chindi*), half-melted giants (*The Shaman*), dream-dolls (*Kachina*), golden-eyed mini-killers (*Shadoweyes*), Aztec alchemists (*The Silver Skull*), cannibal dwarves (*Ten Little Indians*), and silver-coated rabbit gods (*When Spirits Walk*).

The Man behind the Manitou

Seventeen-year-old Graham Masterton started out as a newspaper reporter in his native Scotland. He soon became the editor of *Mayfair*, a men's magazine, and then moved over to *Penthouse*. At the tender age of twenty-five he wrote the sex instruction book *Acts of Love*; since then he has written close to thirty more lovemaking manuals. In 1975 he took a break from nookie advice to write *The Manitou*, the novel that launched his fiction career. He has written more than seventy books, including historical sagas, humor collections, and movie novelizations.

Critics write reviews of Masterton's books in a stunned, slack-jawed daze. "Be warned," a still-reeling reviewer for *Kirkus* wrote of *Master of Lies* in 1992, "Masterton's newest . . . opens with what may be the single most sadistic scene in horror history. . . . The excruciating detail here seemingly acknowledges no bounds and culminates in a soul-draining depiction of a giant mutilating the penis of a renowned psychic."

But Masterton isn't out simply to shock. He is obeying his one commandment, stated in "Rules for Writing" on his website: "Be totally original. . . . Invent your own threats." And so he wrote *Feast* (1988), about gourmet cannibal cults. The story opens with the immortal line: "'Well, then,' said Charlie, his face half hidden in the shadows. 'How long do you think this baby has been dead?'" Turns out the baby is a schnitzel served at the Iron Kettle, a crummy joint in upstate New York that Charlie is reviewing for a food and lodging guide. His three-week trip is ostensibly designed so that he and his teenage son Martin can spend time together. But Charlie is a lousy dad—selfish, hapless, and loaded to the gills with failure. By chapter 4, Charlie's obsessed with Le Reposoir, an exclusive French dining club in the middle of nowhere that refuses to book him a table. After picking up a floozy and spending a very dirty night at his hotel, he returns to his room to find Martin is missing. Most books hoard their plot twists, but Masterton has more twists up his sleeve than the average bear. I am spoiling nothing by revealing that Le Reposoir is a front for a cult of devout cannibals named the Celestines and Martin is in their clutches. The first big wrinkle: the Celestines regard being eaten alive as the holiest of acts, and Martin has joined them because he wants to undergo this peak religious experience. Compared to his dad's grubby, pointless life, participating in a transcendent autocannibalism orgy doesn't sound so bad, and the Celestines maintain the moral high ground throughout the book.

Wherever you think this book won't go, Masterton not only goes there, he reports back in lunacy-inducing detail. By the last page we've seen amputee dwarf assassins, flaming dogs, one of the most harrowing scenes of self-cannibalism ever committed to paper, one death by explosive vomiting, and an appearance by Jesus Christ himself. Throughout, Masterton enjoys himself immensely. He cares about his characters. His dialogue is funnier than it needs to be, his gore is gorier, and his sex is more explicit. His books may not be the most tasteful, or consistent, but you feel that Masterson will gladly hang up his hat the minute they're not the most original.

Graham Masterton went where lesser writers feared to tread, chronicling madmen living inside walls (*Walkers*), an apocalyptic grain blight (*Famine*), an evil chair (*The Heirloom*), cannibal cults (*Feast*), and a mirror that witnessed a child's murder (*Mirror*).

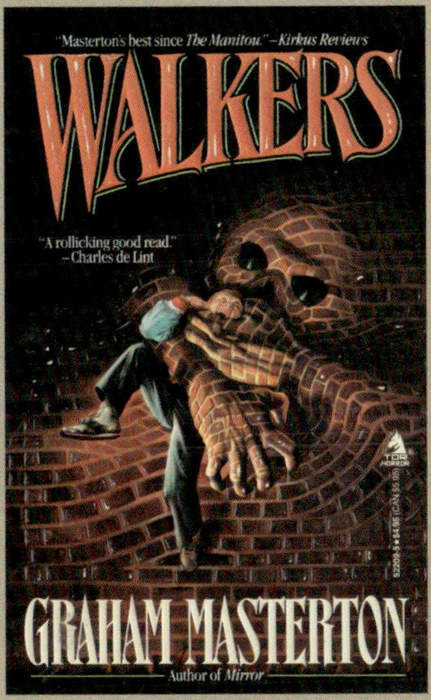

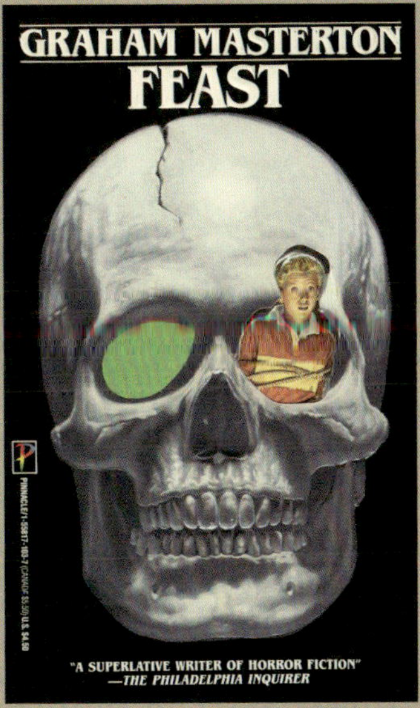

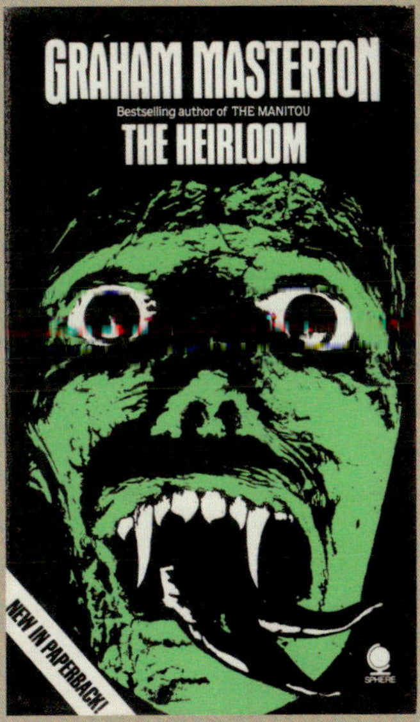

From A to Zebra

If Zebra Books had a mascot, it would be a slipper-clad skeleton sitting atop a crescent moon against the infinite void of space (hello, *Sandman*!). Founded in 1974 by Walter Zacharius and Roberta Grossman, two refugees from paperback house Lancer (whose titles include *Male Nymphomaniac* and *The Man from O.R.G.Y.*), Zebra was the flagship paperback imprint of Kensington Publishing, the independent press Zacharius launched with $67,000.

Grossman was twenty-nine, then the youngest president of a publishing house, and she and Zacharius had no pretensions. Without deep pockets, they had to be smarter and faster. When other publishers went high, Zebra went low. They paid lower royalties (sometimes a mere 2 percent) and smaller advances (as little as $500), and they paid late. They kept a small staff (twenty-two people), but hired smart. Zebra's door was open to talent from other publishers who'd been passed over for promotions or forced to retire. Lacking deep ties to the literary community, Grossman and Zacharius plunged into the slush pile and emerged with titles they thought no one would touch: historical romances. By the early '80s they had built Zebra, and Kensington, into a powerhouse with $10 million in sales annually.

Romance may have built the house of Zebra in the '70s (continuing even into the '90s with loud-sounding gothic romances like *The Shrieking Shadows of Penporth Island* and *The Wailing Winds of Juneau Abbey*), but in the '80s horror made Zebra famous. Its first hit horror author was William W. Johnstone, whose preacher-driven novel *The Devil's Kiss* put the press on the map in 1980. Rick Hautala became a Zebra mainstay, as did that Arkansas granny Ruby Jean Jensen, who never saw a baby that didn't scare the pants off her. Zebra was hungry for

product and became the publisher of last resort for authors like Bentley Little, Ken Greenhall, and Joe R. Lansdale when they couldn't sell a book anywhere else.

Zebra's publishers knew their authors weren't famous enough to sell books on name alone, so they focused instead on covers. They paid their artists well, hiring big names like Lisa Falkenstern (see page 160) and William Teason. Working on the skeleton farm may not have made you proud, but it did earn a paycheck. Always looking for ways to stand out, Zebra published the first hologram cover on a paperback horror novel (Rick Hautala's *Night Stone*) in 1986.

In 1992 cancer claimed the life of Grossman, who had been like a daughter to Zacharius. After her death, Harlequin tried to buy Zebra for the bargain-basement price of $30 million; in the depths of his grief, Zacharius agreed to sell. He backed out at the last minute.

The early '90s saw Zebra flogging the killer-child, Satanic, and animal-attack books that had been so popular in the '70s, giving them increasingly ornate covers. But the death rattle had sounded: in 1993 Zebra reduced its horror output to two titles per month. Three years later one of the last and largest existing horror imprints in America stopped publishing horror titles and focused on romance and suspense instead. An era had ended.

Skulls and bones are familiar cover images for paperback horror. But Zebra Books raised the skeleton cover model to an art form, whether the story was about a devil child (*Sandman*), small-town evil (*Devil's Moon*), Aladdin's lamp (*Smoke*), or an actual walking skeleton (*Wait and See*).

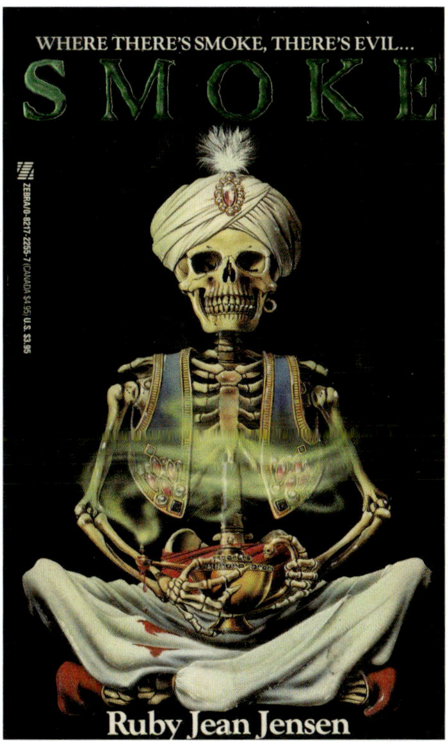

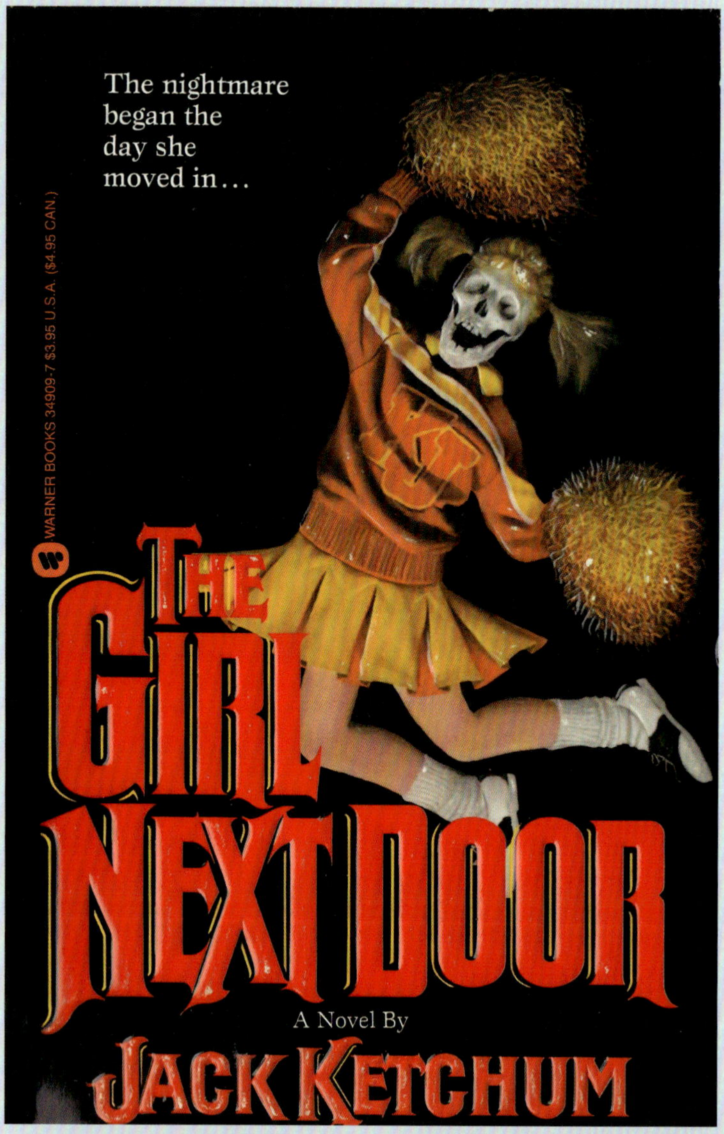

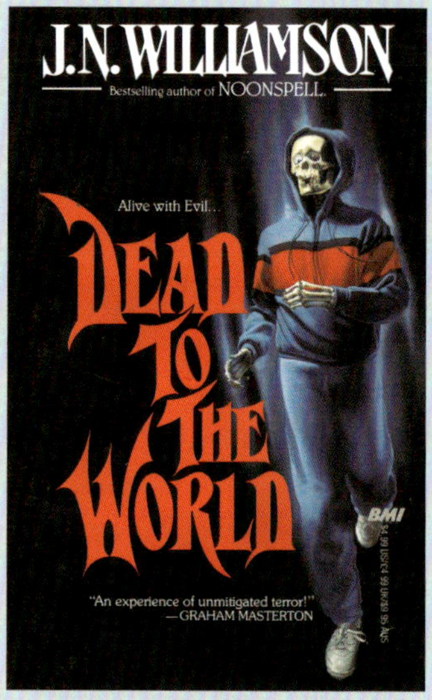

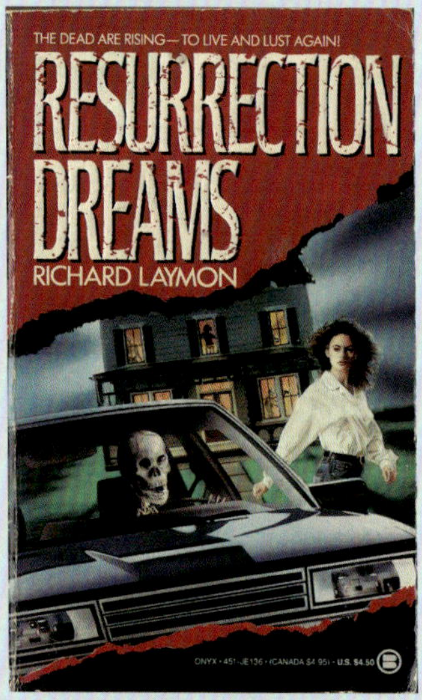

Lazy bones? We think not. Zebra Books and other horror publishers showed us that if they put their minds to it, skeletons could do anything from lead a pep rally to earn an advanced degree.

THE BACKWOODS OF VERMONT HIDES A TWISTED, HIDEOUS SECRET...
GUARDIAN ANGELS
JOSEPH CITRO

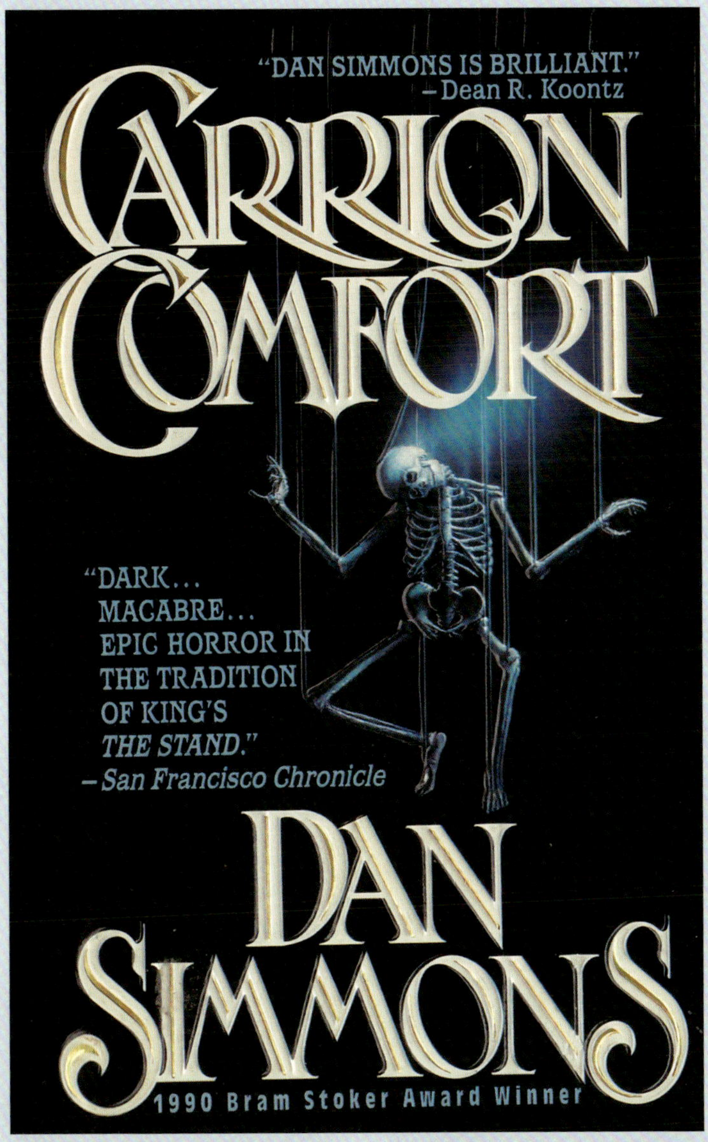
"DAN SIMMONS IS BRILLIANT."
—Dean R. Koontz
CARRION COMFORT
"DARK...
MACABRE...
EPIC HORROR IN
THE TRADITION
OF KING'S
THE STAND."
—San Francisco Chronicle
DAN SIMMONS
1990 Bram Stoker Award Winner

WHEN LITTLE SIMON
PLAYS WITH FIRE,
THE GAME BECOMES
A FUNERAL PYRE
POCKET
62674-4
$3.50
A NOVEL
OF HORROR BY
RUSSELL RHODES
TRICYCLE

Karl Edward Wagner
"JUST ABOUT THE SOLIDEST AND REALEST
HORROR WRITER AROUND." —FRITZ LEIBER
WHY NOT YOU AND I?
—THE PHILADELPHIA
INQUIRER

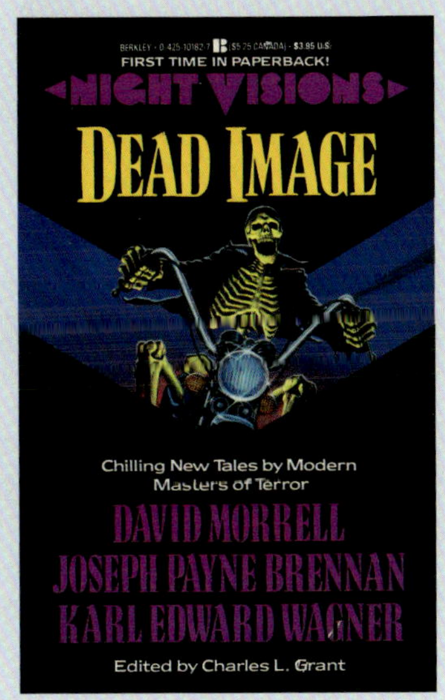
FIRST TIME IN PAPERBACK!
NIGHT VISIONS
DEAD IMAGE
Chilling New Tales by Modern
Masters of Terror
DAVID MORRELL
JOSEPH PAYNE BRENNAN
KARL EDWARD WAGNER
Edited by Charles L. Grant

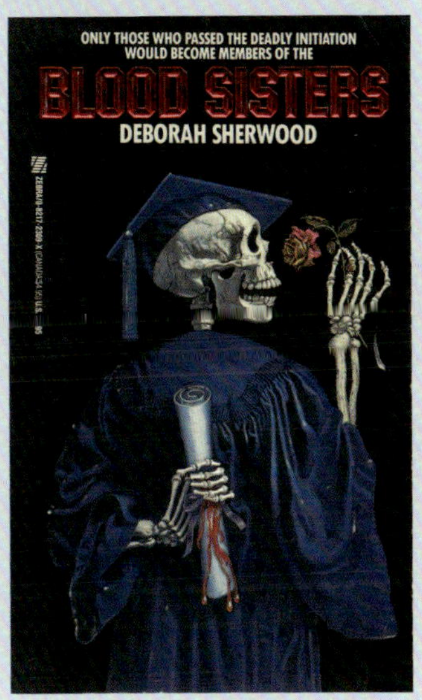
ONLY THOSE WHO PASSED THE DEADLY INITIATION
WOULD BECOME MEMBERS OF THE
BLOOD SISTERS
DEBORAH SHERWOOD

Dark Fantasy and Quiet Horror

For every dancing skeleton who writes a horror novel, there must be a skeleton wrangler, a person who takes that skeleton to NECON (Northeastern Writers' Conference), introduces it to the right editors, publishes its first story. Skeleton wranglers are the grease in the gears that make the pendulum swing; they're the ones who buy the drinks, correct the manuscript, cut the checks.

Often we can spot wranglers by looking at horror periodicals and anthologies. David B. Silva's quarterly magazine *The Horror Show* (1982–91) won a World Fantasy Award, and Silva published early work by future stars like Poppy Z. Brite and Bentley Little. Jeff Conner's Scream/Press published limited editions of Stephen King and Ramsey Campbell and issued the first U.S. hardcover editions of Clive Barker's *Books of Blood* collections. Ellen Datlow was the fiction editor at *Omni* magazine from 1981 to its folding in 1998; she ushered dozens of authors into the spotlight before taking over editing *The Year's Best Fantasy and Horror* and *The Best Horror of the Year*, as well as numerous themed short-fiction anthologies.

But the biggest skeleton wrangler of them all was also one of the genre's best-known editors and most prolific writers: Charles L. Grant. A Vietnam veteran who disliked Lovecraft and hated gore, Grant was a purveyor of what he first called "dark fantasy"—what was later called "quiet horror."

Grant believed in creeping mist and full moons, he loved long titles and characters taking midnight strolls down empty streets. Like fog, he tended to blur lines rather than shatter boundaries. His characters are modern, dreaming of cars they can't afford, and his ghosts go on dates and leave answering-machine messages.

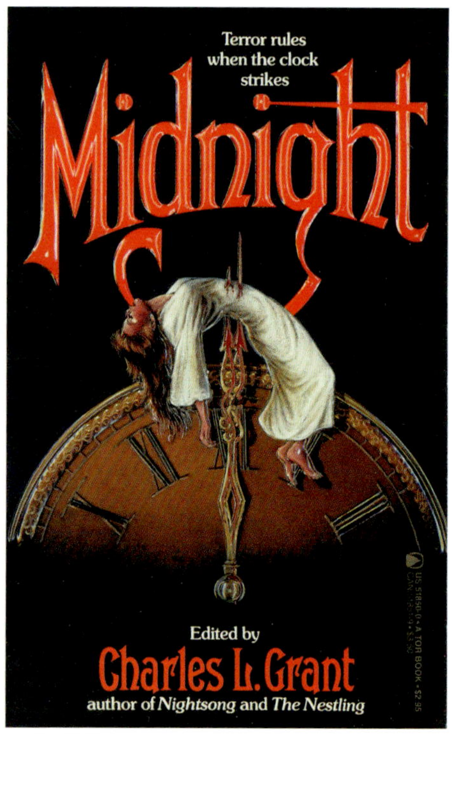

The contents were quiet, but the covers were loud. Grant's books got covers by some of the genre's best artists, like Rowena Morrill (*Night Songs*) and Jill Bauman (*Midnight*).

0-445-04363-6 $1.75

The most terrifying town
since **Salem's Lot**...
"Horror at its finest...guaranteed!"
—Hartford Courant

The Hour of the Oxrun Dead

a novel by C. L. Grant

DON'T LOOK OVER YOUR SHOULDER...
SHADOWS
FEATURING STEPHEN KING
WINNER OF THE WORLD FANTASY AWARD
16751 $2.25

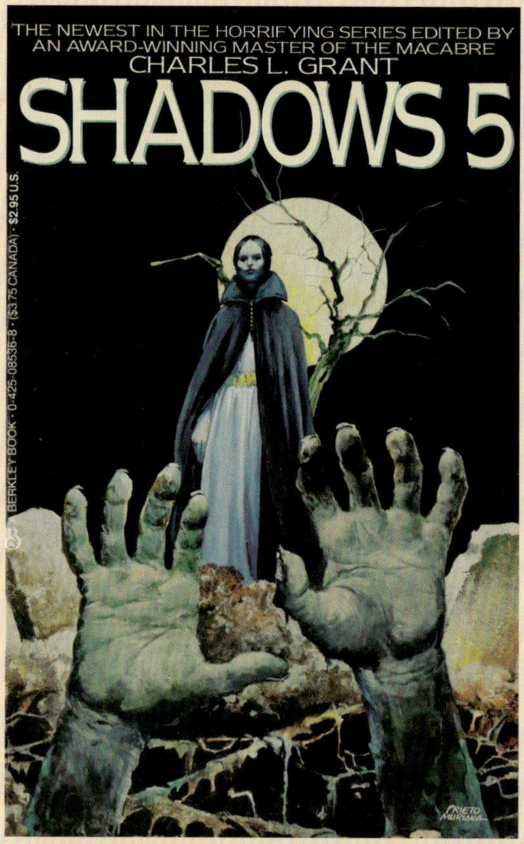
THE NEWEST IN THE HORRIFYING SERIES EDITED BY AN AWARD-WINNING MASTER OF THE MACABRE
CHARLES L. GRANT
SHADOWS 5

THE LATEST IN THE TERRIFYING SERIES EDITED BY AN AWARD-WINNING MASTER OF HORROR
CHARLES L. GRANT
SHADOWS 7

THE NEWEST IN THE TERRIFYING SERIES EDITED BY AN AWARD-WINNING MASTER OF THE MACABRE
CHARLES L. GRANT
SHADOWS 9
R.I.P.

Like John Cheever, he enjoyed writing about suburban ennui, families crumbling under pressure from suspected infidelities, and which child liked which parent best. Four of his fictional New England towns spawned their own series, but the place he kept returning to was the imaginary town of Oxrun Station.

Grant knew everyone, and he made all the introductions. He published more than one hundred novels and wrote uncountable short stories under the pen names Felicia Andrews and Lionel Fenn, among others. But what made Grant the ultimate skeleton wrangler was *Shadows*.

Launched in 1978, *Shadows* was an anthology in which Grant tolerated no traditional monsters and no gore. Instead he published work by Alan Ryan, Chelsea Quinn Yarbro, Al Sarrantonio, and a couple of Stephen King's quieter stories. As contributor Thomas Monteleone said, "If your stories weren't appearing in *Shadows*, then you just weren't cutting it."

A truism is that horror functions best in short stories. Horror is about character and mood. Some of its most effective concepts felt a little threadbare stretched to a few hundred pages, and many of horror's best writers (Dennis Etchison, Robert Aickman, Ramsey Campbell) did their finest work in the short form.

More than any other genre, horror kept short stories alive. In the early '90s, as publishing collapsed, anthologies still sold well. So every few years someone decided to produce an anthology proving that horror could be literature, too. The first, and most important, came from superagent Kirby McCauley, who was inspired by Harlan Ellison's game-changing *Dangerous Visions* science-fiction anthology from 1967. McCauley bundled together stories by Stephen King ("The Mist"), Dennis Etchison (then best known as the short-story writer's short-story writer), Ramsey Campbell, Joyce Carol Oates, and Isaac Bashevis Singer for his landmark 1981 book, *Dark Forces*.

Etchison edited his own cutting-edge anthology called, natch, *Cutting Edge* (1986). Critic Douglas E. Winter did it with *Prime Evil* in 1988, and Monteleone took a stab with *Borderlands* in 1990. Even as the horror market collapsed in the early '90s, themed anthologies stayed strong in paperback. But if ever there was a canary in the coal mine for the horror boom, it died in 1989 when Grant announced he was ending *Shadows* after ten volumes because the quality of the submissions had dropped "drastically." After that, Grant wrote some media tie-ins for *The X-Files*, and then silence. As the industry descended into darkness, so, too, did Charles L. Grant.

Anthologies featured some of the best horror fiction of the '70s and '80s, from the spooky tales in Charles Grant's taste-making *Shadows* to Dennis Etchison's rule-breaking *Cutting Edge.*

SPLATTE
SERIAL
& SUPER

CHAPTER EIGHT

RPUNKS, KILLERS, CREEPS

THE
KILLRIFF
DAVID J. SCHOW

In 1986, war was declared. War on metal!

"The cassette or CD player in too many teens' rooms is an altar to evil, dispensing the devil's devices to the accompaniment of a catchy beat," warned televangelist Bob Larson. In the 1983 book *Backward Masking Unmasked*, author Jacob Aranza warned that Queen's song "We Are the Champions" was "the unofficial national anthem for gays in America." Larson listed all the satanic bands out to seduce our children, balancing the usual suspects—Led Zeppelin, AC/DC, Black Sabbath—with Electric Light Orchestra, the Beatles, and the Eagles, as well as the Beach Boys (transcendental meditators), Bee Gees (believers in reincarnation), and John Denver (once tried aikido). Fueled by *Michelle Remembers* (see page 42), James Egbert III's disappearance (page 76), and other sinister claims, by the mid-'80s the Satanic Panic was in full swing, possibly because the threat of secret satanists was a welcome distraction from the real dangers threatening to kill us all, like a foreign policy based on mutual assured destruction.

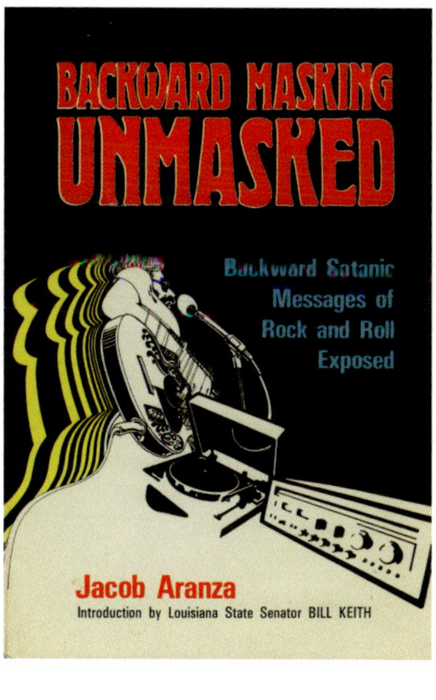

Pop culture was the battlefield in this new holy war, and heavy metal music was on the front lines. In 1985, the Parents Music Resource Center (PMRC) issued their "Filthy 15" blacklist of objectionable bands, whose only real effect was to guide curious kids to the smuttiest music on the market. Made up of the wives of power brokers and politicians in Washington, D.C., the PMRC publicly demanded that record labels reassess the contracts of musicians who performed violent or sexualized stage shows. They managed to hold Senate hearings on explicit lyrics and "porn rock," which accomplished little except to show Americans that Twisted Sister's Dee Snider was more levelheaded and informed than

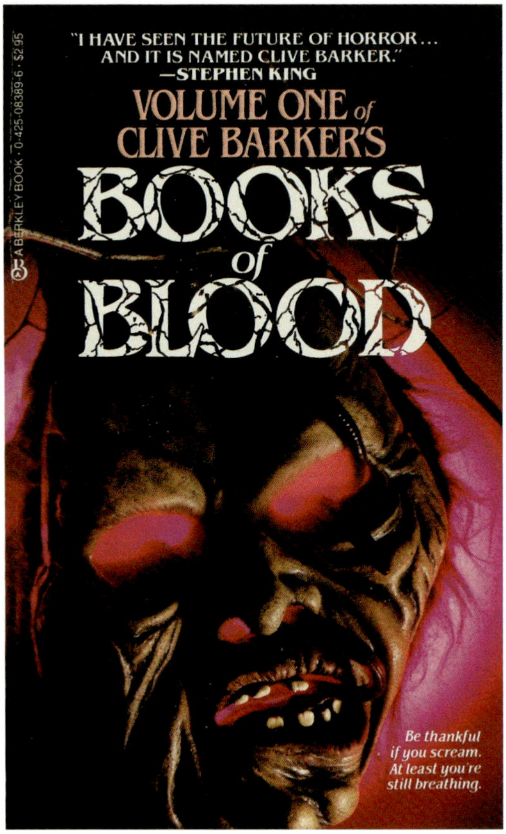

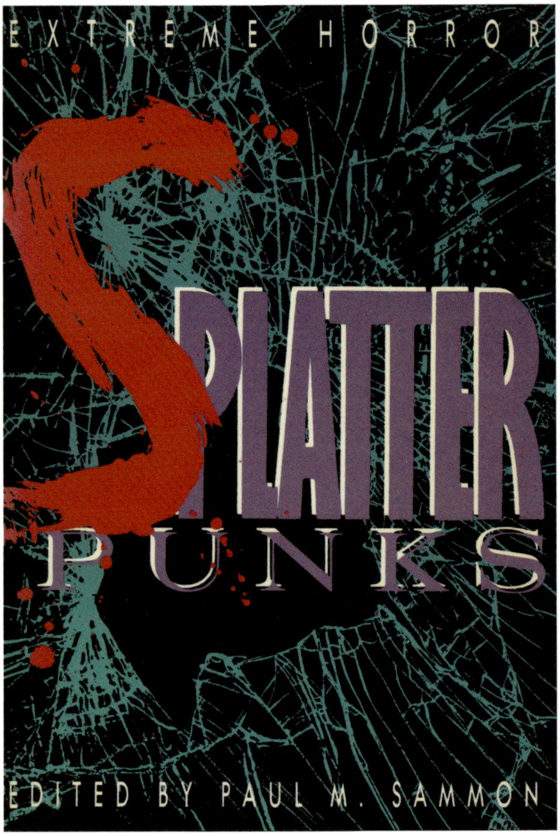

Clive Barker (*far left*) made a name for himself with his debut multivolume short-story collection, inspiring the splatterpunk movement of gory horror fiction. David Schow coined the term, and John Skipp and Craig Spector were among its founding fathers (*right*).

Tipper Gore. The group's only lasting impact was the explicit lyrics sticker on CDs and cassettes, immediately making those recordings one hundred times more desirable to kids.

Horror responded in the most metal way possible. When televangelists denounced horror movies, books, and games as causing cannibalism, murder, suicide, depression, and domestic violence, horror writers and metal bands doubled down, firehosing ever-more-offensive content into the faces of conservatives. In Providence, Rhode Island, at the 12th World Fantasy Convention in 1986, this weaponized brattitude took horror fiction one step closer to extinction when *Fangoria* columnist David Schow coined the term *splatterpunk*, named for a new school of fiction oozing out of the crypt. At the vanguard was Clive Barker, whose debut six-volume short story collection *The Books of Blood*, published in the U.K. in 1984, was released in the U.S in 1986 in the form of six terrible-looking paperbacks.

There had always been American writers, like Jack Ketchum, who refused to blink when describing gore, but the complete conviction, serious craft, and forensic eye for grotesque detail that Barker brought to his stories, about zombie actresses giving blowjobs and an army of disembodied hands declaring war on the human race, unleashed the beast. All at once, a pack of young dudes— Ray

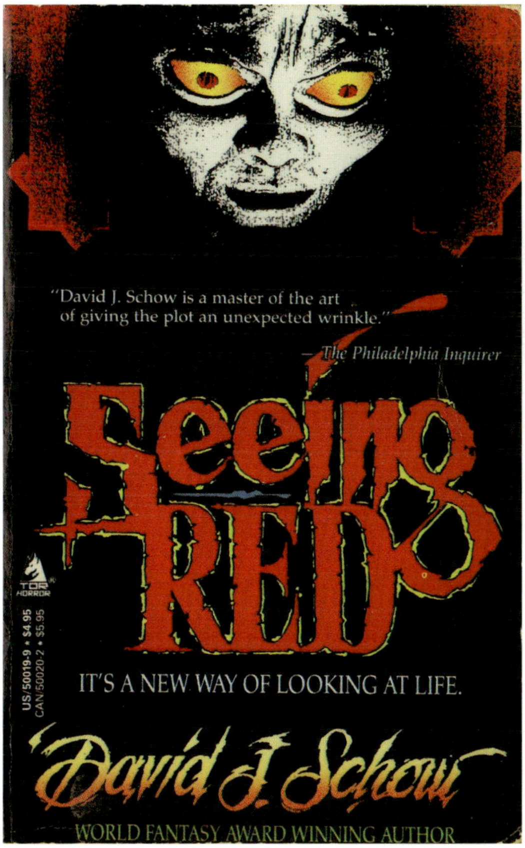

Garton, Joe R. Lansdale, Richard Christian Matheson, John Skipp, Craig Spector, and Schow—were delivering bloody books featuring all the ways a human body could be folded, spindled, curb stomped, flayed, eaten alive, castrated, blow torched, pierced, meat hooked, and mutilated. Powered by a rejection of literary style and an embrace of short, sharp, stripped-down sentences, these edgelords rejected God, America, Reagan, romance, and even the splatterpunk label, which they took great pains to denounce at every opportunity (even within the pages of anthologies with the word *splatterpunk* on the cover). Almost exclusively a boys' club (the most prominent female purveyor of splatterpunk, Poppy Z. Brite, is a trans man), and deeply white-bread (the PMRC targeted gangsta rap as hard as heavy metal, but no writers took up that torch), splatterpunk started as a trickle of short stories before erupting into a mudslide of novels, zines, and anthologies.

The only thing as stupid and outrageous as splatterpunk was rock. Heavy metal was being hit with hard cultural radiation in the '80s, and although hair metal and arena rock dominated, in underground chambers, music was mutating into death metal, thrash, and grindcore as bands like Cannibal Corpse, Rigor Mortis, and Megadeth clawed their way toward daylight. Splatterpunk and metal were a match made in hell, both genres delivering attention-seeking spurts of juvenile nihilism alongside gleeful gushers of gore.

Much like the multiplying subgenres of metal, splatterpunk was not just a marketing label but a movement. Its advocates felt they were the future of horror, a resistance pushing back against the Moral Majority, confronting humankind

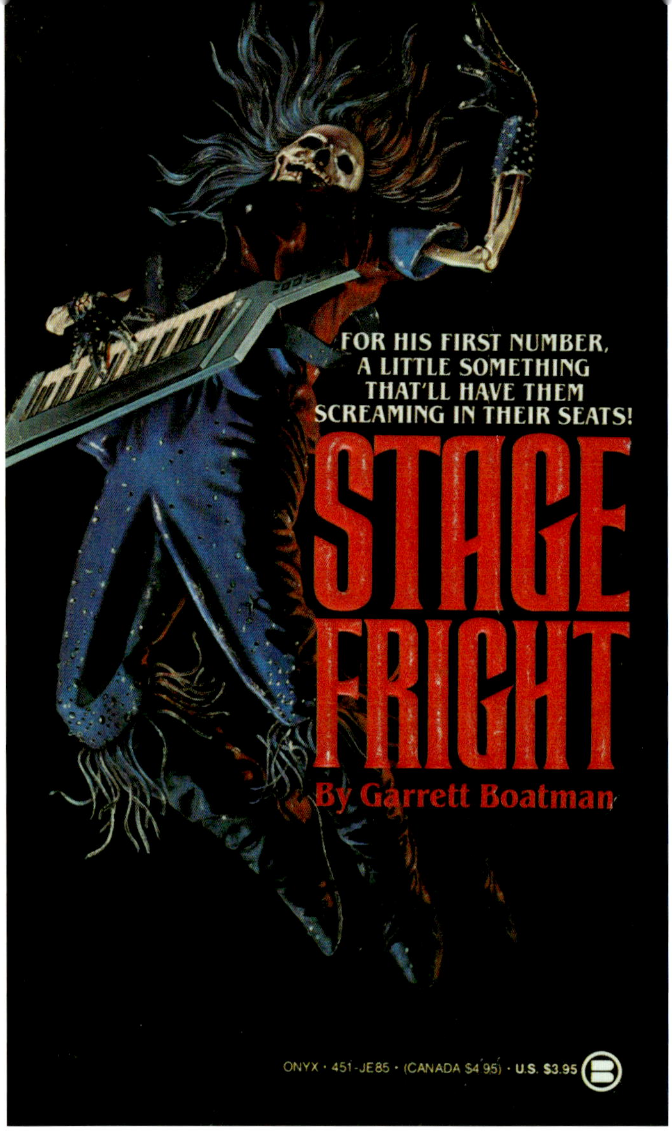

Horror fiction and heavy metal were a match made in hell, thanks to books like *Stage Fright* and *The Scream* (notable for the Stan Watts mini pull-out poster concealed behind the paperback's cover).

with our bleakest impulses and offering a community for the freaks and geeks left behind by Reagan's America. But more than a movement, they wanted to be a band. The splatterpunk authors could picture nothing cooler than being in a punk band (and a few of them were, notably John Shirley, as well as John Skipp and Craig Spector). They made sure they were photographed together as often as possible, worked together on anthologies, and cited one another's work in articles.

Schow lived out both his splatterpunk and rock fantasies in *The Kill Riff* (1987; see page 194), whose narrative did not star the novelty shotgun guitar depicted on the cover but did feature an unfortunately named metal band, Whip Hand, who disbanded after thirteen kids were killed in a riot at one of their concerts. Among the dead was angelic Kristen, whose dad, Lucas Ellington, was (regressively enough) a Vietnam War veteran. After he spends a year in an asylum "resting," his therapist Sara pronounces him cured, although she worries about his occasional nightmares. No biggie. Once Lucas is out in the world, murdering the members of Whip Hand (who have splintered into solo acts), his bad dreams clear right up.

The most important element in rock 'n' roll–splatterpunk books is mega-gore.

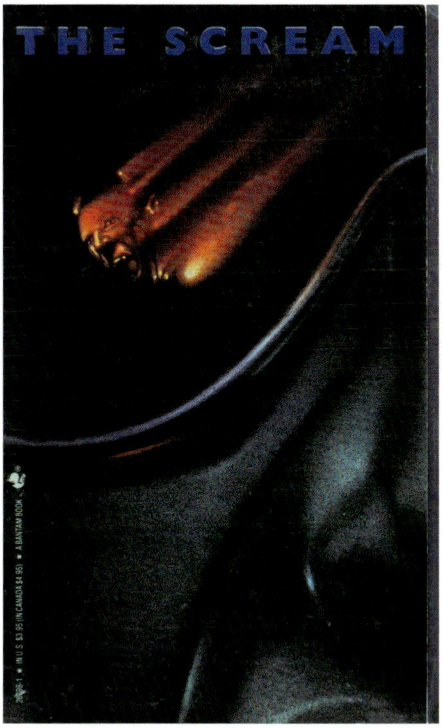

The band's former rhythm guitarist Jackson Knox gets shredded by a claymore mine planted in his monitor speaker ("It looked as though someone had pushed the guitarist through a tree shredder."). Ex-keyboardist Brion Hardin is stabbed to death ("Hardin's tongue bulged out, rimmed with saliva bubbles."), and the rhythm section is picked off from Lucas's sniper perch ("It would be fast and easy to plant a slug right into his mouth, which was now hanging open in a black oval . . ."). Don't worry about anyone running out of weapons. The former lead singer, Gabriel Stannard, lives in what a thirteen-year-old boy imagines to be decadent luxury, complete with a collection of katanas and an archery range in the basement sporting cop-shaped targets.

Splatterpunk books had no good guys and no bad guys, only a swarm of indistinguishable jerks dressed in black leather and camo. *The Kill Riff*'s revelation that Lucas was engaged in an incestuous affair with his daughter proves that the world is all just shades of gray, man. The book makes much of Lucas mourning his wife's suicide and then gleefully springs the news that in fact he murdered his wife after she discovered the incest. Later, Lucas rescues a young woman from her abusive boyfriend, only to beat her to death with a log. Life is darkness.

The next crucial element in rock 'n' roll–splatterpunk books is the obligatory authorial revelation of his own impeccable musical tastes through his characters, who congratulate one another for liking the right bands. This is often paired with denunciations of greedy labels, concert promoters, MTV, and sellout bands. Then there's the mandatory mockery of the Christian right and "Moral Majoritroids." Some of these denunciations ramble on for entire chapters. In these books, all Bible thumpers are hypocrites who barely have time to attend church between their busy schedules of burning albums, having sex with children, and getting high. But this thin layer of macho attitude—bristling with Uzis, crossbows, leather pants, and cocaine—conceals a surprisingly conservative core. Whether it's *Stage Fright*'s dark god of metal who plays the Dreamatron, a piece of tech that lets him beam his vividly imagined dreams into the audience's minds, or *The Scream*'s "postmetal cyber thrash band" that worships Satan (both books 1988), rock was portrayed exactly as it was shown in Christian scare pamphlets. Lead singers were spoiled brats and junkies, hooked on bondage, torture, or drugs made from the blood of schizophrenics. Hell looked exactly like an Iron Maiden album cover. And women were the devil.

Sputtering Out

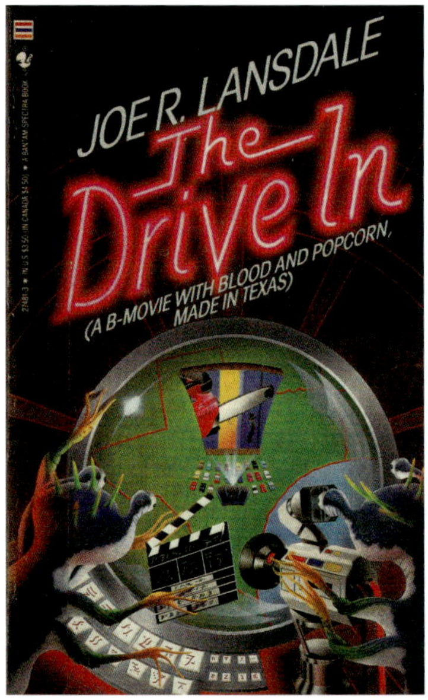

E. T. Steadman's cartoony covers didn't prepare readers for the wild 'n' wooly weirdness inside.

The first female character in *The Scream* is introduced to readers as we're invited to look up her skirt. The second is "all tits and tan and perfect even teeth." Then she's murdered. Not even female dogs are safe from being gang raped, and women spend an inordinate amount of time stripping down and hopping in the shower. The authors might have been inadvertently revealing too much about their personal hang-ups when they named the evil group out to emasculate rock 'n' roll M.O.M. (Morality over Music). But just in case you had doubts, they dub the ultimate evil demon out to destroy the world Momma. She's a 30-foot-tall, rotting, pregnant, hermaphroditic corpse that eats people with her vagina and has a touching vulnerability to rocket launchers.

Splatterpunk fizzled in the mid-'90s because it delivered too much splatter, not enough punk, but it was shockingly fertile before it folded. The late '80s and early '90s spawned an overflowing dump truck's worth of splatterpunk anthologies and magazines. *Fangoria* magazine split off the edgier *Gorezone*, while *Fear* magazine debuted in the U.K. and soon spun off its own fiction mag, *Frighteners*.

Graham Masterton dominated the first cover of *Frighteners* with his outrageous cannibal-kid story "Eric the Pie," which evoked instant outrage. The publisher pulled the magazine from newsstands, and it limped through two more issues before shutting down. *Fear* closed shortly thereafter, followed by *Gorezone* in 1994. Some splatter zines went bust without publishing a second issue.

But there were survivors. Joe R. Lansdale's first serial killer novel, *Act of Love*, slithered out of Zebra Books in 1981. He followed with a few limited-edition books before publishing *The Drive-In* and its sequel, *The Drive-In 2*. Set in a drive-in movie theater that's suddenly and supernaturally cut off from the rest of the world, these shaggy dog stories owe a big debt to Stephen King's "The Mist." But Lansdale is a better writer than a lot of his compatriots, and he wields his down-home folksy drawl like a straight razor. His early novel *The Nightrunners* wasn't published until much later because, when he wrote it, most publishers didn't know what to do with it. A recently raped woman and her husband retreat to the country to heal after the attack, but are tracked down by the reincarnation of her rapist. It's one part *Straw Dogs* and one part Texas noir. But the story offers insight into the psychology of trauma that a book like *The Kill Riff* lacks, offering compassion for its victims, rather than mere high-fives to its cool-dude perpetrators.

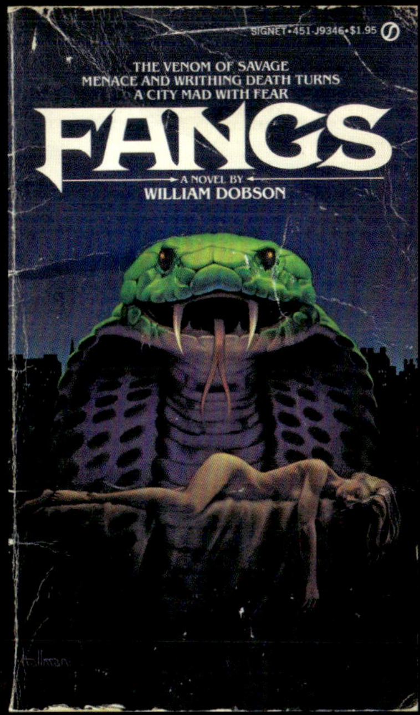

Artist Tom Hallman spent almost two years courting art director James Plumeri at New American Library before getting his first assignment for a nonfiction book called *Masquerade: The Amazing Camouflage Deceptions of World War II*. After that he worked almost exclusively for Plumeri, learning from his mentor how to make a book's cover stand out from a rack, how to do more with less, how the strong simple visual statement was the most powerful.

One thing that Plumeri believed with all his heart was that digital tools could never do what cover artists did using traditional media. But as the graphics editing program Adobe Photoshop gained wider use in the 1990s, Hallman realized this software was going to change his industry forever. Artists like him who learned to use it found that they could speed up production but still be paid their usual rates, allowing them to rake in the bucks. Then publishers caught on. First the rates for the artists fell because the powers that be reasoned that something done quickly should be done cheaply. Then marketing departments started demanding artists to revise finished art because digital tools made last-minute changes easier to execute. Production schedules sped up and turnaround times were cut.

But despite the massive, disruptive impact, digital tools weren't all bad.

"What's internal to me is kept," Hallman says. "And I don't miss mixing paint. Besides, the way I painted, I'd be dead by now. It ruined my back."

Stage Fright

Ah, the deceptive lure of show business. Hollywood may seem glamorous, but it's not all salads served with imported Norwegian crackers and closets full of stylish silver jumpsuits. Breaking in is hard, and it can go wrong in so many ways. First, consider the pitfalls of securing financing. Say, for instance, you're making an independent movie about a serial killer. There is a larger than average chance that your only backers will be serial killers who want to use your movie to conceal their crimes. Even worse, not only do they want script input, they also want to trick you into raping and murdering your son on camera (*Below the Line*, 1987).

And yet, the lure of show business is hard to resist, and that was especially so in the '80s, when even a book about a snuff film like *Below the Line* spends much of its time laying out film financing and tax shelters in enough detail for any wannabe Bruckheimer to follow. The greatest show-biz seductress of them all was Judi Miller, the Aaron Spelling of horror novels. Both of her show-business slasher novels—*Save the Last Dance for Me* (1981) and *Phantom of the Soap Opera* (1988)—are aspirational movie-of-the-week catalogs of dreams seemingly designed to lure tourists to New York City, get them jobs in the entertainment industry, and murder them.

The only difference between the two books is that one is set in the world of ballet and the other is set in the world of daytime soap operas, which turn out to be remarkably similar. Each features psychopathic killers stalking the skinny and the beautiful, multiple red herrings, and guess-the-murderer plots. Soap opera stars take business meetings in the Russian Tea Room, drink strawberry margaritas, and order "the latest Thai delicacies." Directors have their shirts unbuttoned to the navel and necks draped with gold chains. Wedding cakes are six feet tall, the best goodbye gift you can give your ballet teacher is a dramatic black cape, and if you've made it to the top, you probably have a heart-shaped bed.

It's a sealed-off, snow-globe world of '80s decadence, and it makes the killers seem even tackier. When we learn in *Save the Last Dance* that the psycho is murdering ballet students because his domineering mother grew too fat to be a ballerina, we nod because of course she did. Then we shiver as this loony takes his latest victim to Queens and makes her dance in a cold basement. She'll ruin her feet! Then he makes her eat raw meat, lectures her for smoking, and forces her to learn terrible choreography, teaching every aspiring ballet dancer that the only fate worse than death is being trapped in one of the outer boroughs.

Behind every successful soap star and ballerina is a controlling skeleton who doesn't understand personal space and gets 15% of everything she makes.

FICTION
POCKET
83650-1
$2.75
"A TENSE TERRIFYING THRILLER I COULDN'T PUT DOWN...READ IT!"
—V.C. ANDREWS, AUTHOR OF FLOWERS IN THE ATTIC
SAVE THE LAST DANCE FOR ME
JUDI MILLER

HE HAD A SURPRISE FOR TV'S MOST BEAUTIFUL DAYTIME STARS— THE KISS OF DEATH...
PHANTOM OF THE SOAP OPERA
JUDI MILLER
DELL • 20058-X • U.S. $3.95 CAN. $4.95

JARON SUMMERS
Bestselling Author of Safety Catch
To make his movie, he pledged his children as collateral and signed his life away.
BELOW THE LINE
LEISURE • 2434 • $3.95 US/$4.95 CAN

THE MILLION-COPY BESTSELLER BY
THOMAS HARRIS
AUTHOR OF THE SILENCE OF THE LAMBS
RED DRAGON
27522-4 ★ IN U.S. $4.95 (IN CANADA $5.95) ★ A BANTAM BOOK

Hello, Clarice

By the late '80s, horror fiction was walking down an empty street, all alone, late at night, stalked by a maniac that would prove to be its doom: the serial killer. The FBI had been using the term *serial killer* since 1961, and books about psychotic killers have a long history, dating back at least to Robert Bloch's *Psycho* in 1959. In 1970, Lawrance Holmes's novel *A Very Short Walk* introduced us to a killer narrating the story of his own murderous alienation, starting as an angry fetus stewing in amniotic rage juice. Judith Rossner's 1975 novel *Looking for Mr. Goodbar*, about a woman who picks up a stranger in a bar and gets murdered for her trouble, was a cultural touchstone that inspired a million magazine think pieces.

But 1981 was the dawn of something new. That was the year the term *serial killer* entered the mainstream. And that was the year that saw the publication of the book Stephen King called "probably the best popular novel to be published since *The Godfather*." Genre historian Douglas E. Winter wrote that, although many established novelists may have written the second-best book of the year, there was no doubt that "the best horror novel of the early eighties" was from a relatively obscure thriller writer named Thomas Harris. The book was *Red Dragon*.

Deeply literary, informed by the latest thinking on forensics and criminal profiling, *Red Dragon* was a writer's book that inspired dozens of copycats but never quite broke into the mainstream. Even its ultra-'80s movie adaptation *Manhunter* (1986) didn't help sales. However, the book and the film did introduce a minor character named Hannibal Lecter, who was willing to wait for his turn in the spotlight. It wouldn't be long before the culture caught up to him. According to the FBI, there were only 19 serial murders in the '60s, while the '70s saw a flood of 119, and the '80s yielded 200. The country watched in stunned fascination as one unshaven white man with a supervillain name after another was arrested for inhuman crimes: the Hillside Strangler, Son of Sam, the Freeway Killer, the Vampire of Sacramento, the Green River Killer, the Sunset Strip Killer, the Midtown Slasher.

The seemingly sudden surge of serial killers took everyone by surprise, and in a flash the scariest motive for murder was no motive at all. A deranged falconer terrorizes Manhattan with his killer peregrine falcon in *Peregrine* (1981) for no other reason than he thinks it's a challenge. In *Horror Story* (1979; page 208), a disgraced general starts an end-times cult in rural Connecticut, abducts a family of lost tourists, and drops off the husband in Boston with a .357 magnum and instructions to execute a random black family before 11 p.m. or his wife and child die. The general's motive? Absolutely nothing. Robert Bloch's agent suggested he write *Psycho II* (1982), and Bloch complied, submitting a book in which Norman Bates is not so bad. But the therapist who thinks he can rehabilitate him, and the movie producers making a film about his killings, are the ones truly off the deep end.

As the '80s progressed, supernatural horror felt exhausted, with the same old writers dishing out the same old books. Horror movies were all campy slaughter, aimed at teens in on the joke. But the serial-killer book walked the line between crime fiction and horror novel, bringing in new—and in some cases, better—writers, or at least writers whose tricks weren't familiar to exhausted audiences. Informed by the splatterpunk movement, these writers felt like they had permission to upset readers. A lot.

Thomas Tessier's placid prose lured readers out on the ice, which then cracked, plunging them into a nightmare abyss where alcoholic plastic surgeons babbled about the Marquis de Sade to living human torsos shorn of limbs and locked in cages. One of the few horror novelists to spin his fear out of adult sexual relationships, rather than slopping sex on top of his stories like a mountain of Reddi-wip, Tessier's books feel more mature, and therefore much darker, than a lot of what was on the market. In Tessier's *Shockwaves* (1982), a disappointed wife learns that the man she married isn't just a career-obsessed bore; he is truly dangerous. *Rapture* (1987) is about a man obsessed with his old high school crush, who's now married and has a daughter who looks exactly like Mom did in her glory days.

A kind of Fight Club for the hot tub set, Eric C. Higgs's *The Happy Man* was a short, minimalist novel of suburban ennui written in disaffected prose that could pass as a Brett Easton Ellis novella if it contained less cannibalism. A bunch of middle-aged yuppies trapped in California cul-de-sacs work identical mindless jobs in the aerospace industry, numbing themselves on weekends with expensive liquor and top-shelf grass. Armored in thick plates of boredom, their shells can be cracked only by a new neighbor who brings violence and illicit humping to their cocktail parties. At first, the newcomer seems to offer entrance into a bold new world of Authentic Experience, but then someone mentions the Marquis de Sade and suddenly machine guns and torture are on the menu. Surprisingly, the book

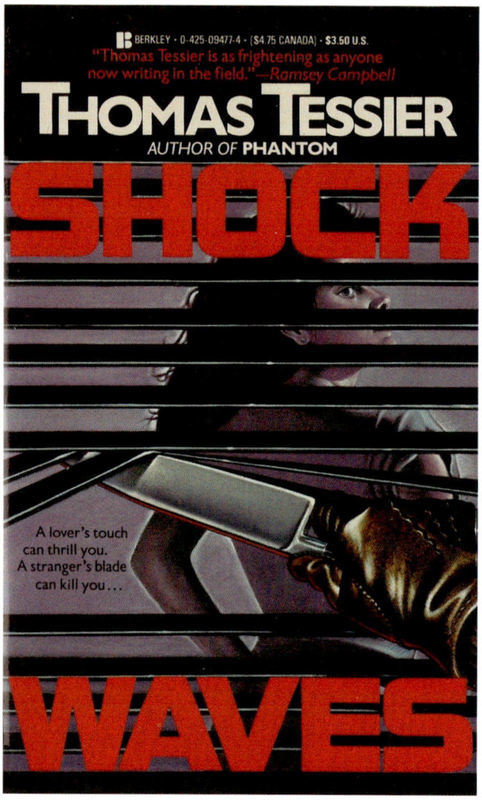

ends on a note of unexpected faith in human decency, albeit one that's earned by switching this literary assault rifle into full auto mode and squeezing the trigger until the last cartridge hits the ground.

The language of horror novels even infected true crime books. Flora Rheta Schreiber, author of the best-selling 1973 multiple personality best seller *Sybil*, delivered a true-crime account of the murders committed by Joseph Kallinger in a book called *The Shoemaker*—which sports a die-cut cover like a V. C. Andrews novel, lurid marketing copy, and breathless prose about how this sad killer was "pursued by Demons" possessed by "Satanic evil" and haunted by the "ghosts of his past."

All the strands were converging: serial killers, true crime, splatterpunk, sympathy for the monster. The hangman's noose was knotted in 1988 when Thomas Harris's second novel, *The Silence of the Lambs*, debuted and won the genre's two biggest honors: the World Fantasy Award and the Bram Stoker Award. A few years later, in 1991, the movie adaptation won five Academy Awards. Suddenly, Hannibal Lecter was a household name. This was the moment horror editors and agents had been eagerly awaiting for more than twenty years. This was the next *Exorcist*. This was Rosemary's second baby. And the first thing it did was strangle its older sibling.

Straight razors, butcher knives, steak knives, and leatherworking knives all conveyed the same message: this book is dangerous.

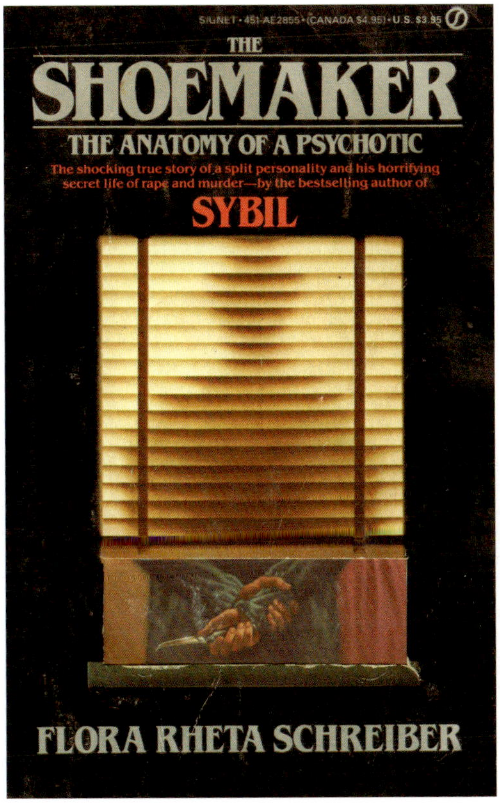

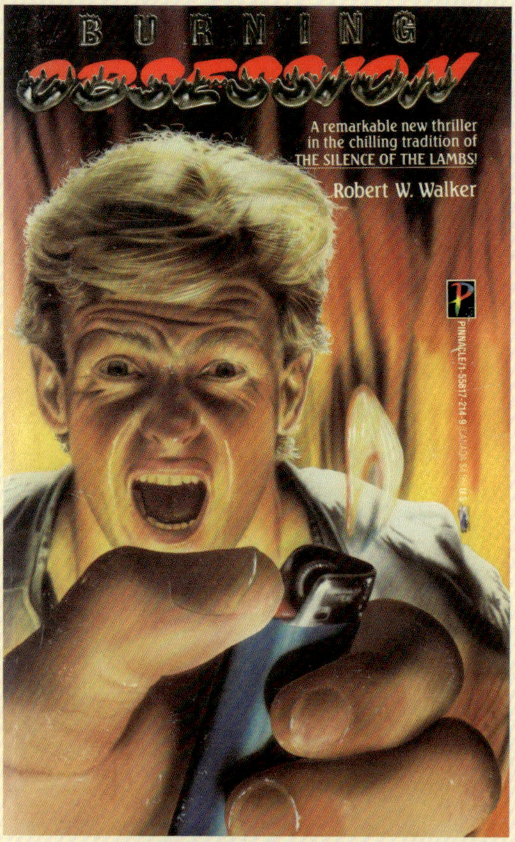
BURNING
OBSESSION
A remarkable new thriller
in the chilling tradition of
THE SILENCE OF THE LAMBS!
Robert W. Walker

OLIVER McNAB
HORROR-STORY
'Perfect bedtime reading
except you'll never get to sleep'
-Andrew Coburn, author of The Babysitter

DYING BREATH
In the terrifying tradition of
THE SILENCE OF THE LAMBS
PINNACLE/1-55817-261-0/CANADA $4.95/U.S. $3.95
Robert W. Walker

A scalpel flashes in the moonlight...
and another victim dies!
RAZOR'S
EDGE
Robert W. Walker

In serial-killer horror, fire is a tool of killers, not Satan (*Burning Obsession*); masks conceal madmen, not mutants (*Horror Story*, *The Hood*); breath is stolen by asphyxiation, not aliens (*Dying Breath*); blood is spilled by knives, not fangs (*Razor's Edge*); and office parties are awkward (*Office Party*, also real life).

Nails in the Coffin

Horror was out. Serial killers were in. The horror-fiction market of the late '80s was glutted, and the inevitable crash was happening fast. Imprints collapsed like punctured lungs, publishers shoveled books onto store shelves faster than readers could buy them, and returns flooded into warehouses. Customers stayed away in droves. Writers begged their editors to market their books as thrillers instead of horror.

Gore ruled the market. Splatterpunk still seemed like a badge of authenticity, and readers greedy for guts were rewarded by *Fangoria* magazine's *Gorezone* spinoff in 1988. Paul Dale Anderson's *Instruments of Death* series ignored its human characters in favor of their titular methods of mutilation: *Claw Hammer*, *Pickaxe*, *Icepick*, and *Meat Cleaver*. Redheads were popular, or at least scalping them on the book's first page was, as in *Razor's Edge*. But nothing tracked the rise and decline of horror better than Rex Miller's Chaingang novels. Hailed as a bold new chapter in the gospel of splatterpunk, Miller's *Slob* appeared in 1987 to much sweaty-palmed page-turning.

Hannibal Lecter hadn't made serial killers a supertrend yet, but writers already knew they had to offer different flavors of sociopath to hook their readers. Miller gave them Daniel "Chaingang" Bunkowski, a 469-pounder who defied all logic as his creator tried to meet market demands. Bunkowski prowled the Midwest, murdering at random, committing sex crimes against women, and pulping the skulls of men who annoyed him. The man determined to bring him down was a tough Chicago cop named Jack Eichord, who happened to be an expert in the new science of profiling serial killers. The first Chaingang book felt almost like an attempt to put the pathetic squalor of the actual serial killer on the page. Bunkowski was a junk-food-addicted monstrosity who put away forty egg rolls at a time and whose breath smelled like "stale burritos, wild onions and garlic, bad tuna, and your basic terminal halitosis." But then *The Silence of the Lambs* won all those Academy Awards.

Miller had already elevated Bunkowski above the typical unskilled, blue-collar serial killer by making him the product of a secret government research program to produce super-killers for the Vietnam War. But in the wake of Dr. Lecter's success, serial killers needed to be collectors of fine art, avengers of the weak, men of taste and refinement. Miller was happy to oblige. Chaingang Bunkowski began as nothing more than a murderous slob, but Miller was nothing if not flexible, and over the course of *Chaingang* (1992), *Savant* (1994), and *Butcher* (1994) he turned Bunkowski into a superhero.

First, Miller made sure readers knew that his killer "warped every curve, deviated from every chart . . . he was that rare human being called the physical precognitive." He was "an autodidact, a self-taught killer whose alarming proclivity for violence was surpassed only by what appeared to be a genius intellect." He had a photographic memory, the ability to detect the presence of human life in a house, an understanding of "the role of the mystagogue in televangelistic fund-raising, cellular phenomena, theoretical fluid mechanics" and "noncyclical phylogeny," whatever that is. He was "a master at camouflaged doublespeak," much like his author, able to make anyone believe anything with almost no effort. He possessed "the natural skills of a consummate actor: keen powers of observation and mimicry, a predisposition for thorough preparation, the ability to instantly summon up stored emotion, and the feel for a character's center." He knew how to make "a smart bomb activated by an ordinary kitchen food timer. A device for starting an undetectable fire." He was immune to poison ivy. Miller transformed Bunkowski from a psychopath who killed at random into a good guy who killed people who deserved it: drug dealers, evil psychiatrists, cold-blooded psychotic snipers sporting micropenises and armed with futuristic ray guns, who happened to have graduated from the same government black-ops program as Bunkowski did. That happened in *Savant*, the last of the Chaingang novels, which revealed that Chaingang had to destroy the other assassins in his old super-psychopath program because they killed indiscriminately and had sex with prostitutes. Unlike Chaingang, who, by this point, was only killing the people who abused him as a child or were mean to puppies.

Horror fiction of the late '80s seemed more interested in the killer's weapons than in the killer.

By the end of *Savant*, Chaingang—whom we met in the first book raping a woman, ejaculating on her face, then breaking her neck—had developed the ability to turn invisible in darkness by regulating his respiration and heart rate like a ninja. He had mailed a teeny tiny possum heart to the government doctor who created him and had adopted five adorable puppies. The serial killer was no longer a menace. He wasn't even a cartoon. He had become a hero.

But as the '80s rolled into the '90s, even a hero couldn't save horror publishing. Canada's mass-market paperback publisher, Paperjacks, stalled drastically in 1989; Tudor Books disappeared that same year. Mass-market paperbacks were replaced by larger and more lucrative trade paperbacks. Magazines died suddenly and without warning; *Twilight Zone* magazine shuttered in 1989, *Fear* magazine ceased publication in 1991, and *Omni* magazine became online-only in 1995. Paper costs were rising, distribution was becoming more difficult, and things were looking grim. In the late '80s, St. Martin's cut back its horror line, followed by Tor, then Pinnacle; Avon went on hiatus. Finally, in 1996, Zebra closed its skeleton farm.

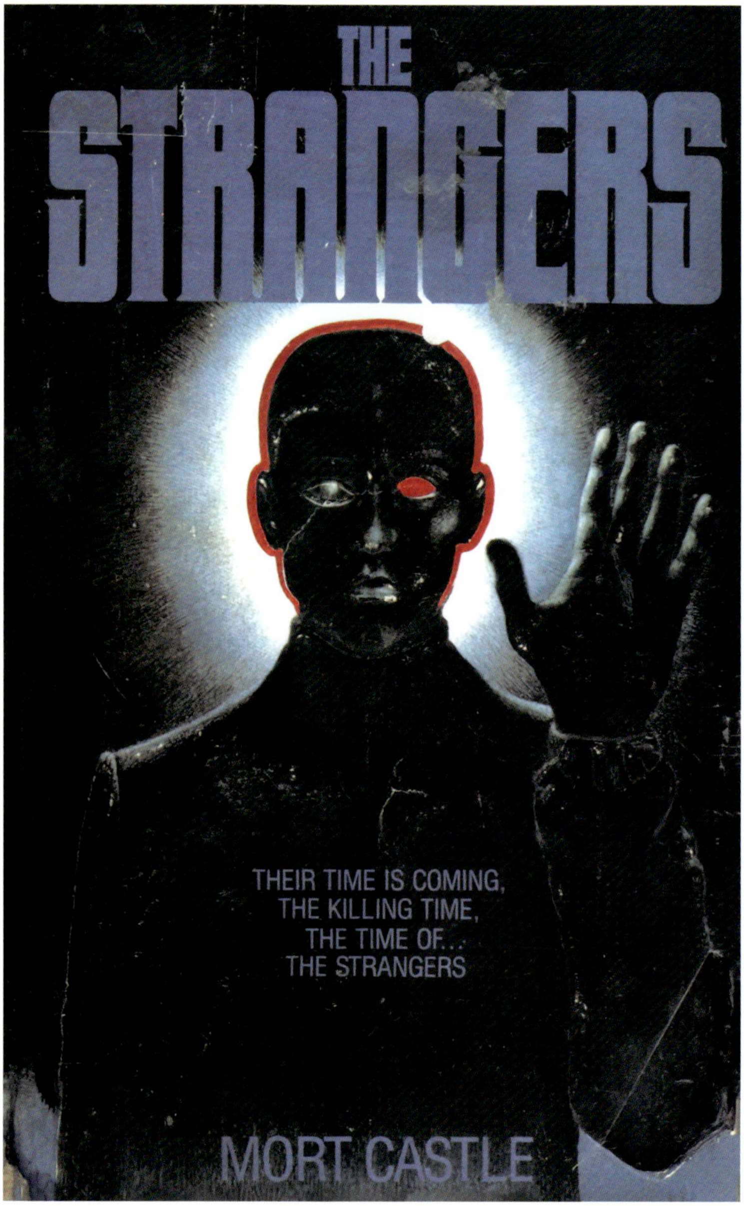

Serial killers can be anybody, but likely suspects include cemetery caretakers (*Joyride*), punk rock bands (*Ghoul*), and anyone swathed in black (*Headhunter*). They could also be everybody, as in *The Strangers*, in which secret sociopaths stage a revolution and take over the world.

Won't Somebody Think of the Children?

As horror for adults gasped its last breaths, the genre found new life in a younger generation. Horror fiction for kids had been around for decades, whether it was Joan Aiken's ersatz gothics like *The Wolves of Willoughby Chase* (1962, a forerunner of Lemony Snicket's *Series of Unfortunate Events*) or thrillers like Lois Duncan's *Killing Mr. Griffin*. Duncan, the queen of young-adult suspense, had started turning out teen thrillers in 1966, including *I Know What You Did Last Summer* (1973), *Stranger with My Face* (1981), and the cult classic *Daughters of Eve* (1979). But after the murder of her daughter in 1989, she seemed to lose her taste for fictional horror and devoted the rest of her life to chronicling the search for the girl's killer.

Horror hit its stride with a hungry teenage audience in the '80s, first with slasher films and then with books. Dell launched its teen occult horror series, Twilight, in 1982, complete with gruesome corpse exhumations and relatively graphic and goopy gore. Bantam countered with its less gory but more timely Dark Forces series in 1983, which was like the Satanic Panic for teens; its books were full of video games that unleashed Satan as an end-level boss, unholy heavy metal bands, and role-playing games that summoned the Prince of Darkness.

The late '80s were a growing nightmare for adult horror writers. Author after author failed to earn out advances, and agents unleashed tornadoes of bad advice that ripped through the trailer park of publishing, leaving destruction in its wake: "Write big fat novels because that's what sold last week." "Write like Michael Crichton." "Write like Stephen King." But the market was glutted and returns were often at 60 percent. The industry was trying everything to stop the bleeding, but the patient wouldn't leave the table alive.

As the '90s approached, the seemingly insatiable kid's market emerged as horror's last hope. R. L. Stine launched his teen horror series *Fear Street* in 1989, which included seasonal offerings like *Silent Night*. Around the same time Christopher Pike began turning out Lois Duncan–esque teen thrillers, proving to publishers that kids had a ravenous hunger for horror. Adult readers were left in the dust, while Stine and Pike went on to found the best-selling series *Goosebumps* in 1992 and *Spooksville* in 1995, respectively. At long last, Whitney Houston's words rang true: the children were the future.

Horror titles aimed at kids tended to feature young people's interests on the covers: hangin' at the beach, rock and roll, computer games, peering into creepy mirrors, and gazing over the edge of a cliff.

Dark Forces
THE BARGAIN
REX SPARGER

Dark Forces
BEAT THE DEVIL
SCOTT SIEGEL

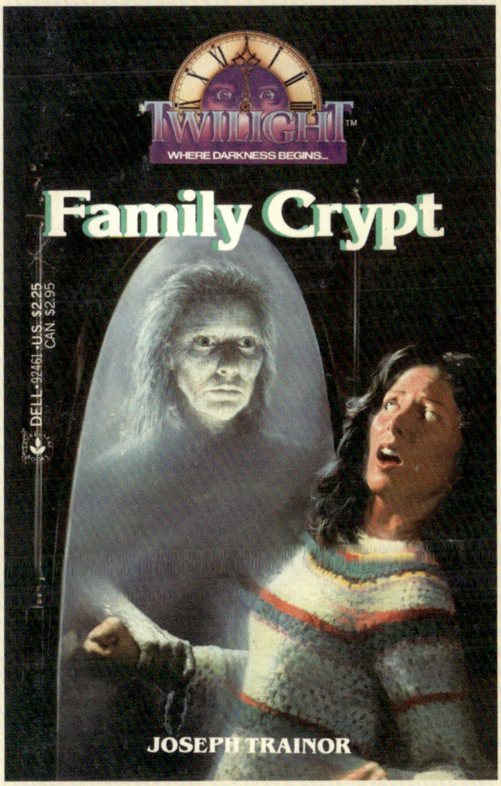
TWILIGHT
WHERE DARKNESS BEGINS...
Family Crypt
JOSEPH TRAINOR

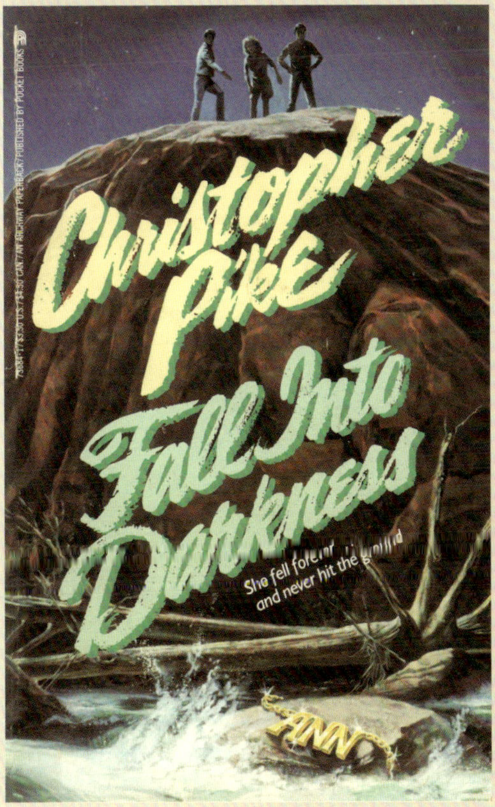
Christopher Pike
Fall Into Darkness

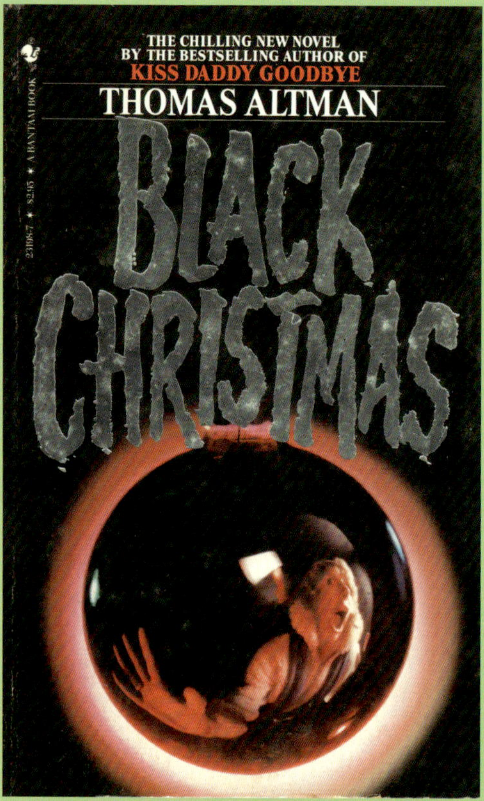
THE CHILLING NEW NOVEL
BY THE BESTSELLING AUTHOR OF
KISS DADDY GOODBYE
THOMAS ALTMAN
BLACK CHRISTMAS

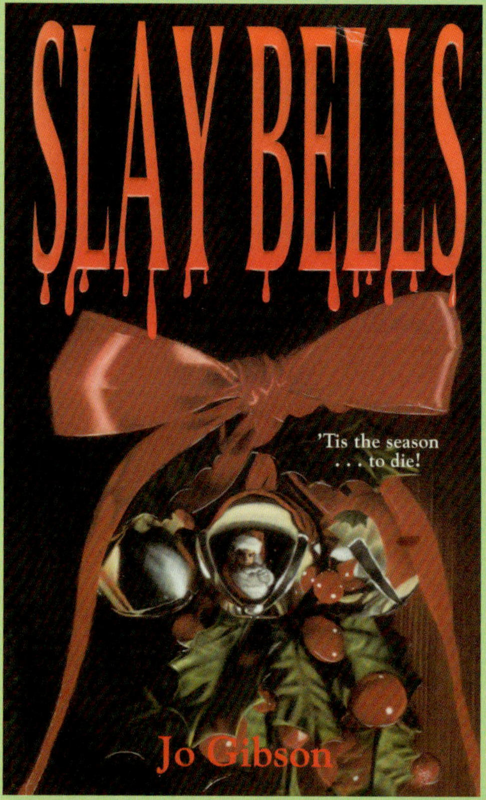
SLAY BELLS
'Tis the season
. . . to die!
Jo Gibson

Christmas Babies
Red hair,
green eyes,
sheer terrors . . .
Christopher Keane
and
William D. Black, M.D.

It was eight years later,
and it was happening again . . .
CHRISTOPHER PIKE
Slumber Party

Hang Your Stockings and Say Your Prayers

It's the night before Christmas and all through the town, someone is chopping up pregnant coeds, stabbing babysitters in the brain, and decapitating divorced ladies. Even more so than Halloween, Christmas is horror's favorite holiday, full of psycho Santas leaving red-and-green-wrapped heads under each and every Christmas tree.

Black Christmas (1983) is an Italian giallo-style thriller, with a faceless black-gloved killer terrorizing a tiny snowbound town. Its stalk 'n' slash set pieces can be stopped only by inexperienced Sheriff Bud Dunsmore, who is not only overwhelmed by the murders, he hasn't even bought his daughter a Christmas present yet. *Slay Bells* (1994) ups the yuletide ante with a deranged lunatic dressed like Santa stalking a snowed-in shopping mall, where he murders teens to avenge his grandfather's defeat in a long-ago fly-fishing tournament.

But, mostly, holiday paperback horror turned out to be that terrible boyfriend who wraps an Applebee's coupon in a Tiffany's box or slides a subscription to *Ladies' Home Journal* into an iPhone case. Its savagely seasonal covers concealed a distinct lack of Christmas carnage inside. No enraged, fire-shrouded snowmen appear in *Slumber Party*. And not only are no evil elf-babies born in *Christmas Babies* (1991), but the novel takes place in February. In Florida.

Books that delivered true seasonal slaughter typically didn't advertise that fact on their covers. Christmas is the most wonderful time of the year for WASPs, and WASP horror novels (you remember them from chapter 2) include plenty of Christmas carnage for every boy and girl.

Weirdly enough, it was by way of Christmas that the Satanic Panic spread its infection from heavy metal and role-playing games to horror movies. In 1984 TriStar Pictures released *Silent Night, Deadly Night*, and television ads for this touching tale—about a tiny orphan who dons a Santa suit and murders everyone in sight—featured a bloody St. Nick waving an ax. That image earned so many protests, and resulted in so many tots picketing movie theaters with WE LOVE SANTA signs, that the distributor pulled the film from theaters after barely a week. It was a lesson that horror writers learned well: mess with Santa and risk getting axed.

While *Black Christmas* and *Slay Bells* are indeed set during the holidays, there's no yuletide terror to be found in *Christmas Babies* or *Slumber Party*.

Death Rattle

By the early '90s, the coroner had called it and the medical examiner was zipping up horror's body bag. But one last twitch was left in the corpse.

In 1990, a sales rep at Dell claimed there was room for more paperback horror because everyone was getting out of the market. This would be like someone in *Jaws* noting there's plenty of space on the beach. Barely thirty years old, editor Jeanne Cavelos was bored of cursed Indian burial mounds and imitation Stephen King, so when her boss asked her to pitch a horror line, she was ready.

Unable to afford big names, with even B-listers off-limits because at that time they rarely earned out their advances, Cavelos had the idea of making the line the star. Abyss would be a home for genuinely new voices in horror, punk rock writers with something to say beyond "Serial killers are scary." She didn't want the same old books with thirtysomething male protagonists wading through piles of naked and mutilated female corpses. She hunted down artists to paint covers that looked like nothing on the market.

In February 1991 the first Abyss book, *The Cipher* by Kathe Koja, hit the racks. A sharply observed slice of early-'90s bohemia, it was about a couple of starving artists in a dying Rust Belt city who find a hole in their storage space. Dubbing it the Funhole (the original title of the book), they discover that anything organic fed into the Funhole comes out disturbingly mutated. So these art scene bottom-feeders use the Funhole to get themselves a gallery show.

The Cipher was anything but typical horror. The main action was psychological, and the Funhole is never explained, but readers were ready for something new. The book shared that year's Stoker Award for best first novel with another Abyss title, Melanie Tem's *Prodigal*, about dead children, social workers, and psychic vampires.

Abyss published Koja's next novel, *Bad Brains*, about an artist whose sustains a minor head injury at a party that unleashes apocalyptic hallucinations, seizures, and extradimensional silver snot dripping over everything he sees. Then his paintings start coming to life. Relentlessly interior, unfolding in dreams, visions, and nightmares, reading the book is like being trapped

Die-cut covers that teased gruesome art was nothing new for horror paperbacks, but these strikingly creative Abyss covers look like nothing that had come before.

inside William Blake's worst headache. Abyss's brand of psychological horror avoided creepy kids, real estate nightmares, and Satanic cults, and their books gave off a whiff of opium and absinthe. Nancy Holder's *Dead in the Water* is her riff on William Hope Hodgson's early-twentieth-century Sargasso Sea stories, only in her version a clutch of shipwreck survivors is picked up by a hellish cruise ship helmed by an undead buccaneer and his phantasmal pirate crew.

Not every Abyss book was a heavy, hallucinatory, psychological drama. Coming right on the heels of *The Cipher* was Abyss's second novel, *Nightlife* by Brian Hodge, which was basically a cross between *Crocodile Dundee* and *Miami Vice*. A Yanomamö warrior tracks the newest drug, Skullflush, from his home in Venezuela to Tampa, where it's getting sold in nightclubs as a bright-green cocaine alternative. A flashy horror thriller for the MTV generation, it's all were-piranha gangbangers, drug dealers nailed to yachts with arrows, and an AK-47-powered climactic car chase across Tampa's three-mile-long Howard Frankland Bridge.

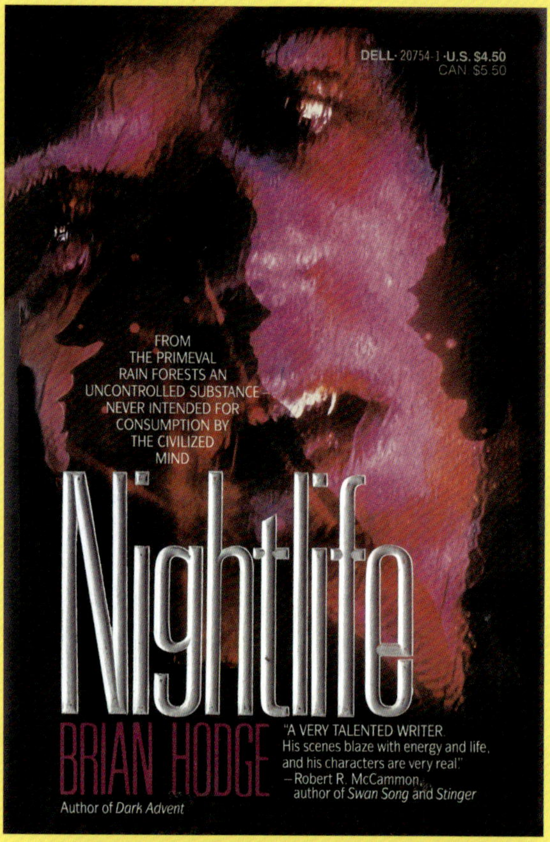
DELL·20754-1·U.S. $4.50
CAN. $5.50
FROM
THE PRIMEVAL
RAIN FORESTS AN
UNCONTROLLED SUBSTANCE—
NEVER INTENDED FOR
CONSUMPTION BY
THE CIVILIZED
MIND
Nightlife
BRIAN HODGE
"A VERY TALENTED WRITER.
His scenes blaze with energy and life,
and his characters are very real."
—Robert R. McCammon,
author of Swan Song and Stinger
Author of Dark Advent

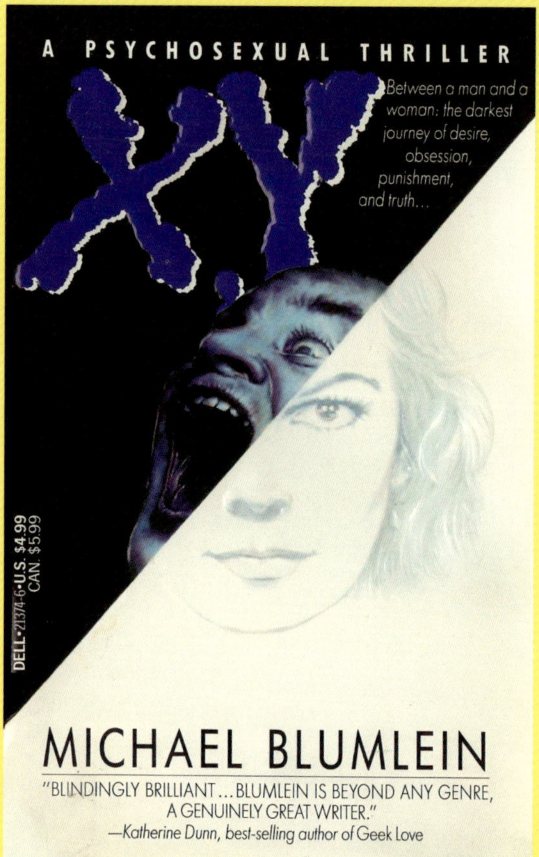
A PSYCHOSEXUAL THRILLER
XY
Between a man and a
woman: the darkest
journey of desire,
obsession,
punishment,
and truth...
DELL·21374-6·U.S. $4.99
CAN. $5.99
MICHAEL BLUMLEIN
"BLINDINGLY BRILLIANT...BLUMLEIN IS BEYOND ANY GENRE,
A GENUINELY GREAT WRITER."
—Katherine Dunn, best-selling author of Geek Love

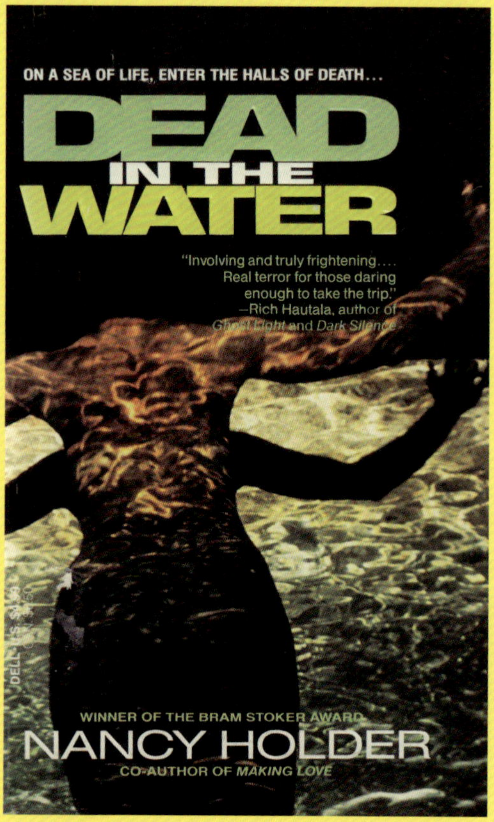
ON A SEA OF LIFE, ENTER THE HALLS OF DEATH...
DEAD
IN THE
WATER
"Involving and truly frightening....
Real terror for those daring
enough to take the trip."
—Rich Hautala, author of
Ghost Light and Dark Silence
WINNER OF THE BRAM STOKER AWARD
NANCY HOLDER
CO-AUTHOR OF MAKING LOVE

"A MAJOR NEW VOICE IN HORROR FICTION...
AN ELECTRIC STYLE AND NO SHORTAGE OF NERVE." —BOOKLIST
POPPY Z.
BRITE
AUTHOR OF
DRAWING BLOOD
VAMPIRES...
THEY ACHE,
THEY LOVE,
THEY THIRST FOR
THE FORBIDDEN.
THEY ARE YOUR FRIENDS
AND LOVERS,
AND YOUR WORST FEARS
LOST
SOULS

Written in chilly, precise, clinical prose, Michael Blumlein's *X, Y* feels like the fruit of a collaboration between J. G. Ballard and David Cronenberg. The only thing tying it to the old-school horror market is the fact that its main character is a stripper. After she passes out onstage and wakes up convinced that she's a man, Blumlein dives into the complicated swamp of gender difference, territory that no other horror novel had broached. Rather than worrying about identity politics or liberation narratives, he boils everything down to biology. And then he keeps on boiling. By the time he's finished, Blumlein has made a case that our assumptions about our identities aren't built on bedrock but on ever-shifting sand. It's probably the only book to cite the *Journal of Neuro-Medical Mechanics* in its endnotes, and it's also more dark science fiction than flat-out horror, much like Lisa Tuttle's quantum narrative *Lost Futures*, about a woman who begins to simultaneously experience all the lives she could have led.

Abyss's breakout star was Poppy Z. Brite, whose *Lost Souls* was the line's first hardcover book; it earned Brite a six-figure, three-book deal with Dell. His books revolve around the fictional town of Missing Mile, North Carolina, which is populated by sensitive psychic musicians, bisexual vampires, runaway waifs, serial killers, and cannibals. Dripping with graphic sex and violence, refusing to pay lip service to conventional *tsk-tsk*ing over runaway kids, Brite's books are the R-rated, younger, sexier, more rebellious version of Anne Rice's gothic vampire epics. His characters ditch the lives and families they'd been assigned at birth to build their own stronger, braver, more inclusive families on the margins. Brite had been associated with the splatterpunk movement, but he had something that eluded most of that gang, and he used it wisely: restraint.

For the next three years, Abyss published one new horror title every month. Financially, the line was moderately successful, but its books won awards and were unlike anything on the market. Dennis Etchison published with the line, as did Lisa Tuttle, Kristine Kathryn Rusch, and even Michael McDowell. Their books didn't set the world on fire, but they did set individual readers' minds ablaze.

In July 1994, Jeanne Cavelos left Abyss to focus on her own writing and teaching. She was supposed to be replaced by a new editor, but never was. An editorial assistant took over and Dell lost confidence in the line, refusing to publish the third title on Brite's contract, *Exquisite Corpse*, due to its "extreme" content. Abyss, with around forty-five titles on its list, withered and died shortly thereafter. And with it went the last echo of the horror boom.

Abyss proved that horror fiction still had room for original voices telling new stories about everything from psychoactive plants (*Nightlife*) to gender identity (*X, Y*) to Poppy Z. Brite's re-re-reinvention of vampires (*Lost Souls*), and Nancy Holder's hallucinatory sea story (*Dead in the Water*).

EPILOGUE

The lesson horror teaches us is that everything dies. The horror fiction boom of the 1970s and '80s became roadkill on the superhighway of the '90s. Authors disappeared, cover artists found new outlets, and this publishing *Titanic* hit an iceberg, split apart, and released its cargo into the cold, dark waters to wash up on the shores of thrift stores and used paperback emporiums for years to come.

Things change, flesh rots, houses decay and fall into disrepair—there's no point complaining. But the lost creativity makes you want to scream and pound on the inside of your coffin lid as it's being nailed into place. If we forget about these books, where else will we find a town invaded by killer clowns (*Dead White*), Prometheus chained to a rock in an abandoned New York City subway station (*Night Train*), an army of killer jellyfish (*Slime*), a Satan who is obsessed with anal sex (*The Nursery*), an Alabama family welcoming a river monster into its ranks (The *Blackwater* series), an army of six-inch-tall Nazi leprechauns (our beloved classic *The Little People*)?

Darkness may have fallen over the hellscape these books once illuminated, but there are still some candles burning out there in the night, a handful of lonely bonfires kindled on windswept beaches along the coastline of the Internet. There aren't many, but they're enough to steer by if you care to explore this dark and fascinating world further. Reach out and you'll find websites, some books, a few nerds and freaks like me and Will, some professors and academics, each one a lone lighthouse keeper for the legacy of these paperbacks.

We know we can't make these authors famous again. We know we can't give their titles another chance at the best-seller list. But for those who love these impossible, unpredictable books, it's enough for us to imagine that somewhere out there, underneath the vast dome of the night, a few people are curled up on their couches, nestled in their beds, riding the bus or the train, holding a copy of *When Darkness Loves Us*. Or maybe *The Voice of the Clown*. Or *Elizabeth*. Or *The Auctioneer*. Or *Feast*. Or *The Happy Man*.

We can't be certain that anyone is reading these books anymore. But we can hope. Because after all the monsters have flown away, hope is what's left at the bottom of the box.

The sunken continent of horror paperbacks occasionally disgorges new treasures that float ashore like messages in a bottle. One of them is this never-before-published Les Edwards cover for the pigs-gone-wild classic *The City*, which was senselessly cropped back in 1986 for its mass-market release.

APPEN

DIXES

SELECTED CREATOR AND PUBLISHER BIOGRAPHIES

Avon Books (founded 1941) Established to challenge paperback powerhouse Pocket Books, Avon issued paperback reprints for the mass market, which means lots of mysteries, westerns, and nurse romances. The *New Yorker* called them "one of the most resolutely down-market of the major paperback imprints." In 1969 they started printing original fiction. Their first blockbuster hit was Kathleen Woodiwiss's bodice-ripper *The Flame and the Flower*, which sold 2.5 million copies. Avon was bought by Harper Collins in 1999.

Bantam Books (founded 1945) Ian and Betty Ballantine were sent by Penguin UK to found Penguin in the United States. After parting ways with owner Allen Lane, they founded Bantam as the paperback arm of Grosset & Dunlap. In 1952 they were fired because the line was foundering. Oscar Dystel was hired and quickly turned things around, grabbing paperback rights to blockbusters like *Catcher in the Rye*, *Jaws*, and *The Exorcist* (he sold the hardcover rights to Blatty's book to Harper & Row). By 1980 Bantam was the largest publisher of paperbacks in America. In 1998 it was merged into Random House.

Ballantine Books (founded 1952) The next stop for Ian and Betty Ballantine, this paperback house was founded to release paperback and hardcover editions simultaneously but became famous for their fantasy and science fiction lines. Based on a recommendation from their switchboard operator, they picked up the paperback rights to *The Lord of the Rings* and got rich. Ballantine was acquired by Random House in 1973 and absorbed Fawcett in 1982.

Barker, Clive (born 1952) This British-born author's 1984 six-volume short story collection *The Books of Blood* rocked the horror market. He went on to direct *Hellraiser* and *Nightbreed*, both films based on his writings, and to write a lot of super-long dark fantasy novels like *Weaveworld* and *The Great and Secret Show*.

Berkley Books (founded 1955) The editor-in-chief and the vice-president of Avon Books broke away and started this rival paperback company that became known for science fiction. In 1965 they became G. P. Putnam's paperback arm. In 1982, Berkley struck gold with *The Hunt for Red October* and began publishing military thrillers.

In 1996, Putnam was acquired by Penguin; Berkley is now an imprint of Penguin Random House.

Bloch, Robert (1917–1994)

The youngest of H. P. Lovecraft's acolytes, Bloch was an enormously prolific writer, turning out hundreds of short stories, dozens of novels, and scripts for the original *Star Trek* and *Alfred Hitchcock Presents* TV shows. He wrote crime and horror but is best remembered for his 1959 novel *Psycho*, based on real-life murderer Ed Gein, a book that pioneered the psychological serial killer story.

Brautigam, Don (1946–2008)

Most famous for his Stephen King paperback covers, Brautigam delivered striking, iconic, sophisticated covers for *Cujo*, *Firestarter*, *The Stand*, and *'Salem's Lot*, plus the hand full of eyeballs on the paperback *Night Shift*. He's also the man behind the album covers of Metallica's *Master of Puppets* and Mötley Crüe's *Dr. Feelgood*.

Conner, Jeff (born 1956)

After starting his career in a southern California record store, Conner launched his Scream/Press imprint in 1981, delivering beautiful limited-edition volumes of works by Stephen King, Richard Matheson, Ramsey Campbell, and Dennis Etchison, which often featured extensive illustrations. He was the first to publish Clive Barker's *Books of Blood* in hardcover in the United States. Scream/Press wound down in 1992 as the horror market died.

Coyne, John (born 1937)

After writing a stack of unpublished novels, Coyne studied *The Exorcist* and delivered *The Piercing* (1979), a carefully calibrated knockoff about stigmata. Before its release, he wrote the novelization for the lukewarm 1978 horror movie *The Legacy*, which sold two million copies. *The Piercing* became a best seller in paperback, as did *The Searing*. His next book, *Hobgoblin* (1981), was a paperback original whose cover featured his name above the title. After *The Shroud* (1983), he married the editor of *The Piercing* and declared he was done with horror. He delivered the family saga *Brothers and Sisters* in 1986 before returning to horror for three books, and then he took a seventeen-year break from publishing. His next books were golf novels, published in 2007 and 2009.

Daniels, Les (1943–2011)

Between 1978 and 1991, Daniels wrote five historical vampire novels about Don Sebastian de Villanueva, a delightfully evil Spanish nobleman who keeps witnessing horrible historical events that make his vampirism seem comparatively benign (*The Black Castle*, *The Silver Skull*, *Citizen Vampire*, *Yellow Fog*, *No Blood Spilled*). Daniels is most famous as one of the first and best chroniclers of comic book history, possibly the result of his mom having thrown out his comic book collection when he was nine years old.

Dell Books (founded 1942)

One of the largest magazine and pulp publishers, Dell entered the paperback field under the guidance of long-term employee Helen Meyer, the first female president of a publishing house. It had several enormous hits (including *Peyton Place*); the company launched the Dial hardcover imprint to provide itself with source material. Dell was sold to Doubleday in 1976.

Eulo, Ken (born 1939)

The first book in this playwright-turned-novelist's "stone" trilogy, *The Brownstone* (1980), feels like reheated *Amityville* but sold in the ballpark of one million copies and spawned two sequels, *The Bloodstone* (1981) and *The Deathstone* (1982). After Pocket Books dropped its horror line, Eulo published a few more horror paperback originals for Tor while also working as a staff writer for TV shows like *The Golden Girls* and *Benson*. He stopped publishing in the mid-'90s.

Farris, John (born 1936)

One of the B-list superstars of the '70s and '80s, Farris wrote lots of paperbacks (and a few hardcovers), including a trio of dark thrillers, before Playboy Press published his hit ESP novel *The Fury* in 1976. Brian De Palma directed the film adaptation two years later. Heralded for his mature style in books like *All Heads Turn When the Hunt Goes By* (1977) and *Minotaur* (1985), Farris is the very definition of the reliable, journeyman genre author with the occasional over-the-top touch, like a priest turned pro wrestler turned exorcist named Irish Bob O'Hooligan in *Song of Endless Night*.

Fawcett (founded 1919)

Originally a magazine publisher and distributor, Fawcett turned out lowbrow pulps and comics, until a 1945 deal with NAL to distribute their paperback reprints gave them the idea to publish their own paperback originals for casual readers. They started Gold Medal in 1950 to do just that, horrifying the guardians at the gates of culture. By paying higher royalties than the competition, Fawcett became the number two paperback publisher in America, with books by Vladimir Nabokov and Kurt Vonnegut on their list. In 1977 they were bought by a diversifying CBS, who sold their backlist in 1982 to Ballantine, effectively dismantling the company.

Gray, Linda Crockett (born 1943)

Writing under several different names, Gray has published about ten horror novels and five Harlequin romances. Her first book was *Satyr* (1979) for Playboy Press, and her stories veer wildly from sedate to lurid. Injuries from a car accident in 1990 curtailed her writing career, and she now teaches.

Jensen, Ruby Jean (1927–2010)

A constant presence in Zebra's catalogue, Jensen was born in Missouri and started writing for Warner in 1974 with *The House That Samael Built*. After four gothic romances for them, she jumped to Manor Books and turned out three occult novels in 1978. Her horror novels, *Hear the Children Cry* (1981) and *Such a Good Baby* (1982), were published by Leisure and Tor, respectively, and in 1983 she settled down with Zebra Books for a 20-book run that started with *Mama*. A fairly perfunctory writer specializing in evil children, she was rewarded with Zebra's first all-hologram cover (*House of Illusions*, 1988).

Klein, T.E.D. (born 1947)

Editor of *Twilight Zone* magazine from 1981 to 1985, Klein was an influential member of the northeastern horror community, like a less productive Charles L. Grant (page 188). Much less. His 1984 novel *The Ceremonies* took him five years to write and was hailed as a modern classic. His short story collection, *Dark Gods*, contains four novellas including the much-anthologized "Black Man with a Horn" and "Children of the Kingdom." It is rumored that one day he'll publish his long-delayed second novel, *Nighttown*, which was originally announced for publication in 1989.

Lory, Robert (born 1936)

Writing for Lyle Kenyon Engle's book mill Book Creations, Lory delivered the eleven-installment men's adventure series *John Eagle: The Expeditor* before writing *The Dracula Horror Series,* starting in 1973. In it, Dracula is forced to work for the forces of good thanks to the splinter of stake lodged next to his heart. In 1974 Lory pitched Engle a book of horror short stories about the zodiac, but Engle sold the Horrorscope series (page 130) to Pinnacle as standalone novels. Lory didn't enjoy writing them and Pinnacle canceled the series at book four. Lory's day job is in advertising and consulting.

Martin, George R. R. (born 1948)

Before *Game of Thrones* Martin was, like Thomas Monteleone and Charles L. Grant, a science fiction guy who got into horror when the market was booming. His disconcerting 1979 novella *Sandkings* won the Hugo and Nebula awards, and his 1982 vampire novel, *Fevre Dream*, is considered a modern classic. *Armageddon Rag*, his 1983 novel about an occult '60s band reuniting in the '80s, was a commercial failure that temporarily ended his career as a novelist and sent him to Hollywood to become a television writer.

Manor Books (founded 1972)

One of the original giants of the true-confession magazine market, Macfadden Communications bought Hillman Publications in 1961 and begrudgingly absorbed its paperback publishing arm, which it then sold as Manor Books in 1972. Manor published cheap paperbacks, men's adventure, and paranormal gothics until ceasing operations in 1981.

Matheson, Richard (1926–2013)

A more prolific and pulpier Ray Bradbury, Matheson is one of the cornerstones of twentieth-century American horror, with twenty-seven novels and more than one hundred short stories to his credit. He wrote teleplays for all the essentials—*Star Trek*, *Alfred Hitchcock Presents*, and *The Twilight Zone*—and his three novels, *I Am Legend*, *The Shrinking Man*, and *The Legend of Hell House*, have all been adapted as movies. He's written films for Roger Corman's AIP and Britain's Hammer Films, and Anne Rice and Stephen King have cited him as an influence.

Monteleone, Thomas F. (born 1946)

A chance encounter led to Monteleone and Charles L. Grant signing on as two of future super-agent Kirby McCauley's first clients. Monteleone wrote a fistful of sci-fi paperback originals in the '70s before turning to horror (at Grant's prodding) in the '80s. His nutty but effective genre mash-ups—particularly 1984's *Night Train* (page 120) and his 1987 werewolves-versus-the-mafia book, *Fantasma*—made him a midlist regular. In the early '90s, Melissa Singer at Tor advised him to write a hardcover, and the result was *Blood of the Lamb* (1992), a high-concept thriller that hit big and rebranded Monteleone as a thriller writer.

Morrell, David (born 1943)

This Canadian novelist rocketed to attention with his debut *First Blood* (1972), which was denounced by *Time* magazine as "carnography" and made into a movie starring Sylvester Stallone. His next novel was the harrowing revenge thriller *Testament* (1975). Although his books contained only brief horrific elements, Morrell was considered part of the horror family throughout the '70s. *The Totem* (1979) was his first "true" horror novel.

New American Library (founded 1948)

Established during the post–World War II paperback boom, NAL started as American Penguin but was bought and rebranded after Penguin gave up on the American market. Considered the intellectual publishing house, it nonetheless made a mint on Mickey Spillane's Mike Hammer novels and turned James Bond into a literary franchise. In 1987 NAL merged with Penguin, and as of 2016 they only publish nonfiction under the merged Penguin Random House. Their imprints included Signet and Onyx.

New English Library (founded 1961)

When the Times Mirror Company of Los Angeles acquired NAL in 1960, they merged British paperback houses Ace and Four Square to form NEL. When Gareth Powell became managing director in 1964, they hit overdrive, pumping out pulpy books aimed at teenagers looking for cheap kicks. NEL milked the horror craze and teen market hard (their eighteen-volume Skinheads series ran from 1970 to 1980) with beautifully lurid covers. In 1981, they were sold to Hodder & Stoughton and became that publisher's mass-market imprint until being discontinued in 2004.

Paperjacks (founded 1971)

The massive Canadian publishing and distribution company General Publishing launched Paperjacks to print mass-market fiction and nonfiction by Canadian authors. By 1978, it was releasing five books per month, including some American imports. By the mid-'80s Paperjacks was releasing four to six horror and science-fiction books each year. In 1989, the company was set to be acquired by Zebra Books, who pulled out of the sale at the last minute. Paperjacks was never heard from again.

Playboy Press (founded 1963)

Originally established to dump *Playboy* magazine joke books onto the market, Hugh Hefner's book outfit hired Mike Cohn from NAL in 1971 to beef up its publishing program, ultimately releasing about thirty mass-market paperbacks per month. Founded with a focus on books for male readers, the line remained dormant until 1976, when it abandoned men and began targeting female readers with horror novels and bodice rippers. In 1982, Hefner's daughter Christie became president of Playboy Enterprises and immediately sold the book business to Putnam.

Pinnacle Books (founded 1969)

Started by Dallas-based Michigan General Corporation (a mobile home and concrete pipe manufacturer), constantly cash-strapped Pinnacle specialized in romance and men's adventure. Their first big hit was Don Pendleton's *The Executioner* series (now on its 434rd installment). Throughout the '70s, they were hobbled by disputes over ownership of the character, an FTC-vetoed merger with Harlequin Books, and an ill-fated four-year move to Los Angeles;

in 1985, the company declared bankruptcy. Its backlist was bought by Windsor Publishing in 1988, and that same year Zebra revived Pinnacle as a horror imprint. It published a monthly horror title until Zebra discontinued that program around 1994. Pinnacle is now an imprint of Kensington, specializing in westerns and true crime.

Pocket Books (founded 1938)

Pioneer of the paperback revolution in America, Pocket made mass-market paperbacks cheap by dropping their size to the 4-by-7-inch format used today and substituting sewn binding with glue. These were the first paperbacks sold in drugstores and newsstands, and they were roundly mocked by the industry until their stellar sales figures came in. Simon & Schuster acquired Pocket in 1966 and made it the paperback imprint.

Popular Library (founded 1942)

Established as a mystery-only paperback house by pulp publisher Ned Pines, Popular Library was known for racy covers throughout the '40s and '50s. The first paperback house bought by CBS in 1971, it was sold to Warner Books in 1982.

Ptacek, Kathryn (born 1952)

Although born in Nebraska, Ptacek attended university in New Mexico, and many of her nineteen novels deal with the Southwest, Native Americans, and giant gila monsters, among them *Gila!* (1981, written as Les Simons), *Shadoweyes* (1984), and *Kachina* (1986). She was married to Charles L. Grant until his death and, like him, also works as an editor.

Russell, Ray (1924–1999)

Before *The Exorcist*, there was Russell's inferior but eerily similar *The Case against Satan* (1963). His 1961 short story "Sardonicus" became the famous William Castle film *Mr. Sardonicus*, and his novel *Incubus*, about a demon killing women with his enormous penis, was made into the 1980 film *Incubus*, starring John Cassavetes.

Ryan, Alan (1943–2011)

Originally a book reviewer for the *New York Times*, Ryan entered the horror world when his short story "Sheets," based on his Christmas temp job at Macy's as a sheet salesman, was reprinted in the 1980 *Year's Best Horror* anthology. Encouraged by Charles L. Grant, as well as his friends Thomas Monteleone and Jill Bauman, Ryan wound up selling his first paperback original, *Panther!* (1981), on proposal for $6,000. That was followed by *The Kill* (1982), *Dead White* (1983), *Cast a Cold Eye* (1984), and numerous short stories. He went silent in 1990 until 2011, when his novel *Amazonas* came out immediately before his death.

Saul, John (born 1942)

A paperback originals writer, Saul was a struggling playwright and staff member at a Wisconsin drug treatment facility in 1976 when Dell rejected one of his novels but asked if he'd write a psychological thriller instead. They bought his outline and he wrote *Suffer the Children* in twenty-eight days. Published in paperback, supported by a huge television ad campaign, it sold 1.2 million copies. Since then, Saul has published a best-selling book each year, usually about either children in peril or children killing people. His books typically sell about a million copies each.

Schoell, William (born 1951)

Between 1984 and 1989, Schoell wrote six paperback originals for Leisure (*Bride of Satan*, *Saurian*, *The Dragon*, *Shivers*, *Late at Night*, and *Spawn of Hell*), which remain C-grade delights, although he regretted the generic titles Leisure slapped on them. Schoell moved to St. Martin's for *The Pact* (1988) and *Fatal Beauty* (1990), two titles that were left out in the cold when St. Martin's closed its horror line almost overnight. Now Schoell writes nonfiction, including *The Rat Pack* (1998) and *I Can Do Anything: The Sammy Davis Jr. Story* (2004).

Sharman, Nick (born 1952)

Norwegian-born Scott Grønmark was head of publicity for NEL before writing eight books for them under his Nick Sharman pen name, starting with *The Cats* in 1977. Plotted more like murder mysteries than traditional horror, his last horror novel was *Next!* (1986), after which he began working for BBC Radio.

Straub, Peter (born 1943)

Similar in prominence to Stephen King in the '70s and '80s, Straub wrote big, fat books that became big, fat paperback best sellers, and he blurbed plenty of other horror writers. He began his career writing literary fiction but started writing horror with his third book, the ghost story *Julia* (1975); and his fifth book, *Ghost Story* (1979), was a huge hit. The massive sales are unusual for an elegant, understated writer whose prose is some of the most polished in horror fiction.

Teason, William (1922–2003)

One of the best-loved and most prolific cover artists in the business, Teason got his first big break when Dell hired him to paint a cover for one of its Agatha Christie titles. Dell was contractually forbidden from depicting the book's characters on the cover, but Teason's clue-based still life won approval and he wound up painting about 150 Christie covers for Dell. A master craftsman, sometimes called one of the best American illustrators nobody knows, he painted everything from fine art that hung in galleries to skeletons for Zebra Books.

Tem, Melanie (1949–2015)

After Melanie Kubachko and writer Steve Rasnic were married, both she and her husband adopted the surname Tem. Her early novels were all published by the Abyss line: *Prodigal* (1991), *Blood Moon* (1992), *Wildling* (1992), and *Revenant* (1994). Her work focuses on the horror found within families. She has fifteen novels to her name.

Tor Books (founded 1980)

When Tom Doherty left science-fiction publisher Ace Books, he immediately founded Tor, a paperback originals house with a focus on sci-fi. Tor was publishing 137 books a year by 1986, when it was sold to St. Martin's Press due to cash-flow problems after its paperback distributor, Pinnacle Books, declared bankruptcy. Doherty stayed on at Tor, and the company remains a science-fiction imprint under Macmillan.

Tuttle, Lisa (born 1952)

Like a lot of writers of her generation, Tuttle started in science fiction as a respected short story writer, coauthoring *Windhaven* in 1981 with George R. R. Martin, and then moved to horror after one of her stories was included in Kirby McCauley's groundbreaking *Dark Forces* anthology. Since then she's bounced back and forth, with well-written novels like *Familiar Spirit* (1983) and *Gabriel* (1987) and her short story collection, *Nest of Nightmares* (1986). She remains the only person ever to refuse a Nebula Award.

Wallace, Patricia (born 1949)

Patricia Wallace wrote exclusively for Zebra between 1982 and 1992, turning out eleven titles that are either medical thrillers or children in peril novels (or sometimes both at the same time), including *The Taint*, *The Children's Ward*, *Monday's Child*, and *The Water Baby*. Between 1988 and 1994 she also wrote four Sydney Bryant mysteries about a private investigator. Her real name is Patricia Wallace Estrada.

Wheatley, Dennis (1897–1977)

With his first occult novel, *The Devil Rides Out* (1934), Wheatley established himself as the great British horror author of the '30s, '40s, and '50s selling a million copies every year. His novels, including *To the Devil a Daughter* (1953) and *The Haunting of Toby Jugg* (1948), have been made into films and are frequently reprinted with updated covers (*The Devil Rides Out* was reissued in paperback twelve times between 1969 and 1991). Wheatley was a deeply conservative snob who feared Britain would become a socialist state after his death.

Williamson, J. N. (1932–2005)

Gerald "Jerry" Neal Williamson was a prolific writer who never saw a trend he couldn't imitate. He wrote forty novels, mostly for cellar-dwellers like Leisure and Zebra. His work included haunted house books (*Ghost Mansion*, 1981), creepy kid books (*Playmates*, 1982), and UFO books (*Brotherkind*, 1982), most of which were overwritten and underdeveloped pastiches of other novels. Occasionally one achieved a kind of lunatic grandiosity, mostly by accident (*The Premonition*, 1981; *Brotherkind*).

Wright, T. M. (1947–2015)

Terrance "Terry" Michael Wright started his career with the novel *Strange Seed* (published in hardcover in 1978 and as a paperback in 1980), which earned an enthusiastic blurb from Stephen King. Wright developed a midlist cult following over the course of twenty-four novels. His *Manhattan Ghost Story* (1984) and five Strange Seed books weave a quiet, off-kilter spell that may not appeal to all readers but is certainly disquieting

Yarbro, Chelsea Quinn (born 1942)

Named a Grand Master at the World Horror Convention in 2003, Yarbro is best known for her Saint-Germain vampire novels. Her Count Saint-Germain is a 4,000-year-old bloodsucker who is romantic and sexy, a gothic pinup boy whose convoluted chronology is tracked from ancient Egypt to postwar Paris over the course of approximately twenty-five novels, starting with *Hotel Transylvania* in 1978.

AFTERWORD
Recommended Reading
By Will Errickson

While reading *Paperbacks from Hell*, you may have compiled a lengthy to-read list. Or you may feel like I did, decades ago, on the first day at my job at a dusty used bookstore with the entire horror section to myself: *Where do I start?*

Ease your way into horror fiction the way I did, by rereading novels in the genre that you've read before, and then turning to the ones you remember from when they were first released but never read. When I did this, I found that Stephen King's *'Salem's Lot* and *Pet Sematary*, John Farris's *All Heads Turn When the Hunt Goes By*, and Peter Straub's *Ghost Story* still hold up (no surprise). Ray Garton's *Live Girls*, a sleazy '80s NYC vampire tale, is lots of fun today. The rollicking splatter-punky tales collected by David J. Schow in *Silver Scream* are a terrific blast from the past; Thomas F. Monteleone's series of 1990s anthologies, *Borderlands*, blend real-life horror with the surreal and the absurd in a way that continues to be effective.

Writers I dug in their '80s heyday—Clive Barker, Dennis Etchison, T.E.D. Klein, Karl Edward Wagner—are even more enjoyable to me as an older, more experienced reader. Michael Blumlein's icy short works, collected in 1990's *The Brains of Rats*, reveal a talent unfettered by horror conventions but still within the parameters.

Thomas Tessier is a mature, intelligent writer who threads together sex and horror like nobody's business. *Finishing Touches* and *Rapture* are near-masterpieces of the era, and his werewolf novel *The Nightwalker* is a penetrating psycho-thriller set in punk-era London. His short stories, scattered in various anthologies, are well worth searching out as well.

As you explore further, you'll discover overlooked writers like Michael McDowell, Alan Ryan, and Graham Masterton. Two of my favorite novels from the pre–Stephen King '70s are William H. Hallahan's *The Search for Joseph Tully* and Joan Samson's *The Auctioneer*. Fantastic stuff! Hallahan's novel is a chilling work of fate and vengeance across the ages that remains enigmatic and melancholy; Samson's story of quiet, polite small-town life slowly upended by the mysterious appearance of the titular character is compulsively readable and psychologically adept.

You may be tempted to dismiss some subgenres depicted in this book . . . don't! I looked down on "animal attacks" books (see chapter 3) until I found *The Cormorant*, British author Stephen Gregory's 1986 debut novel. Critically lauded upon release, it's a doom-laden journey as the protagonist inherits the titular avian. Obsession and tragedy follow. *Feral* is a light-footed affair about marauding felines; author Berton Roueche's understated prose subtly evokes humanity's complicit guilt in the matter. At the opposite pole is Gregory A. Douglas's nasty *The Nest*, which gleefully runs roughshod over taste and decorum, as though the author had dared himself to make his writing grosser and grosser. He was a pulp writer getting paid a penny a word, and he worked for it. This hopeless, despairing book featuring mutant cockroaches, but with the courage of its trashy convictions, may make one wish that more Zebra titles had been so committed.

If you hunger for vampire thrills, try *Fevre Dream*, George R. R. Martin's bloodthirsty nineteenth-century tale of night creatures on a Mississippi River steamboat, with lively characterizations and historical detail. The late Michael Talbot's cult novel *A Delicate Dependency* contains almost no bloodshed but is rife with opulent dressing and intellectual debate; collectors pay ridiculous prices for it (and yet I found a copy at a library sale for a single dollar). For tawdrier, cheaper vampire fun, try Lee Duigon's *Lifeblood*, Marc Eliot's *How Dear the Dawn*, and Leslie Whitten's crime procedural mystery/horror *Progeny of the Adder*. Whitten's title comes from a Baudelaire poem, but the story isn't so high-minded; its grim matter-of-factness prefigures both Stephen King's *'Salem's Lot* and television's *The Night Stalker*.

Love stories can offer much to horror: *Lovers Living, Lovers Dead* is a loopy Freudian mystery in which a middle-aged professor tries to plumb the depths of his young wife's mental state; author Richard Lortz's arty pretensions and casual '70s sexism elicits some groans, but the bizarre basis for the woman's instability is a stunner. Joan Chambers, a lesbian playwright, produced *The Burning*, which links two present-day women to the tragic fate of lovers condemned as witches in the past. Sensitively wrought and suffused with a kind of free-floating heartache, the paperback novel was adorned with a lurid Rowena Morrill cover that may have turned off non-genre readers who otherwise might have been drawn to the tragic story.

Domestic horrors come full flower in *A Nest of Nightmares*, a paperback collection of short stories by American Lisa Tuttle, published only in Great Britain in 1986. Her work showcases women's lives and heightens their anxieties to deadly degrees. Melanie Tem's *The Prodigal* has a child protagonist trying to make sense of an adult world in which two of her siblings go missing. The very nature of friendship is rent asunder in the creepily excellent *Spectre*, from Stephen Laws, in which a group of British college mates confront their long-ago secrets and memories.

Some of the best horror titles cannot be classified. *The Happy Man*, by Eric C. Higgs, introduces Marquis de Sade–style pleasures into a precisely-wrought suburban background. French surrealist Roland Topor's *The Tenant* from 1964 oozes paranoia and humiliation, its moody euro-intellectualism a refresher compared to the less subtle horror offerings. Another title that's hard to classify but not to be missed is *Gwen, in Green*; the book features one of my favorite covers, by George

Ziel. As an eco-horror novel with tendrils of then-current pseudoscience and female sexual liberation, Hugh Zachary's utterly '70s novel charms with its datedness and its explicitness.

I hope you find some of the books and authors mentioned here to your liking. Before long, you may find that your horror paperback collection, like mine, keeps growing, almost of its own volition. Personally, I wouldn't have it any other way.

Will Errickson collects and reviews vintage horror literature and celebrates its resplendent paperback cover art at TooMuchHorrorFiction.blogspot.com. He provided many of the cover images for this book from his own collection.

CREDITS

Listed below is publisher and cover artist information for each book reproduced in *Paperbacks from Hell*. We have tried to include complete and accurate names, titles, and dates. Please contact the publisher to correct omissions or errors in attribution. All artwork copyright of the artists.

FRONTISPIECE
Total Recall by Peg Case and John Migliore (Paperjacks, 1987), cover art by Tom Hallman

TABLE OF CONTENTS
Child of Hell by William Dobson (Signet Books, 1982), cover art by Tom Hallman

PAGE 6
The Little People by John Christopher (Avon Books, 1966), cover art by Hector Garrido

PAGE 11
Rod Serling's Triple W: Witches, Warlocks, and Werewolves edited by Rod Serling (Bantam Books, 1963), cover artist unknown
Unholy Trinity by Ray Russell (Bantam Books, 1967), cover artist unknown
We Have Always Lived in the Castle by Shirley Jackson (Popular Library, 1963), cover art by William Teason

PAGE 12
Something Evil by Arthur Hoffe (Avon Books, 1968), cover art by Bob Foster
The Haunting of Hill House by Shirley Jackson (Fawcett Popular Library, 1977), cover artist unknown

PAGE 13
The Devil's Dreamer by Alice Brennan (Magnum, 1971), cover art by George Ziel
Fire Will Freeze by Margaret Millar (Signet Books, 1967), cover artist unknown

PAGE 15
The Guardians #2: Dark Ways to Death by Peter Saxon (Berkley Medallion, 1968), cover art by Catherine Jeffrey Jones
The Guardians #3: The Haunting of Alan Mais by Peter Saxon (Berkley Medallion, 1969), cover art by Catherine Jeffrey Jones
The Guardians #4: The Vampires of Finnistere by Peter Saxon (Berkley Medallion, 1970), cover art by Catherine Jeffrey Jones

PAGE 18
Rosemary's Baby by Ira Levin (Dell Books, 1967), cover art by Paul Bacon

PAGE 19
The Other by Thomas Tryon (Fawcett Crest, 1971), cover art by Paul Bacon
The Exorcist by William Peter Blatty (Bantam Books, 1971), cover art by Bill Gold

PAGE 20
The Dowry by Maggie Gould (Pyramid Books, 1949), cover artist unknown

PAGE 21
To the Devil a Daughter by Dennis Wheatley (Ballantine Books, 1972), cover artist unknown
The Devil Finds Work by Michael Delving (Leisure Books, 1969), cover art by Jack Thurston

PAGE 22
Falling Angel by William Hjortsberg (Warner Books, 1978), cover artist unknown

PAGE 24
Isobel by Jane Parkhurst (Jove Books, 1977), cover by Rowena Morrill
The Colour Out of Space by H. P. Lovecraft (Jove Books, 1978), cover by Rowena Morrill
The Dunwich Horror by H. P. Lovecraft (Jove Books, 1978), cover by Rowena Morrill

PAGE 25
The Satan Sleuth #1: Fallen Angel by Michael Avallone (Warner Books, November 1974), cover art by Charles Sovek
The Satan Sleuth #2: The Werewolf Walks Tonight by Michael Avallone (Warner Books, December 1974), cover art by Charles Sovek
The Satan Sleuth #3: Devil, Devil by Michael Avallone (Warner Books, January 1975), cover art by Charles Sovek

PAGE 26
The Night Visitor by Laura Wylie (Critic's Choice, 1987), cover art by Paul Stinson
The Succubus by Kenneth Rayner Johnson

(Dell Books, 1980), cover artist unknown
Satan Sublets by Jack Younger (Carlyle Books, 1979), cover art by Stephen Shub
Dark Advent by Brian Hodge (Pinnacle Books, 1988), cover art by Bob Larkin

PAGE 27
The Stigma by Trevor Hoyle (Sphere Books, 1980), cover artist unknown
Exorcism by Eth Natas (Lexington House, 1972), cover artist unknown
Incubus by Ray Russell (Dell Books, 1976), cover artist unknown
Son of the Endless Night by John Farris (Tor Books, 1985), cover art by John Melo

PAGE 28
The Inner Circle by Jonathan Fast (Dell Books, 1980), cover artist unknown
The Sacrifice by Henry Sutton (Charter Books, 1978), cover artist unknown
The Closed Circle by Barney Parrish (Playboy Press, 1976), cover art by Ron Sauber

PAGE 29
The Transformation by Joy Fielding (Playboy Press, 1976), cover art by Ron Sauber

PAGE 31
The Black Exorcist by Joseph Nazel (Holloway House, 1974), cover art by Ruben De Anda

PAGE 32
The Sentinel by Jeffrey Konvitz (Ballantine Books, 1974), cover art by Judith Jampel

PAGE 33
The Guardian by Jeffrey Konvitz (Bantam Books, 1979), cover art by Bob Larkin

PAGE 34
Shrine by James Herbert (New English Library, 1983), cover artist unknown

PAGE 35
In the Name of the Father by John Zodrow (Dell Books, 1980), cover artist unknown
Night Church by Whitley Strieber (Pocket Books, 1983), cover art by Bill Klimy and Maurine Klimy

PAGE 36
Legion by William Peter Blatty (Pocket Books, 1983), cover art by Lisa Falkenstern
Dark Angel by Sean Forestal (Dell Books, 1982), cover artist unknown
Dagon by Fred Chappell (St. Martin's Press, 1987), cover art by Dave Ross
Unholy Communion by Adrian Savage (Pocket Books, 1988), cover artist unknown

PAGE 37
The Gilgul by Henry Hocherman (Pinnacle Books, 1990), cover art by Jim Thiesen

PAGE 38
The Keep by F. Paul Wilson (Berkley Books, 1982), cover artist unknown
Red Devil by David Saperstein (Berkley Books, 1989), cover art by Mark Gerber and Stefanie Gerber

PAGE 39
The Tribe by Bari Wood (Signet Books, 1981), cover artist unknown

PAGE 40
Satan's Love Child by Brian McNaughton (Star Books, 1977), cover art by Gino D'Achille

PAGE 41
Satan's Mistress by Brian McNaughton (Star Books, 1978), cover artist unknown
Satan's Seductress by Brian McNaughton (Star Books, 1980), cover artist unknown

PAGE 42
Michelle Remembers by Michelle Smith and Lawrence Pazder, M.D. (Pocket Books, 1980), cover artist unknown
Michelle Remembers by Michelle Smith and Lawrence Pazder, M.D. (Pocket Books, 1983), cover artist unknown

PAGE 43
Michelle Remembers by Michelle Smith and Lawrence Pazder, M.D. (Pocket Books, 1980), cover artist unknown

PAGE 44
The Desecration of Susan Browning by Russell Martin (Playboy Press, 1981), cover artist unknown
The Education of Jennifer Parrish by Russell Martin (Tor Books, 1984), cover art by John Melo
The Obsession of Sally Wing by Russell Martin (Tor Books, 1983), cover artist unknown
The Possession of Jessica Young by Russell Martin (Tor Books, 1982), cover artist unknown
Rhea by Russell Martin (Playboy Press, 1980), cover artist unknown
The Resurrection of Candy Sterling by Russell Martin (Jove Books, 1982), cover artist unknown

PAGE 48

The Omen by David Seltzer (Signet Books, 1976), cover artist unknown

PAGE 50

Damien: Omen II by Joseph Howard (Signet Books, 1978), cover artist unknown

Omen III: The Final Conflict by Gordon McGill (Signet Books, 1980), cover artist unknown

PAGE 51

Omen IV: Armageddon 2000 by Gordon McGill (Signet Books, 1982), cover artist unknown

Omen V: The Abomination by Gordon McGill (Signet Books, 1985), cover artist unknown

PAGE 52

Crib by Harold Lee Friedman (Pocket Books, 1982), cover art by Lisa Falkenstern

PAGE 53

Embryo by Daniel M. Klein (Fawcett Popular Library, 1981), cover artist unknown

The Jonah by James Herbert (New English Library, 1981), cover artist unknown

Premature by Mary L. Hanner (Signet Books, 1981), cover artist unknown

The Reaping by Bernard Taylor (Leisure Books, 1982), cover artist unknown

PAGE 55

Spawn by Shaun Hutson (Leisure Books, 1983), cover artist unknown

PAGE 56

Childmare by A. G. Scott (Signet Books, 1981), cover artist unknown

The Moonchild by Kenneth McKenney (Avon Books, 1979), cover artist unknown

Prissy by Clifford Hanley (Fontana Books, 1978), cover artist unknown

PAGE 57

The Next by Bob Randall (Warner Books, 1981), cover art by Dario Campanile

Kate's House by Harriet Waugh (St. Martin's Press, 1987), cover artist unknown

The Sky Children by Donald Olson (Avon Books, 1975), cover artist unknown

PAGE 58

The Children by Charles Robertson (Bantam Books, 1982), cover art by Max Ginsburg

Seed of Evil by Edmund Plante (BMI, 1988), cover art by Mark Gerber and Stephanie Gerber

PAGE 59

Piper by Brett Rutherford and John Robertson (Zebra Books, 1987), cover art by Lisa Falkenstern

Lupe by Gene Thompson (Ballantine Books, 1978), cover artist unknown

PAGE 60

Nursery Tale by T. M. Wright (Playboy Press, 1982), cover art by Hector Garrido

The Godsend by Bernard Taylor (Avon Books, 1976), cover artist unknown

Judgment Day by Nick Sharman (Signet Books, 1982), cover art by Tom Hallman

The Little Girl Who Lives Down the Lane by Laird Koenig (Bantam Books, 1975), cover artist unknown

Harriet Said by Beryl Bainbridge (Signet Books, 1974), cover artist unknown

The Sendai by William Woolfolk (Fawcett Popular Library, 1981), cover artist unknown

PAGE 61

Strange Seed by T. M. Wright (Tor Books, 1987), cover art by Hector Garrido

The Accursed by Paul Boorstin (Signet Books, 1977), cover art by Michael Presley

Mama's Little Girl by George McNeill (Bantam Books, 1983), cover art by Lisa Falkenstern

The Savior by Marvin Werlin and Mark Werlin (Dell Books, 1978), cover artist unknown

Smart as the Devil by Felice Picano (Dell Books, 1976), cover artist unknown

PAGE 62

Let's Go Play at the Adams' by Mendal W. Johnson (Bantam Books, 1974), cover artist unknown

PAGE 63

Let's Go Play at the Adams' by Mendal W. Johnson (Bantam Books, 1974), cover artist unknown

PAGE 64

Halo by Chet Day (Pocket Books, 1987), cover art by Peter Caras

PAGE 65

Such Nice People by Sandra Scoppettone (Fawcett Crest, 1981), cover artist unknown

The Sibling by Adam Hall (Playboy Press, 1979), cover art by Martin Hoffman

PAGE 66

Elizabeth by Jessica Hamilton (Popular Library, 1976), cover artist unknown

Hell Hound by Ken Greenhall (Zebra Books, 1977), cover art by Luke Ryan

PAGE 67
Childgrave by Ken Greenhall (Pocket Books, 1982), cover art by Lisa Falkenstern

PAGE 68
Ghost Child by Duffy Stein (Dell Books, 1982), cover art by Peter Caras
After Midnight edited by Charles L. Grant (Tor Books, 1986), cover art by Jill Bauman

PAGE 69
Dead White by Alan Ryan (Tor Books, 1983), cover artist unknown

PAGE 70
Possession by Celia Fremlin (Pocket Books, 1969), cover artist unknown
Dark Companions by Ramsey Campbell (Tor Books, 1985), cover art by Jill Bauman
The Doll Castle by Martha Monigle (Beagle Books, 1975), cover artist unknown

PAGE 71
The Surrogate by Nick Sharman (Signet Books, 1980), cover art by Don Brautigam
Somebody Come and Play by Clare McNally (Tor Books, 1987), cover artist unknown
Keeper of the Children by William H. Hallahan (Avon Books, 1978), cover art by George Ziel

PAGE 72
The Voice of the Clown by Brenda Brown Canary (Avon Books, 1982), cover art by Don Brautigam
The Kill by Alan Ryan (Tor Books, 1982), cover art by Jill Bauman

PAGE 73
Cast a Cold Eye by Alan Ryan (Dark Harvest, 1984), cover art by Jill Bauman
A Glow of Candles by Charles L. Grant (Berkley Books, 1981), cover art by Jill Bauman

PAGE 75
Abracadabra by Stephen Gresham (Zebra Books, 1988), cover art by Richard Newton

PAGE 76
Mazes and Monsters by Rona Jaffe (Dell Books, 1982), cover art by Peter Caras

PAGE 77
Hobgoblin by John Coyne (Berkley Books, 1982), cover art by Mark Gerber and Stefanie Gerber

PAGE 80
Jaws by Peter Benchley (Bantam Books, 1974), cover art by Roger Kastel

PAGE 82
The Rats by James Herbert (New English Library, 1974), cover art by W. F. Phillips

PAGE 83
The Fog by James Herbert (New English Library, 1975), cover art by Stuart Bodek

PAGE 84
Rabid by David Anne (Dell Books, 1977), cover artist unknown
The Dogs by Robert Calder (Delacorte Press, 1976), cover art by Bob Antler

PAGE 85
The Pack by William Essex (Leisure Books, 1987), cover art by Brian Kotzky
The Long Dark Night by David Fisher (Ballantine Books, 1976), cover artist unknown
Dog Kill by Al Dempsey (Tor Books, 1987), cover art by Jon Ellis
The Haven by G. R. Diamond (Playboy Press, 1977), cover art by Wayne McLoughlin
The Blood Snarl by Ivor Watkins (Signet Books, 1980), cover artist unknown

PAGE 86
The Cats by Nick Sharman (New English Library, 1977), cover art by David McAllister
Satan's Pets edited by Vic Ghidalia (Manor Books, 1972), cover artist unknown
Night Shriek by Michael Wolfitt (Granada Publishing, 1983), cover artist unknown

PAGE 87
Panther! by Alan Ryan (Signet Books, 1981), cover art by Tom Hallman
Panther! unused cover art by Jill Bauman

PAGE 88
The Folly by David Anne (Pan Books, 1978), cover art by Lynn Duncombe

PAGE 89
The Farm by Richard Haigh (Granada Publishing, 1984), cover art by Les Edwards
The Predators by Mark Washburn and Robert Webb (Stein and Day, 1985), cover artist unknown

Taurus by George Wells (Signet Books, 1982), cover artist unknown

PAGE 90
Orca by Arthur Herzog (Pan Books, 1977), cover art by John Berkey

PAGE 91
Fleshbait by David Holman and Larry Pryce (New English Library, 1979), cover artist unknown
Pestilence by Edward Jarvis (Hamlyn Publishing Group, 1983), cover artist unknown
Slime by John Halkin (Hamlyn Publishing Group, 1984), cover art by Terry Oakes
Killer by Peter Tonkin (Signet Books, 1979), cover art by Ken Barr

PAGE 92
Killer Crabs by Guy N. Smith (Signet Books, 1978), cover artist unknown
Crabs on the Rampage by Guy N. Smith (Dell Books, 1981), cover art by Rowena Morrill
Crabs' Moon by Guy N. Smith (Dell Books, 1984), cover art by Rowena Morrill

PAGE 93
Crabs: The Human Sacrifice by Guy N. Smith (Dell Books, 1988), cover artist unknown

PAGE 94
Maggots by Edward Jarvis (Arrow Books, 1986), cover art by Terry Oakes
Slugs by Shaun Hutson (Leisure Books, 1982), cover art by John Holmes
The Ants by Peter Tremayne (Signet Books, 1980), cover artist unknown

PAGE 95
Eat Them Alive by Pierce Nace (Manor Books, 1977), cover artist unknown

PAGE 96
Squelch by John Halkin (Critic's Choice, 1985), cover artist unknown
Blight by Mark Sonders (Ace Books, 1981), cover artist unknown

PAGE 97
Croak by Robin Evans (Hamlyn Publishing Group, 1981), cover artist unknown
Slither by John Halkin (Hamlyn Publishing Group, 1980), cover artist unknown

PAGE 98
Gila! by Les Simons (Signet Books, 1981), cover art by Tom Hallman
Gila! cover sketch by Tom Hallman
Black Horde by Richard Lewis (Signet Books, 1980), cover artist unknown
Creatures by Richard Masson (Pocket Books, 1979), cover art by Roger Kastel

PAGE 99
Blood Worm by John Halkin (Guild Press, 1988), cover artist unknown
The Nest by Gregory A. Douglas (Zebra Books, 1980), cover artist unknown
Scorpion by Michael R. Linaker (New English Library, 1980), cover art by David O'Connor
Scorpion: Second Generation by Michael R. Linaker (New English Library, 1982), cover artist unknown

PAGE 100
Garden of Evil by Edmund Plante (Leisure Books, 1988), cover art by Jill Bauman
Disembodied by Robert W. Walker (St. Martin's Press, 1988), cover art by Ken Barr

PAGE 101
Gwen, in Green by Hugh Zachary (Fawcett Gold Medal, 1974), cover art by George Ziel
The Plants by Kenneth McKenney (Golden Apple Publishers, 1984), cover art by Norman Adams
Moonbog by Rick Hautala (Zebra Books, 1982), cover artist unknown
Cherron by Sharon Combes (Zebra Books, 1980), cover artist unknown

PAGE 104
Burnt Offerings by Robert Marasco (Dell Books, 1973), cover art by Paul Bacon

PAGE 106
Hell House by Richard Matheson (Bantam Books, 1972), cover art by Morgan Kane
The House Next Door by Anne Rivers Siddons (Ballantine Books, 1979), cover artist unknown

PAGE 107
The Intruders by Pat Montandon (Fawcett Crest, 1975), cover artist unknown, lenticular cover by Vari-Vue
The Architecture of Fear edited by Kathryn Cramer and Peter D. Pautz (Avon Books, 1989), cover art by Tim O'Brien

PAGE 108
Amityville: The Final Chapter by John G. Jones (Jove Books, 1984), cover artist unknown

PAGE 109

The Amityville Horror II by John G. Jones (Warner Books, 1982), cover art by Dennis Luzak

Amityville: The Evil Escapes by John G. Jones (Tudor Publishing, 1988), cover art by Dennis Luzak

PAGE 110

Witch House by Evangeline Walton (Ballantine Books, 1979), cover art by Michael Herring

Walls of Fear edited by Kathryn Cramer (Avon Books, 1991), cover art by Jim Warren

The Woman Next Door by T. M. Wright (Playboy Press, 1981), cover artist unknown

PAGE 111

666 by Jay Anson (Pocket Books, 1981), cover art by Lisa Falkenstern

PAGE 112

Cat's Eye by William W. Johnstone (Zebra Books, 1989), cover art by Richard Newton

Toy Cemetery by William W. Johnstone (Zebra Books, 1987), cover artist unknown

PAGE 113

The Devil's Cat by William W. Johnstone (Zebra Books, 1987), cover artist unknown

Cat's Cradle by William W. Johnstone (Zebra Books, 1986), cover art by Richard Newton

PAGE 114

The Stepford Wives by Ira Levin (Random House, 1972), cover art by Paul Bacon

PAGE 115

The Searing by John Coyne (G. P. Putnam's Sons, 1980), cover art by Gillian Hills

The Turning by Justin Scott (Dell Books, 1978), cover art by John Melo

The Curse by Carl Sherrell (Pageant Books, 1989), cover art by Hector Garrido

Effigies by William K. Wells (Dell Books, 1980), cover art by Peter Caras

PAGE 116

Harvest Home by Thomas Tryon (Fawcett Crest, 1973), cover art by Melvyn Grant

The Auctioneer by Joan Samson (Simon & Schuster, 1975), cover art by Wendell Minor

Maynard's House by Herman Raucher (G. P. Putnam's Sons, 1980), cover art by Wendell Minor

PAGE 117

The Abyss by Jere Cunningham (Panther Books, 1981), cover art by Terry Oakes

PAGE 118

A Manhattan Ghost Story by T. M. Wright (Tor Books, 1984), cover artist unknown

Fort Privilege by Kit Reed (Ace Books, 1985), cover art by Alan Gutierrez

Rooftops by Tom Lewis (Signet Books, 1981), cover artist unknown

PAGE 119

Death Tour by David J. Michael (Signet Books, 1978), cover art by Don Ivan Punchatz

PAGE 120

Night Train by Thomas F. Monteleone (Pocket Books, 1984), cover art by Lisa Falkenstern

Cellars by John Shirley (Avon Books, 1982), cover art by Neil Slovin

Our Lady of Darkness by Fritz Leiber (Berkley Books, 1977), cover art by Richard Powers

PAGE 121

The Children of the Island by T. M. Wright (Jove Books, 1983), cover art by Hector Garrido

Ghost Train by Stephen Laws (Tor Books, 1986), cover art by Jim Bandsuh

The Glow by Brooks Stanwood (Fawcett Crest, 1979), cover artist unknown

Urban Horrors edited by William F. Nolan and Martin H. Greenberg (DAW Books, 1993), cover art by Ashley Pearce

PAGE 122

The Parasite by Ramsey Campbell (Pocket Books, 1980), cover artist unknown

PAGE 123

The Influence by Ramsey Campbell (Tor Books, 1988), cover artist unknown

The Face That Must Die by Ramsey Campbell (Tor Books, 1979), cover art by Jill Bauman

PAGE 126

Coma by Robin Cook (Little, Brown, 1977), cover art by Paul Bacon

PAGE 128

The Tulpa by J. N. Williamson (Leisure Books, 1981), cover artist unknown

Light Source by Bari Wood (Signet Books, 1984), cover artist unknown

Heads by David Osborn (Bantam Books, 1985), cover art by Richard Newton

Next by Nick Sharman (Signet Books, 1986), cover artist unknown

PAGE 129

Slime by William Essex (Leisure Books, 1988), cover artist unknown
Fatal Beauty by William Schoell (St. Martin's Press, 1990), cover artist unknown

PAGE 130

Home to the Night by Julia Thatcher (Ballantine Books, 1975), cover art by George Ziel
The Carnelian Cat by Jean DeWeese (Ballantine Books, 1975), cover art by Charles Gehm

PAGE 131

Horrorscope #1: The Green Flames of Aries by Robert Lory (Pinnacle Books, 1974), cover art by John Holmes
Horrorscope #2: The Revenge of Taurus by Robert Lory (Pinnacle Books, 1974), cover art by John Holmes
Horrorscope #3: The Curse of Leo by Robert Lory (Pinnacle Books, 1974), cover art by John Holmes
Horrorscope #4: Gemini Smile, Gemini Kill by Robert Lory (Pinnacle Books, 1975), cover art by John Holmes

PAGE 132

The Fury by John Farris (Popular Library, 1977), cover artist unknown
The Nightmare Candidate by Ramona Stewart (Dell Books, 1980), cover artist unknown
The Mesmerist by Felice Picano (Dell Books, 1977), cover art by Peter Caras
Psychic Spawn by Ryder Syvertsen and Adrian Fletcher (Popular Library, 1987), cover art by Mark Gerber and Stephanie Gerber

PAGE 133

The Scourge by Nick Sharman (Hamlyn Publishing Group, 1980), cover artist unknown
Brain Watch by Robert W. Walker (Leisure Books, 1985), cover artist unknown
Mind War by Gene Snyder (Playboy Press, 1979), cover artist unknown

PAGE 134

Majestic by Whitley Strieber (Macdonald & Co., 1990), cover artist unknown
The Hunters by Burt Wetanson and Thomas Hoobler (Playboy Press, 1978), cover art by V. Segrelles
Earth Has Been Found by D. F. Jones (Dell Books, 1979), cover artist unknown

PAGE 135

Brotherkind by J. N. Williamson (Leisure Books, 1982), cover artist unknown

PAGE 136

The Children's Ward by Patricia Wallace (Zebra Books, 1985), cover art by Lisa Falkenstern
Allison's Baby by Mike Stone (Dell Books, 1988), cover art by Joe Burleson

PAGE 137

Twice Blessed by Patricia Wallace (Zebra Books, 1986), cover artist unknown

PAGE 139

Hot Blood: Tales of Provocative Horror edited by Jeff Gelb and Lonn Friend (Pocket Books, 1989), cover art by Richard Newton
Nocturnal by Ken Eulo (Pocket Books, 1983), cover artist unknown
The Mall by Steve Kahn (Pocket Books, 1983), cover art by Don Brautigam
Black Magic by Whitley Strieber (Corgi Books, 1982), cover art by Melvyn Grant

PAGE 140

The Shadow Man by Stephen Gresham (Zebra Books, 1986), cover art by Lisa Falkenstern
The Hacker by Chet Day (Pocket Books, 1989), cover art by Peter Caras

PAGE 141

Bugs by Theodore Roszak (Pocket Books, 1981), cover artist unknown
Little Brother by John McNeil (New English Library, 1983), cover artist unknown

PAGE 142

PIN by Andrew Neiderman (Pocket Books, 1981), cover art by Lisa Falkenstern
Night Howl by Andrew Neiderman (Pocket Books, 1986), cover art by Lisa Falkenstern
Teacher's Pet by Andrew Neiderman (Zebra Books, 1986), cover art by Lisa Falkenstern

PAGE 143

Brainchild by Andrew Neiderman (Pocket Books, 1981), cover art by Lisa Falkenstern

PAGE 146

Flowers in the Attic by V. C. Andrews (Pocket Books, 1979), cover art by Gillian Hills

PAGE 149

Garden of Shadows by V. C. Andrews (Pocket Books, 1987), cover art by Steve Huston

PAGE 150

Interview with the Vampire by Anne Rice (Ballantine Books, 1977), cover artist unknown

PAGE 151
Interview with the Vampire by Anne Rice (Ballantine Books, 1979), cover art by Tom H. Hall

PAGE 152
An Old Friend of the Family by Fred Saberhagen (Tor Books, 1987), cover art by Joe DeVito
Dracula in Love by John Shirley (Zebra Books, 1979), cover art by Carlo Jacono

PAGE 153
Nightblood by T. Chris Martindale (Warner Books, 1990), cover art by Greg Winters

PAGE 154
Fevre Dream by George R. R. Martin (Pocket Books, 1983), cover art by Barron Storey
No Blood Spilled by Les Daniels (Tor Books, 1991), cover art by Duncan Eagleson
The Delicate Dependency by Michael Talbot (Avon Books, 1982), cover artist unknown
Live Girls by Ray Garton (Pocket Books, 1987), cover art by Ron Lesser

PAGE 155
How Dear the Dawn by Marc Eliot (Ballantine Books, 1987), cover art by David Palladini
By Blood Alone by Bernhardt J. Hurwood (Charter Books, 1979), cover artist unknown
Vampire Junction by S. P. Somtow (Berkley Books, 1985), cover artist unknown
Darkness on the Ice by Lois Tilton (Pinnacle Books, 1993), cover artist unknown
The Vampire Tapestry by Suzy McKee Charnas (Tor Books, 1980), cover art by Kevin Johnson
Hotel Transylvania by Chelsea Quinn Yarbro (Signet Books, 1979), cover artist unknown

PAGE 157
Jaws by Peter Benchley (Doubleday & Company, 1974), cover art by Paul Bacon

PAGE 159
Dracula Began by Gail Kimberly (Pyramid Books, 1976), cover art by George Ziel
Sweetheart, Sweetheart by Bernard Taylor (Ballantine Books, 1979), cover art by George Ziel
Death Knell by C. Terry Cline Jr. (Fawcett Crest, 1977), cover art by George Ziel
False Idols by Betty Ferm (Fawcett Crest, 1974), cover art by George Ziel
Moon of the Wolf by Leslie H. Whitten (Ace Books, 1968), cover art by George Ziel

PAGE 160
The Nestling by Charles L. Grant (Pocket Books, 1982), cover art by Lisa Falkenstern
The Nestling cover sketch by Milton Charles

PAGE 161
The Longest Night by J. N. Williamson (Leisure Books, 1985), cover artist unknown

PAGE 162
The Amulet by Michael McDowell (Avon Books, 1979), cover artist unknown

PAGE 163
The Elementals by Michael McDowell (Avon Books, 1981), cover artist unknown
The Blackwater series by Michael McDowell (Avon Books, 1983), cover art by Wayne Barlow

PAGE 164
Halloween Horrors edited by Alan Ryan (Sphere Books, 1987), cover artist unknown
The Alchemist by Les Whitten (Zebra Books, 1986), cover artist unknown
The Manse by Lisa W. Cantrell (Tor Books, 1987), cover art by Bob Eggleton
Usher's Passing by Robert R. McCammon (Avon Books, 1985), cover artist unknown
Pranks by Dennis J. Higman (Leisure Books, 1994), cover artist unknown

PAGE 165
The October Country by Ray Bradbury (Ballantine Books, 1969), cover art by Bob Pepper

PAGE 166
Black Ambrosia by Elizabeth Engstrom (Tor Books, 1986), cover art by Bob Eggleston

PAGE 167
When Darkness Loves Us by Elizabeth Engstrom (William Morrow, 1985), cover art by Anthony Greco
When Darkness Loves Us by Elizabeth Engstrom (Tor Books, 1986), cover art by Jill Bauman

PAGE 170
Evil Eye by Ehren M. Ehly (BMI, 1989), cover artist unknown

PAGE 171
Soulmate by Charles W. Runyon (Avon Books, 1974), cover artist unknown
Snowman by Norman Bogner (New English Library, 1977), cover art by David McAllister

PAGE 172
Berserker by Frank Spiering (Sphere Books, 1981), cover art by Les Edwards

PAGE 173
The Shinglo by Alex Kane (Charter Books, 1989), cover artist unknown
Obelisk by Ehren M. Ehly (Leisure Books, 1988), cover art by Ben Perini

PAGE 174
Darker Than You Think by Jack Williamson (Dell Books, 1979), cover art by Rowena Morrill
The Changing by F. W. Armstrong (Tor Books, 1985), cover art by Joe DeVito

PAGE 175
Birthpyre by Larry Brand (Corgi Books, 1980), cover art by Terry Oakes
The Bamboo Demons by Jory Sherman (New English Library, 1979), cover art by Ian Miller
The Djinn by Graham Masterton (Pinnacle Books, 1977), cover art by Ed Soyka

PAGE 176
The Manitou by Graham Masterton (Pinnacle Books, 1976), cover art by Ed Soyka
Crooked Tree by Robert C. Wilson (Berkley Books, 1980), cover art by Dario Campanile

PAGE 177
Totem by Ehren M. Ehly (Leisure Books, 1989), cover art by Ben Perini

PAGE 178
Chumash by Gary Thompson (Leisure Books, 1986), cover artist unknown

PAGE 179
Skeleton Dancer by Alan Erwin (Dell Books, 1989), cover artist unknown

PAGE 180
Bearwalk by Lynne Sallot and Tom Peltier (Paperjacks, 1977), cover artist unknown
The Chindi by Brad Steiger (Dell Books, 1980), cover art by John Melo
The Shaman by Frank Coffey (Playboy Press, 1982), cover art by Les Katz
Kachina by Kathryn Ptacek (Tor Books, 1986), cover art by Paul Stinson

PAGE 181
Shadoweyes by Kathryn Ptacek (Tor Books, 1984), cover artist unknown
The Silver Skull by Les Daniels (Ace Books, 1983), cover art by Ian Craig
Ten Little Indians by E. Patrick Murray (Zebra Books, 1988), cover art by Lisa Falkenstern
When Spirits Walk by Christine Gentry (Critic's Choice, 1988), cover artist unknown

PAGE 183
Famine by Graham Masterton (Ace Books, 1981), cover art by Carlos Ochagavia
Walkers by Graham Masterton (Tor Books, 1989), cover art by Joe DeVito
Mirror by Graham Masterton (Tor Books, 1989), cover art by Jim Thiesen
Feast by Graham Masterton (Pinnacle Books, 1988), cover art by Bob Larkin
The Heirloom by Graham Masterton (Signet Books, 1981), cover artist unknown

PAGE 184
Sandman by William W. Johnstone (Zebra Books, 1988), cover art by Richard Newton
Devil's Moon by William M. Carney (Zebra Books, 1988), cover artist unknown

PAGE 185
Smoke by Ruby Jean Jensen (Zebra Books, 1988), cover artist unknown
Wait and See by Ruby Jean Jensen (Zebra Books, 1986), cover artist unknown

PAGE 186
The Girl Next Door by Jack Ketchum (Warner Books, 1989), cover art by Lisa Falkenstern
Dead to the World by J. N. Williamson (BMI, 1988), cover art by Mark Gerber and Stefanie Gerber
Resurrection Dreams by Richard Laymon (Onyx Books, 1989), cover artist unknown
Wild Violets by Ruth Baker Field (Zebra Books, 1980), cover art by William Teason
Chain Letter by Ruby Jean Jensen (Zebra Books, 1987), cover artist unknown

PAGE 187
Guardian Angels by Joseph Citro (Zebra Books, 1988), cover art by Richard Newton
Carrion Comfort by Dan Simmons (Warner Books, 1990), cover art by Don Brautigam
Tricycle by Russell Rhodes (Pocket Books, 1983), cover art by Lisa Falkenstern
Why Not You and I? by Karl Edward Wagner (Tor Books, 1987), cover art by J. K. Potter
Night Visions: Dead Image edited by Charles L. Grant (Berkley Books, 1987), cover art by James Warhola
Blood Sisters by Deborah Sherwood (Zebra Books, 1988), cover art by William Teason

PAGE 188
Night Songs by Charles L. Grant (Pocket Books, 1984), cover art by Rowena Morrill
Midnight by Charles L. Grant (Tor Books, 1985), cover art by Jill Bauman

PAGE 189
The Hour of the Oxrun Dead by Charles L. Grant (Popular Library, 1979), cover artist unknown

PAGE 190
Shadows edited by Charles L. Grant (Playboy Press, 1980), cover artist unknown
Shadows 5 edited by Charlest L. Grant (Berkley Books, 1986), cover art by Prieto Muriana
Shadows 7 edited by Charles L. Grant (Berkley Books, 1987), cover art by Prieto Muriana
Shadows 9 edited by Charles L. Grant (Berkley Books, 1988), cover artist unknown

PAGE 191
Cutting Edge edited by Dennis Etchison (St. Martin's Press, 1987), cover art by Linda Fennimore

PAGE 194
The Kill Riff by David J. Schow (Macdonald & Co., 1987), cover artist unknown

PAGE 195
Backwards Masking Unmasked by Jacob Aranza (Huntington House, 1983), cover artist unknown

PAGE 196
Books of Blood vol. 1 by Clive Barker (Berkley Books, 1986), cover artist unknown
Splatterpunks edited by Paul M. Sammon (St. Martin's Press, 1990), cover artist unknown

PAGE 197
Seeing Red by David J. Schow (Tor Books, 1990), cover art by Tom Canty
Animals by John Skipp and Craig Spector (Bantam Books, 1993), cover art by Joe DeVito

PAGE 198
Stage Fright by Garrett Boatman (Onyx Books, 1988), cover artist unknown

PAGE 199
The Scream by John Skipp and Craig Spector (Bantam Books, 1988), cover art by Stan Watts

PAGE 200
The Drive-In by Joe R. Lansdale (Bantam Books, 1988), cover art by E. T. Steadman
The Drive-In 2 by Joe R. Lansdale (Bantam Books, 1989), cover art by E. T. Steadman

PAGE 201
Judgment Day by Nick Sharman (Signet Books, 1982), cover art by Tom Hallman
Fangs by William Dobson (Signet Books, 1980), cover art by Tom Hallman

PAGE 203
Save the Last Dance for Me by Judi Miller (Pocket Books, 1981), cover art by Lisa Falkenstern
Phantom of the Soap Opera by Judi Miller (Dell Books, 1988), cover artist unknown
Below the Line by Jaron Summers (Leisure Books, 1987), cover artist unknown

PAGE 204
Red Dragon by Thomas Harris (Bantam Books, 1981), cover art by Hiram Richardson

PAGE 206
Shock Waves by Thomas Tessier (Berkley Books, 1987), cover artist unknown
Rapture by Thomas Tessier (Warner Books, 1987), cover art by Sonja Lamut and Nenad Jakesevic

PAGE 207
The Shoemaker by Flora Rheta Schreiber (Signet Books, 1983), cover art by Tom Hallman
The Happy Man by Eric C. Higgs (Paperjacks, 1985), cover art by Peter Maher

PAGE 208
Burning Obsession by Robert W. Walker (Pinnacle Books, 1989), cover art by Broeck Steadman
Horror Story by Oliver McNab (Penguin Books, 1979), cover artist unknown
Dying Breath by Robert W. Walker (Pinnacle Books, 1989), cover art by Broeck Steadman
Razor's Edge by Robert W. Walker (Pinnacle Books, 1989), cover art by Broeck Steadman

PAGE 209
The Hood by David Scannell (Avon Books, 1984), cover artist unknown
Office Party by Michael A. Gilbert (Pocket Books, 1984), cover artist unknown

PAGE 210
Slob by Rex Miller (Signet Books, 1987), cover artist unknown

PAGE 211
Claw Hammer by Paul Dale Anderson (Pinnacle Books, 1989), cover artist unknown

PAGE 212
The Strangers by Mort Castle (Leisure Books, 1984), cover artist unknown

PAGE 213
Joyride by Stephen Crye (Pinnacle Books, 1983), cover art by Sonja Lamut and Nenad Jakesevic
Ghoul by Michael Slade (Signet Books, 1989), cover artist unknown
Headhunter by Michael Slade (Onyx Books, 1986), cover artist unknown

PAGE 214
The Lifeguard by Richie Tankersley Cusick (Scholastic, 1991), cover artist unknown

PAGE 215
The Bargain by Rex Sparger (Bantam Books, 1983), cover art by Stanley S. Drate
Beat the Devil by Scott Siegel (Bantam Books, 1983), cover artist unknown
Family Crypt by Joseph Trainor (Dell Books, 1984), cover artist unknown
Fall into Darkness by Christopher Pike (Pocket Books, 1990), cover artist unknown

PAGE 216
Black Christmas by Thomas Altman (Bantam Books, 1983), cover artist unknown
Slay Bells by Jo Gibson (Pinnacle Books, 1994), cover artist unknown
Christmas Babies by Christopher Keane and William D. Black, M.D. (Pocket Books, 1991), cover art by Lisa Falkenstern
Slumber Party by Christopher Pike (Hodder & Stoughton, 1990), cover artist unknown

PAGE 217
Silent Night 2 by R. L. Stine (Pocket Books, 1991), cover artist unknown

PAGE 218
Prodigal by Melanie Tem (Dell Books, 1991), cover artist unknown
Bad Brains by Kathe Koja (Dell Books, 1992), cover art by Marshall Arisman

PAGE 219
The Cipher by Kathe Koja (Dell Books, 1991), cover art by Marshall Arisman

PAGE 220
Nightlife by Brian Hodge (Dell Books, 1991), cover artist unknown
X, Y by Michael Blumlein (Dell Books, 1993), cover artist unknown
Dead in the Water by Nancy Holder (Dell Books, 1994), cover artist unknown
Lost Souls by Poppy Z. Brite (Dell Books, 1993), cover art by Miran Kim

PAGE 223
The City by Richard Haigh (Grafton, 1986), cover art by Les Edwards

ACKNOWLEDGMENTS

An enormous expression of thanks is due to the crew at Abyss. Jeanne Cavelos, Kathe Koja, and Michael Blumlein are all exceptionally busy individuals, but they were willing to give me a lot more time than I deserved to help with this book. I interviewed them all early in its writing and they had an enormous influence on my thinking about the paperback publishing boom and, especially, its end.

Elizabeth Hand was the first person I interviewed for this book, and she was also one of my teachers at Clarion Writers' Workshop back in 2009. I wouldn't have written this book without her encouragement.

I have rarely interviewed someone who tells as many great stories as well as Thomas Monteleone. I stole several of his jokes.

Ellen Datlow has always been one of the nicest people in the business, and the time she gave me was valuable beyond words.

One of the great honors of this book was getting to meet Agnes Greenhall, the widow of Ken Greenhall. I hope in some small way this book helps him finally receive the readers he deserves.

You can't judge a book by its cover, but a huge debt of gratitude is owed to the cover artists whose work appears in this book. I tried my best to identify everyone, but please let me know if I missed someone, got something wrong, or if you have a credit for an uncredited cover.

Special thanks to Lisa Falkenstern who was as lovely as her paintings and far more generous with her time than I ever could have expected.

Jill Bauman is as funny and off-center as her art would lead you to believe, but she was also enormously kind and told some of the best stories.

Vincent Di Fate now teaches at the Fashion Institute of Technology and everything I know about the history of cover illustration comes from him. The wisdom is his, the mistakes are mine. He was also instrumental in helping me contact the Society of Illustrators who were an invaluable resource. If you don't support their work, you should.

Tom Hallman was as gracious as he is talented, and Richard Newton was frank, straightforward, and this book would be poorer without his insights.

Jane Frank at Worlds of Wonder Art opened up the world of British cover illustration to me, and I would not have Terry Oakes's mind-melting artwork in this book if not for her. Also, Val and Les Edwards were tremendously helpful and kind.

Zebra Books art director Patty Pecoraro gave generously of her time and insight, which was invaluable.

Almost as important as the writers and artists are the fans, many of whom have become historians of a world that would otherwise be lost.

This book would not exist if not for Will Errickson and his Too Much Horror Fiction blog. No one has worked harder to read the unreadable, champion the unchampioned, and identify the unidentified than Will.

Enormous thanks go also to Darrin Venticinque. Besides Will, no one has done more to preserve the art of cover illustration than Darrin, and he was always happy to do some sleuthing to figure out who painted which cover, if he didn't already own the original and have it hanging in his Gallery of Gloom.

For information about the British horror paperback industry, check out the Vault of Evil ProBoards forum, or Justin Marriott's Paperback Fanatic. And there would not be a chapter about the gothic revival in horror paperbacks if not for Jennifer F. and her astounding website, The Complete V. C. Andrews.

Finally, my apologies to Amanda Cohen. That vacation was supposed to be a celebration of the completion of this book. Who knew that those leprechauns would turn out to be Nazis? And so hungry?

INDEX

Library of Congress Cataloging in Publication number: 2016957818

ISBN: 978-1-59474-981-0

Printed in China
Typeset in ITC Benguiat, ITC Korinna, and Sabon
Designed by Timothy O'Donnell
Production management by John J. McGurk

Full publisher and artist credits appear on page 237. All illustrations in this book are copyrighted by their respective copyright holders (according to the original copyright or publication date) and are reproduced for historical purposes. Any omission or incorrect information should be transmitted to the author or publisher, so it can be rectified in any future edition of this book.

Quirk Books
an imprint of Andrews McMeel Publishing
a division of Andrews McMeel Universal
1130 Walnut Street, Kansas City, Missouri 64106
quirkbooks.com

The authorized representative in the EEA is Simon and Schuster Netherlands BV, Herculesplein 96 3584 AA Utrecht, Netherlands. (info@simonandschuster.nl)

10 9

FSC
www.fsc.org
MIX
Paper | Supporting responsible forestry
FSC® C144853